ADVANCE PRAISE FOR

# Innovations in Transformative Learning

"Beth Fisher-Yoshida, Kathy Dee Geller, Steven A. Schapiro, and colleagues have gathered together a set of transformative learning offerings that truly expand the boundaries of this field in new and unchartered directions. The field of transformative learning is pressing to widen the space of theory and practice behind its earlier cognitive base and this set of readings does just that. This is a truly important addition to this field."

*Edmund O'Sullivan, Transformative Learning Centre, University of Toronto;*
*Author,* Transformative Learning: Educational Vision for the 21st Century

"Beth Fisher-Yoshida, Kathy Dee Geller, and Steven A. Schapiro bridge the divide between scholars and practitioners to provide us with a provocative collection of applications of transformative learning theory in culturally diverse settings and using multidisciplinary approaches. This engaging and accessible volume is founded on a commitment to social justice and adult learning and development outside of the traditional classroom. Using the themes of creating space for learning, looking through the lens of culture, and promoting learning through the arts, the editors and contributing authors give us a fresh perspective on transformative education."

*Patricia Cranton, Penn State University, Harrisburg;*
*Author,* Understanding and Promoting Transformative Learning

"In a time of racism and widespread racial micro-aggressions, of shameless ideological manipulation, and of uncritical jingoism, we need more than ever to transform the structures and systems within which we learn our identity, create meaning, and live purposefully. *Innovations in Transformative Learning: Space, Culture, and the Arts,* helps us envisage how those things might happen."

*From the Foreword by Stephen Brookfield*

# Innovations in Transformative Learning

# Studies in the
# Postmodern Theory of Education

Joe L. Kincheloe and Shirley R. Steinberg
*General Editors*

Vol. 341

PETER LANG
New York • Washington, D.C./Baltimore • Bern
Frankfurt am Main • Berlin • Brussels • Vienna • Oxford

# INNOVATIONS IN TRANSFORMATIVE LEARNING

## Space, Culture, & the Arts

EDITED BY
Beth Fisher-Yoshida,
Kathy Dee Geller,
& Steven A. Schapiro

WITH A FOREWORD BY STEPHEN BROOKFIELD

PETER LANG
New York • Washington, D.C./Baltimore • Bern
Frankfurt am Main • Berlin • Brussels • Vienna • Oxford

Library of Congress Cataloging-in-Publication Data

Innovations in transformative learning: space, culture, and the arts /
edited by Beth Fisher-Yoshida, Kathy Dee Geller, Steven A. Schapiro.
p. cm. — (Counterpoints: studies in the postmodern theory of education; v. 341)
Includes bibliographical references and index.
1. Transformative learning. 2. Adult learning. 3. Multicultural education.
4. Educational innovations. I. Geller, Kathy Dee. II. Schapiro, Steven A. III. Title.
LC1100.F57   370.11'5—dc22   2008015051
ISBN 978-1-4331-0291-2
ISSN 1058-1634


Bibliographic information published by **Die Deutsche Bibliothek**.
**Die Deutsche Bibliothek** lists this publication in the "Deutsche
Nationalbibliografie"; detailed bibliographic data is available
on the Internet at http://dnb.ddb.de/.

Cover design by Joni Holst


The paper in this book meets the guidelines for permanence and durability
of the Committee on Production Guidelines for Book Longevity
of the Council of Library Resources.

© 2009 Peter Lang Publishing, Inc., New York
29 Broadway, 18th floor, New York, NY 10006
www.peterlang.com

Printed in the United States of America

# Contents

## SECTION 2:
## LOOKING THROUGH THE LENS OF CULTURE, DIFFERENCE, AND DIVERSITY

## SECTION 3:
## ANIMATING AWARENESS THROUGH THE EXPRESSIVE AND PERFORMATIVE ARTS

# Innovations in Transformative Learning: Space, Culture, and the Arts

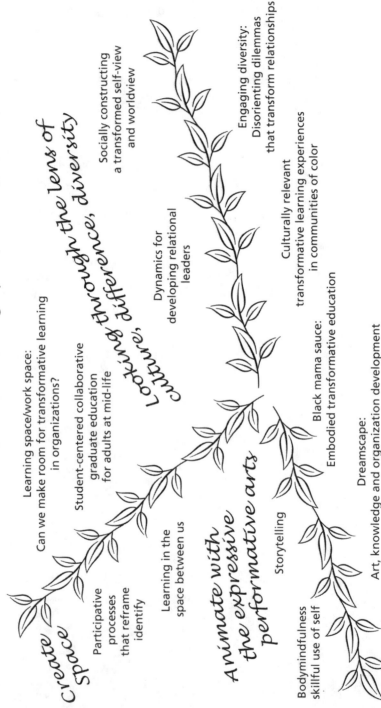

*create space*

Learning space/work space:
Can we make room for transformative learning
in organizations?

Student-centered collaborative
graduate education
for adults at mid-life

Participative
processes
that reframe
identify

Learning in the
space between us

*Animate with
the expressive
performative arts*

Storytelling

Bodymindfulness
skillful use of self

Dreamscape:
Art, knowledge and organization development

*Looking through the lens of
Culture, difference, diversity*

Socially constructing
a transformed self-view
and worldview

Engaging diversity:
Disorienting dilemmas
that transform relationships

Dynamics for
developing relational
leaders

Culturally relevant
transformative learning experiences
in communities of color

Black mama sauce:
Embodied transformative education

# Acknowledgments

This book has been inspired by the transformative learning that all of us have experienced through our involvement with the doctoral program in Human and Organization Development at Fielding Graduate University. We would like to express our deep appreciation to all of our Fielding colleagues—students, faculty, and staff—who have provided us with the space for learning, and the challenge, support, and vision that make transformation possible. In particular, we would like to especially thank the contributors to this volume, from whom we have learned so much, and who have made this project such a rewarding collaborative experience.

*Beth Fisher-Yoshida, Kathy Geller, and Steve Schapiro*
October 2008

# Foreword

About 25 years ago, I became aware of an important adult higher educational stirring on the West Coast. Apparently an institution had been created that was trying to do something obvious but also radical—to teach about adult learning, adult education, and adult development in a way that was consistent with the central principles those disciplines espoused. At the time, I was working on the opposite coast in a program that was attempting the same project—the AEGIS doctoral program in adult education at Teachers College, Columbia University in New York. With my colleagues Jack Mezirow, Victoria Marsick, and Elizabeth Kasl, we were doing our best to practice in a way that was consistent with the field we were studying. For us that meant placing the development of critical reflection at the heart of our work, encouraging the collaborative writing of dissertations, and turning the responsibility for planning doctoral learning, as much as was possible, over to the students. But the AEGIS program was always struggling against the external constraints posed by the college and the larger university. Our experiments took place in a system that did not naturally accommodate our innovations.

On the West Coast, however, the problem of compromising with the wider organizational structure's demands did not occur. This was because the mission of the whole institution concerned was to do across all its programs what we were trying to do in one—to treat learners as the adults they were, recognizing that they brought skill, experience, and knowledge to learning that often exceeded that of teachers or mentors. This institution was, of course, the Fielding Institute.

I remember being in Jack Mezirow's flat in the early 1980s as Fredric Hudson talked excitedly about Fielding. He stressed how influenced he had been by Malcolm Knowles's ideas regarding andragogical ways of working, and how much he saw the experience of entering graduate study in midlife as having all kinds of important developmental dimensions. Before the phenomenon that is now the theory and practice of transformative learning had really got up a head of steam, Fredric was working in a way that was consistent with that idea.

Of course, now Fielding has 35 years of history behind it. From being viewed as the new kid on the block of freestanding graduate institutions working in an adult-centered way, it is now the venerable elder. But age has not brought a dilution of the program's concern to treat people as adults. Its faculty has grown; new programs have been added, and it now has graduates across the world that can attest to the Fielding experience. Just as importantly, however, a cadre of faculty has developed that has consistently conducted a collaborative and critical analysis of their own experiences. This book gives a glimpse into that process.

The book's coeditors and all its contributors are all in some way affiliated with Fielding, and the practices they document reflect the breadth of Fielding's concerns. They bring a wide variety of theoretical perspectives to their understanding of transformative learning and consistently trace its connections to and location in diverse intellectual traditions. The sections on difference and diversity and on the performing arts are particularly noteworthy given that transformative learning has sometimes appeared as a White-dominated area of scholarship and as overly focused on modes of rational analysis. As I read these sections, they extended and sometimes challenged my thinking in a useful way.

In a time of racism and widespread racial micro-aggressions, of shameless ideological manipulation and of uncritical jingoism, we need more than ever to transform the structures and systems within which we learn our identity, create meaning, and live purposefully. *Innovations in Transformative Learning: Space, Culture, and the Arts* helps us envisage how those things might happen.

*Stephen Brookfield*
Minneapolis–St. Paul
March 2008

# Chapter 1

## Introduction: New Dimensions in Transformative Education

*Beth Fisher-Yoshida, Kathy D. Geller, and Steven A. Schapiro*

Transformative learning has been widely embraced as a means of teaching for change through intentional action. While its basic principles have been applied in situations outside the academy, the writings on transformative learning generally have provided little insight into its use in such settings. Rather, these writings have focused primarily on classroom applications and on research and theory. Patricia Cranton (2006) notes, "Oddly, we have few resources for practitioners," and she further queries, "How can transformative learning be encouraged . . . In the workplace? In informal self-help groups? In community development initiatives?" (p. vi). Cranton's question draws attention to the current disconnection between transformative learning theory as espoused and practiced in the academy and the application of transformative learning tenets in the workplace, in communities, and in other non-formal educational settings. This book addresses this disconnection by providing examples and analyses of the application of transformative learning beyond formal classroom settings and by articulating new models of transformative education that integrate transformative learning theory with other models of change and development.

This publication grew out of a series of conversations amongst a diverse group of people drawn together by our mutual belief in the potential power of transformative learning to positively impact individuals, our organizations, our communities, and our society. Following a meeting we had at the Sixth International Transformative Learning Conference, where many of us presented our work, we became very excited about the unique contribution to the field that we could make as a group and began putting together this volume.

We first crossed paths as faculty and students in the doctoral program at the Fielding Graduate University's School of Human and Organization Development. The program, originally designed using the adult learning principles of Malcolm Knowles, has in recent years integrated more collaborative and critical modes of learning. In its current form, this interdisciplinary human development and organizational systems program offers faculty and students the opportunity to work collaboratively on professional and research interests. Faculty members are scholars and practitioners with extensive experience in research, practice, social activism, and policy. Their disciplinary backgrounds include psychology, sociology, anthropology, political science, education, social work, theology, law, and communications. Doctoral students enter at midlife with extensive professional practice—as organizational consultants, lawyers, family therapists, human resource specialists, educators, community activists, and more—and emerge as broadly based scholar-practitioners dedicated to bringing theory to life and adding life to theory in diverse settings. This rich mix of diverse multidisciplinary perspectives and broad professional experience creates a dynamic, challenging, and catalytic learning environment for faculty and students alike.

It has been our lived experience as scholar-practitioners that practitioners often reside on one end of a continuum and scholars on the other. This is evident in how scholars and practitioners frequently communicate—assigning different meanings to the same words or saying the same thing but with different vocabularies and manners of expression. Given the demands of their environmental context, the practitioner generally·works from a sense of urgency and a need for completion in response to client or institutional demands; while the scholar focuses on ensuring the validity and reliability of a research-based approach to concept development. Practitioners tend to operate on tacit knowledge and base their future actions on previous experiences, without necessarily considering the theoretical underpinning of the approach; their range of practice may be broad and eclectic. Alternatively, scholars operate from focused depth and the grounding that theory provides. Theories are dealt with in their purest form with little evidence of the blending characteristics of a more pragmatic approach. It is in the space between—the middle ground—where we as scholar-practitioners reside. As scholar-practitioners, we draw upon the best of the worlds of both theory and practice and act as translators bridging the divide.

The stories presented in this book are drawn from this intermediate space. Individually and collectively working with transformative learning theory and transformative education, the contributors to this volume live and engage in our professional endeavors across a range of global settings. We are a diverse group of people, a mélange of individuals who offer the flavoring of our families of origin, historical roots, ethnicities, learned cultures, and practices.

The work we do is centered in communities, multinational corporations, not-for-profit organizations, governmental agencies, and graduate schools in global locations. What we have in common is an overarching belief in social justice and a commitment to adult learning and development that fosters the conscious use of critical reflection, the personal willingness to challenge assumptions, the recognition of complexity inherent in the situations in which we are engaged, and the willingness to challenge assumptions, question conformity, and embrace difference.

Moving from the traditional university classroom where most research in this area has been conducted, the stories we present in these pages describe transformative learning theory used to create conscious interventions drawing on the expressive and performative arts, applied cross-culturally in graduate education and in leadership development programs in Asia, Africa, and the Middle East and developed through multidisciplinary approaches synergistically integrated with theories of communication, participatory action research, and communities of inquiry and practice.

As we listened to the stories and read each other's work, three overarching themes emerged: (1) creating space for transformative learning; (2) looking through the lens of culture, difference, and diversity; and (3) animating awareness through the expressive and performative arts. These themes became the organizing framework for this volume, with four chapters on each. Before turning to a more detailed introduction to these themes and chapters, we offer a brief overview of the field of transformative learning in order to place this contribution within the literature and to provide a common conceptual foundation for what follows.

## Transformation, Transformative Learning, and Transformative Education

Transformative learning and transformative education are not new phenomena. Although described in those terms only in recent decades, they have been present in probably every culture since at least the beginning of recorded history. From the rites of passage rituals of many indigenous peoples, to medieval monasteries, to feminist consciousness-raising groups, and the freedom schools of the civil rights movement, the intentional use of educational experiences to bring about deep transformations in human consciousness and behavior has existed in many forms throughout history. While an academic discourse using these terms has existed for only the last 30 years or so and has taken place primarily within the North American and European contexts, we believe it is important that we not limit our exploration to just that dominant discourse. We provide below a brief review of the recent literature that uses these terms with the intention of providing a context into which other perspectives will be integrated and discussed.

During the last three decades, transformative learning has taken an increasingly prominent place within the field of adult education. Since 1998, a now biannual international conference has been held, and since 2003, the *Journal of Transformative Education* has been published. During this period, the premises of Jack Mezirow's original theory have been considered, questioned, expanded, and revised; alternative theories and perspectives on transformative learning and transformative education have been articulated; and attempts have been made to identify common ground amongst these various perspectives. In this brief review, we summarize key perspectives and describe the areas of differentiation and integration.

A brief explanation of this ongoing development of transformative theory and practice follows, beginning with a discussion of Mezirow, whose work has been the starting place in how this field has been conceptualized within adult learning and development in higher education. One of the contributions this book makes is to broaden the boundaries of this field by acknowledging and drawing on other theories and practices of change that describe transformation from other perspectives.

Mezirow drew on his 1975 study of adult women returning to college to articulate a process of perspective transformation that he claimed to be a fundamental dynamic of adult learning and adult development, a process that occurs as we attempt to make meaning of our experience (Mezirow, 1978). From this perspective (which he fully articulated in his book *Transformative Dimensions of Adult Learning* [1991]), transformative learning is presented as a process through which adults critically reflect on assumptions underlying their frames of reference and resulting beliefs, values, and perspectives; engage in a reflective rational dialogue about those assumptions; and, as a result, transform their assumptions and frames of reference to make them more inclusive, open, and better justified.

This theory draws on a constructivist perspective about how we humans make meaning of our experience, and on Habermas's theory of communicative action that denotes three kinds of learning: instrumental, communicative, and emancipatory. In these terms, transformative learning emancipates us from the uncritically assimilated assumptions underlying what Mezirow later came to call our "habits of mind" and "points of view" about ourselves and the world, making it possible for us to think and to act in new ways (Mezirow et al., 2000).

Habits of mind are sets of assumptions—"broad, generalized, orienting predispositions that act as filters for interpreting the meaning of experience" (p. 17)—that include (but are not limited to) the following epistemic domains—sociolinguistic, moral-ethical, philosophical, psychological, and aesthetic.

In articulating and refining this theory, Mezirow was not proposing a new kind of learning but rather was describing a process that adults experience as a natural part of living, learning, and developing. By making this process explicit, he opened the door to adult educators to be more intentional in trying to foster this kind of transformation (or development) through planned transformative educational experiences, and for others to critique his theory and to describe other transformative outcomes and other transformative paths. As Carolyn Clark (1993) noted in perhaps the first comprehensive review of transformative learning theory, "The transformation process has been extensively studied by psychologists and by developmental theorists, but it is only in the last 20 years that it has become a subject of interest in adult education and thus conceptualized as a learning process" (p. 48).

Mezirow's broad new theory of adult learning attracted much attention because it helped to explain the process through which many kinds of adult learning experiences and approaches result in deep changes in how we understand ourselves and our world. This broad applicability of the theory was made clear in *Fostering Critical Reflection in Adulthood: A Guide to Transformative and Emancipatory Learning* (Mezirow et al., 1990) which included articles about such diverse practices as action-learning in the workplace, women's consciousness-raising groups, popular education for social change, group psychotherapy, journal writing, autobiography, and reflection on critical incidents. This work made clear how Mezirow's model, with its range of epistemic assumptions from the psychological to the social and ideological, could be useful in explaining and helping us to understand the process of change in these different aspects of our consciousness. The theory as described built upon other representations of transformation first published in the 1970s, ranging from Paulo Freire's (1973) *Education for Critical Consciousness,* to Roger Gould's (1978) *Transformations: Growth and Change in Adult Life.*

While the broad relevance of Mezirow's theory is recognized, the attention also has inevitably brought a variety of critiques about its limitations. Challenges to the theory have focused primarily on two areas. The first area of critique concerns Mezirow's individualistic and psychological conceptualization of transformation as occurring within atomized individual psyches, as opposed to seeing it as a process in which individual transformation happens in specific cultural-political locations and in the context of social action and social transformation (Collard & Law, 1989; Newman, 1994; Tisdell, 2003).

For Mezirow, individual transformation of meaning perspectives may (or may not) lead to social action and transformation. For Freire, individual transformation happens only through praxis, which for him meant an ongoing cycle of collective action and reflection. This critique has focused on both the moral-political domain of those concerned about what they assert as a necessarily social-political mission for adult education, as well as the question of epistemology and of how learning occurs (Schugurensky, 2002).

The second broad area of critique has concerned Mezirow's conceptualization of transformation as a primarily rational process. Others have challenged his exclusion of the emotional, intuitive, and the nonrational aspects of our consciousness as drivers of transformation (Dirkx, 2000; Kasl & Yorks, 2002; Tisdell, 2003).

The growing prominence of Mezirow's theory within the field of adult education led not only to these critiques but also to many efforts to find parallels to and differences from other theories and practices that, while not using the term "transformative learning," describe learning experiences that can result in transformations of various kinds.[1] These comparisons have helped to identify transformations that Mezirow's theory can explain and those that it cannot. They have also helped us to understand other kinds of transformative learning experiences. Before delving into these, it is important to address some definitional and terminological problems that make it difficult to compare and contrast the various theories and practices.

Since different theorists use the terms "transformation, transformative learning, and transformative education" in different ways, the efforts to develop an inclusive and integrative terminology of this field are very challenging. The term "transformative learning" itself is sometimes used by Mezirow and others to refer at once to three different but related ideas: a transformational outcome, a process of learning that is experienced by a learner, and an educational program or event designed to foster learning experiences that result in or catalyze a transformational outcome. As Elizabeth Kasl (2006) pointed out in her reflections on the most recent Transformative Learning Conference: "currently there are three different concepts that have become muddied: learning, transformation, and pedagogical practices" (p. 148). For purposes of this discussion, we would like to suggest that the following terminology may be a helpful way in which to clear these waters.

*Transformation* as an outcome refers to a deep and lasting change, equivalent to what some people term a developmental shift or a change in worldview. As Carolyn Clark (1993) succinctly put it, "Transformative learning shapes people.

---

[1] See Baumgartner, 2001; Clark, 1993; Dirkx, 1998; Taylor, 1998, 2005 for a full discussion.

They are different afterward, in ways both they and others can recognize" (p. 47). In all of the theories, the outcomes are considered to be positive and to have a directionality toward growth, enabling people to move toward habits of mind and habits of being that involve such qualities as greater inclusiveness, openness, wholeness, awareness, choice, wisdom, voice, and/or more power to explain our experiences and the power relations in which we are embedded.

*Transformative learning,* although used at times to refer to outcome, process, and/or pedagogy, is most aptly used to describe the intrapsychic and/or behavioral process of a learner involved in a transformative experience—it is about what the learner does, feels, and experiences. Transformative learning as conceptualized in this way can and does occur through life experience itself, as well as through formal or informal educational programs.

*Transformative education* is a term best used to refer to a planned educational program, experience, intervention, or set of pedagogical practices that are designed to enable people to experience transformative learning and as a result become transformed in some particular way or at least to begin a process of transformation. Transformative education programs could include such diverse practices as personal growth groups, nontraditional graduate education, and popular education for social justice.[2]

We now use this definitional framework to describe the four major and sometimes overlapping streams of theory and practice in transformative learning that have been identified and included under the "transformative learning" umbrella during the past several years.[3]

In the **cognitive rational approach**, *transformation* is defined as a change in meaning perspective; transformative learning involves a process of disorientation, critical reflection on assumptions, dialogue, and action on new meaning perspectives; *transformative education* involves various ways of fostering critical reflection and dialogue on past experience and, at times, catalyzing the process through the intentional introduction of disorienting dilemmas and experiences (Mezirow, 1991; Cranton, 1994, 2006).

**The depth psychology approach** defines *transformation* as individuation, "a fundamental change in one's personality involving conjointly the resolution of personal dilemmas and the expansion of consciousness resulting in greater personality integration" (Boyd cited in Taylor, 1998, p. 13). *Transformative learning*

---

[2] It is important to note that the term transformative education as presented here is different from other representations. It has been used by Boyd and Myers (1988) to refer to education for Jungian individuation, and by Markos and McWhinney (2003) to refer specifically to what they term "fourth order" education for the third quarter of our lives.

[3] See Baumgartner, 2001; Clark, 1993; Dirkx, 1998; Taylor 1998, 2005.

for individuation involves an intuitive process of discernment and receptivity as images and symbols from the individual and collective unconscious are integrated into our consciousness. *Transformative education* in this model can involve group process or guided intrapersonal dialogue with the subconscious and involves the integration of affect, symbol, intuition, and imagination into the learning process (Boyd & Myers, 1988; Dirkx, 2000).

**The structural developmental approach** defines *transformation* as a shift to a different stage of development, sometimes conceptualized as a higher order of consciousness. As described by developmentalists such as King and Kitchener (1994), Kegan (2000), and Belenky et al. (1986), these shifts involve changes in our epistemologies and ways of making meaning toward more inclusive, integrative, and complex ways of knowing. *Transformative learning* in this approach occurs through confronting the limitations of our previous ways of making meaning and exposure to other more satisfactory forms.

*Transformative education* for structural development includes a key role for mentors, teachers, or others in one's life in helping people to engage in a process of whole person learning, of connected knowing as well as separate knowing, and in providing the right balance of affirmation and challenge (Belenky et al., 1986; Daloz, 1999; Kegan, 2000).

While these first three approaches focus on the psychological development (cognitive and/or noncognitive) of individuals (which may or may not lead to social transformation), other approaches see transformative learning as a necessarily integrated process of individual and social transformation.

**The social emancipatory approach** defines *transformation* as the development of critical consciousness. In Freire's words, education for critical consciousness (conscientization) is "the process through which men [*sic*] not as recipients, but as knowing subjects, achieve a deepening awareness of both the sociocultural reality that shapes their lives and of their capacity to transform that reality" (Freire, 1976, p. 27). The *transformative learning* process leading to critical consciousness involves praxis—a continuing process of action, critical reflection, and dialogue. *Transformative education* from this perspective includes various forms of critical pedagogy, ideology critique, and popular education (Brookfield, 1995; Freire, 1970; hooks, 1994; Horton, 1990).

Building on these four major approaches, much recent work in transformative learning has integrated elements of one or more of them. Other more recently articulated approaches integrate elements of the individual and/or social transformation emphasized in these major streams.

**The cultural-spiritual approach** shares much of the goals and process of the social emancipatory perspective but adds recognition of the role of culture, spirituality, symbolic content, nonrational ways of knowing, and narrative in the learning process (Abalos, 1996; Tisdell, 2003).

Another variation of the social emancipatory is **the race-centric approach**, which uses a framework of education for liberation but puts race and power at the center of the analysis, within the learning process itself as well as in the wider sociopolitical context (Johnson-Bailey & Alfred, 2006; Sheared, 1994).

Finally, the integral or **planetary approach**, as articulated by Edmund O'Sullivan and colleagues (2002), presents a vision of *transformative learning* that integrates individual, spiritual, and social transformation in a call for a new cosmology that will fundamentally alter our relationship to the earth as well as to one another. This view advocates a holistic learning process and a movement toward what O'Sullivan describes (O'Sullivan, 1999) as a tripartite vision of *transformative education* involving tools for survival, critique, and vision.

Looking at these perspectives as a group, we can see that their conceptualizations of *transformation, transformative learning,* and *transformative education* vary along such dimensions as psychological versus social, rational versus nonrational, conscious versus subconscious, and universal versus culture-specific. We can also see, as Taylor (2005) points out, that they all share to some degree an emphasis on experience, critical reflection, and dialogue in the learning process.

Moving beyond this necessary effort to differentiate amongst the various perspectives, there has in recent years been a parallel movement toward a more integrative theory and practice of transformative learning that could accommodate or account for some or all of these different perspectives. Cranton and Roy (2003), for instance, find much overlap among the concepts of perspective transformation, individuation, and authenticity. They argue that each involves a process of moving beyond a socially assimilated way of being and conclude that "how people transform or open up their perspectives, grow and develop as persons, and learn to live as their authentic selves" are all ways of talking about different dimensions of a similar process (p. 97). Reviewing all of the major perspectives, they contend that "if we bring these strands together, we can see that the central process of transformative learning may be rational, affective, extra-rational, experiential, or any combination—depending on the individual and the context. . . . One person, depending on psychological preferences, may engage in self-reflection, others may see the journey as imaginative" (p. 90).

Yorks and Kasl (2006) make a similar argument, maintaining that we need to understand more about how various ways of knowing, including expressive ways, can lead to different kinds of transformative learning processes. At the same time, drawing on Heron's work about the phenomenology of experiential learning, Kasl and York argue that all transformations involve our emotions as well as our thinking, our "habits of being" as well as our habits of mind. And they offer a definition to potentially incorporate all of the perspectives that we discussed.

> We define transformative learning as a change in how a person both affectively experiences and conceptually frames his or her experience of the world when pursuing learning that is personally developmental, socially controversial, or requires personal or social healing. (Yorks and Kasl, 2006, p. 45)

That broad definition leaves room for us to continue to expand our understanding of the learning dimensions of many kinds of transformation that people may experience. As we have seen, our understanding of transformative learning has become more comprehensive and complex as it has grown to address the different dimensions of our being; as it is applied to other contexts and integrated with other ways of thinking about learning, change, and transformation, the theory and practice will continue to develop.

The discourse on transformative learning has taken place primarily within the theory and practice of formal adult education. This book builds on that discourse by broadening how we think about and foster transformative learning for adults, consciously creating transformative education approaches to support adult learning across the lifespan. The need for an expanded pragmatic view of transformative learning is a natural progression in the way the theory is being applied. This is especially poignant when we consider the world we live in—a world that is becoming increasingly more complex and in which mobility and information transference and sharing is more widespread.

## We Add to the Conversation on Transformative Learning

In the chapters that follow, we introduce the reader to applications of transformative learning in communities, collaborative partnerships, organizations, and small groups, across cultures and through the visual and performative arts. In exploring the use of transformative learning in more varied contexts, and in relation to other theories and practices of individual, organizational, and social change, it is our hope that this book will contribute to this ongoing conversation. As you wander through the chapters in the book, one of the discoveries you will make is how transformative learning is partnered and integrated with other theories and approaches to develop new ways of looking at the phenomenon of transformation. Some examples of this integration emerge from the focus on creating spaces that are designed to foster transformative learning, as viewed through the lenses of creating student-centered graduate level educational programs, expanding research epistemologies to include collaborative inquiry, and embracing participative processes in areas such as action research.

Another illustration is in the chapters that draw upon *intercultural* experiences as opportunities for transformation. We may or may not intend to be transformed as we engage in encounters with others who are different from ourselves, yet these interactions have ways of surprising us. We may expect a certain response but instead are met with a reaction that is very different from what we envisioned. We have opportunities to become aware of the range of options and the developmental schema for dealing with difference (Bennett and Bennett, 2004). Our contributions here span a range of awareness—from reflecting on our thoughts and words to the bodily sensations we feel when our assumptions are challenged.

The study of *communication* as a vehicle for fostering and understanding transformation is playing a more central role in how some are working with transformative learning in the field and as a source of study in research initiatives. One particular social theory that takes a communication perspective is that of Coordinated Management of Meaning (CMM) originally developed by Cronen and Pearce (1982) and subsequently applied through research and practice in related fields such as therapy, education, conflict, and diversity. CMM is grounded in social constructionism, in which meaning is made in relationship and embedded in multiple contexts. Several of the chapters in this volume discuss the role CMM plays in combination with transformative learning.

As explained above, more recent contributions to transformative literature have expanded on Mezirow's original conception of transformative learning as being primarily a cognitive function to incorporate other realms of existence such as intrapsychic processes and emotions. Some of the contributors in this volume have built on this initial conception and subsequent expansions in the field by including the arts, both expressive and performative, through integrating transformative learning with improvisation, theater of the oppressed, and "bodymindfullness."

## Chapter Summaries

Following are brief descriptions of the chapters in each of the three sections of the book: (1) Creating Space for Transformative Learning; (2) Looking through the Lens of Culture, Difference, and Diversity; and (3) Animating Awareness through the Expressive and Performative Arts.

## Creating Space for Transformative Learning

In *Learning in the Space between Us,* Martin Leahy and Sue Gilly describe what they define as collaborative transformative learning (CTL) and explore how to create the conditions that make such learning possible. They explain the circumstances of their own CTL experience, one that preceded exposure to the transformative learning literature. Building off a two-year interpersonal CTL experience with each other (their subsequent dissertation research into aspects of these experiences, and their work since facilitating CTL experiences for other groups in business organizations and academia), Gilly and Leahy introduce and describe the four commitments that are central to the development of practices to sustain CTL over time: (1) being intentional about creating a certain kind of time and space; (2) being willing to struggle; (3) being together in the space between us; (4) being in inquiry around questions that matter. The foundation for all of these commitments is relationship.

In her chapter, *Learning Space/Work Space: Can We Make Room for Transformative Learning in Organizations?,* Pamela Meyer addresses that question by presenting key findings from her work and research with adults' experiences in learning theatrical improvisation. These findings challenge the assumptions behind much of the prevailing learning practice in organizations and offer recommendations for practitioners to help them create learning spaces that are conducive to transformation in organizational settings. She presents these recommendations in terms of five lessons from improvisation: (1) acknowledge fears and expectations; (2) share responsibility for the learning space; (3) hold the learning space until everyone can hold it for themselves; (4) name the givens; and (5) practice attunement. Using these lessons, she explains how organizational practitioners can respond to their charge to achieve transformational learning outcomes.

Working with a not-for-profit client organization with members who have been convicted of crimes, Beth Fisher-Yoshida, in *Transformative Learning in Participative Processes That Reframe Self-identity,* describes profound transformative learning experiences that occurred through an "appreciative participatory action research" (A-PAR) approach, creating a space for learning through action. The process she introduces encouraged "Second Chance" members to engage at a level of involvement that was deep and profound enough to cause the experience of transformative moments that shifted how they viewed themselves. The members rewrote the stories of who they are, and their identities changed as they began to realize and accept that they were more capable than they previously believed. They took ownership of and led change in their organization.

Drawing on varied experiences in student-centered collaborative education for midlife adult learners (in a research study on adult development and transformative learning, and in the literature), Steve Schapiro presents a model for transformative graduate education in his chapter, *A Crucible for Transformation: The Alchemy of Student-Centered Education for Adults at Midlife.* This crucible serves as a container that (1) holds learners in a safe space and provides a boundary for their learning experience; (2) turns up the heat and the fire that "unfreezes" people and melts their rigid frames of reference and ways of knowing, (3) adds new ingredients to the mix in the form of new paradigms, perspectives, and ways of learning; and (4) provides continuing support as learners "cool down" to solidify a new sense of self as scholar-practitioners. Using Kegan's concept of cultures of embeddedness and the "confirming, contradicting, and continuing functions" of holding environments that support growth, development, and transformation, Schapiro's model adds a fourth function—"creation"—that must follow contradiction if change is to occur.

## Looking through the Lens of Culture, Difference, and Diversity

In *Culture Matters: Developing Culturally Responsive Transformative Learning Experiences in Communities of Color,* her collaborative inquiry into the shared experiences of being a *strong Black woman* provides the context for Charlyn Green Fareed's introduction to a culturally responsive transformative learning model to catalyze transformations within the context of community-based inquiry groups. She offers a powerful design for personal, group, and community learning, presenting a valuable framework for attending to specific cultural learning needs that are vital to successful outcomes. Blending collaborative inquiry, transformative learning perspectives, and participatory action research, Green Fareed introduces a four-goal model inclusive of (1) creating culturally sensitive learning environments; (2) encouraging culturally inclusive learning experiences; (3) creating opportunities for critical reflection and learning through critical questioning on culturally shared meaning; and (4) assessing personal and group learning and change using evaluation methods that allow freedom of expression.

Ann Davis provides insights into an integrated understanding of transformative learning related to culture, communication, and consciousness in *Socially Constructing a Transformed Self-view and Worldview.* She suggests a paradigm for understanding how successful long-term work life experiences in nonnative cultures offer the basis for transformation of individual boundaries and conscious reframing of both one's self-view and worldview. In drawing on her narrative research with expatriates from diverse cultures of origin, Davis introduces evidence of transformative learning's applicability beyond North America. Davis integrates Mezirow's (2000) view of transformative learning with Kim's integrated theory of communication and cross-cultural adaptation, and Pearce's CMM, suggesting a conceptual model for preparing expatriates for success through promotion of reciprocated perception and communication action work with the goal to promoting "global" consciousness in the self/other orientation.

With changing organization demographics in the United States plus the impact of globalization on multinational organizations, Ilene Wasserman and Placida Gallegos in their chapter, *Engaging Diversity: Disorienting Dilemmas That Transform Relationships,* respond to the challenge of creating inclusive workplaces that leverage the value of diversity. Recognizing the innate power of disorienting dilemmas inherent in the challenge to communicate across difference, Wasserman and Gallegos suggest that it is at the point where individuals and workgroups are confused, thrown into uncertain situations, and in conflict that the choice to engage in critical reflection and storytelling in relationship with another may create breakthrough experiences for coworkers and organizations. Synthesizing transformative learning with Pearce's CMM, Kegan and Lahey's seven languages of transformation, and Senge et al.'s exploration of profound change, they introduce the R-E-A-L model for diversity consulting as a proven methodology for organizational learning.

Working with transnational leaders at the middle and senior levels in multinational organizations based in Asia, Africa, and the Middle East, Kathy Geller was charged with creating a leadership curriculum that would prepare global leaders for the exigencies of the twenty-first century. In *Transformative Learning Dynamics for Developing Relational Leaders,* Geller introduces the reader to the confluence of transformative learning, intercultural communication, and transformational leadership as the basis for a new model of relational leadership development in a transnational framework. Building on the work of Taylor, and using content analysis, she introduces and operationalizes six dynamics of transformative learning, suggesting a foundation for increasing levels of reflective action, intercultural appreciation, employee engagement, and ethical action amongst leaders. Her work reflects on the applicability of transformative learning beyond North America and provides a basis for the conscious inclusion of transformative learning interventions for developing leaders.

## Animating Awareness Through the Expressive and Performative Arts

Storytelling as a means of facilitating transformative learning is explored in Annabelle Nelson's chapter, *Storytelling and Transformational Learning.* The ancient oral tradition of storytelling has been used as a means of passing on cultural values and norms to generations in the process of acculturating them into the existing culture. Stories can be used also to transform our consciousness as they may question our current perceptions and cognitive frames and create new frames in their place. Storytelling also calls on the use of metaphor and in so doing connects directly with our subconscious, bypassing our conscious minds and the frames that may be limiting our development. Nelson builds on the links between Piaget and Jung and further connects them to Dirkx and Mezirow as she shows how this psychological development and identity alignment can foster transformative learning.

In the chapter *Bodymindfulness for Skillful Use of Self,* Adair Linn Nagata shows that when we attend to our experiences at multiple levels of body, mind, feelings/emotions, and spirit, we engage with them more holistically, which results in a deeper level of engagement with a more profound understanding of ourselves and the experience. Nagata coined the term *bodymindfulness* based on two concepts: (1) bodymind as a way of paying attention to the systemic nature of lived experiences and (2) mindfulness from the Buddhist practice of developing awareness of self, other, and experience. She used this approach with graduate students in a leading university in Japan with whom she is working and cites their experiences and reflections throughout the chapter. Nagata situates this work in the transformative learning literature that emphasizes extrarational, whole person learning as espoused by Taylor, Boyd, Myers, Dirkx, and others.

*Dreamscape* is an approach that addresses knowledge creation in organizations. In more recent years, there have been socially constructed linguistic turns in knowledge creation. The newest wave, of which dreamscape is a part, is the performative turn, as Tiffany von Emmel describes it in her chapter, *Dreamscape: A Multimedia Collaboration Method.* This performative turn offers a new and refreshing approach to transforming an organization's culture. The author identifies four types of transformation that dreamscape facilitates: (1) connectivity, (2) new meaning, (3) embodiment of values, and (4) adult development. One important characteristic of dreamscape is that it is a participatory process, and it is this participation that is used as a theory of organization development.

In *Black Mama Sauce: Embodied Transformative Education,* Hameed (Herukhuti) Williams uses Theatre of the Oppressed, yoga, and ritual as a means to practice a form of transformative education that is both embodied and decolonizing—a form that he calls "Black Mama Sauce." Williams doesn't claim to have created "Black Mama Sauce," noting that it was created by many cultural workers, activists, revolutionaries, and community organizers. He states that this rich history and tradition of transformative education was present in Black working-class communities in the United States, in the 1960s and 1970s, and that it is yet to be incorporated with the more traditional transformative literature. Williams draws on Black feminist thought, Afrocentricity, and decolonizing queer theory as elements of his theoretical framework. He shares several personal experiences working with groups and organizations that exemplify the application of this theory and the resulting outcomes and consequences that were produced.

Each of the three sections summarized above ends with a discussion of the common threads, the implications for practice, and the questions these authors

raised for further inquiry. In a concluding chapter, we summarize the overarching themes and discuss the contributions of this volume to the theory and
practice of transformative learning and transformative education.

## References

Abalos, D. (1996). *Strategies of transformation toward a multicultural society: Fulfilling the story of democracy.* Westport, CT: Praeger.

Baumgartner, L. M. (2001). An update on transformative learning. *New Directions for Adult and Continuing Education, 89*(Spring), 15–24.

Belenky, M., Clinchy, B., Goldberger, N., & Tarule, J. (1986). *Women's ways of knowing.* New York: Basic Books.

Bennett, J. M., & Bennett M. J. (2004). *Developing intercultural competence: A reader.* Portland, OR: Intercultural Communication Institute

Boyd, R. D., & Myers, J. G. (1988). Transformative education. *International Journal of Lifelong Education, 7*(4), 261–284.

Brookfield, S. D. (1995). *Becoming a critically reflective teacher.* San Francisco: Jossey-Bass.

Clark, M. C. (1993). Transformational learning. In S., Merriam (Ed.), *An update on adult learning theory: New directions for adult and continuing education.* 57. San Francisco: Jossey-Bass.

Collard, S., & Law, M. (1989). The limits of perspective transformation: A critique of Mezirow's theory. *Adult Education Quarterly, 39,* pp. 99–107.

Cranton, P. (1994). *Understanding and promoting transformative learning.* San Francisco: Jossey-Bass.

Cranton, P. (2006). *Understanding and promoting transformative learning,* 2nd edition. San Francisco: Jossey-Bass.

Cranton, P., & Roy, M. (2003). When the bottom falls out of the bucket: Toward a holistic perspective on transformative learning. *Journal of Transformative Education, 1*(2), 86–99.

Cronen, V. E., & Pearce, W. B. (Eds.) (1982). *The coordinated management of meaning: A theory of communication.* New York: Harper and Row.

Daloz. L. (1999). *Mentor: Guiding the journey of adult learners.* San Francisco: Jossey-Bass.

Dirkx, J. (1998). Transformative learning theory in the practice of adult education: An overview. *PAACE Journal of Lifelong Learning. v. 7, 1–14.*

Dirkx, J. (2000). Transformative learning and the journey of individuation. ERIC Digest No. 223. Columbus, OH: ERIC Clearinghouse on Adult, Vocational and Continuing Education.

Freire, P. (1970). *Pedagogy of the oppressed.* New York: Seabury Press.

Freire, P. (1973). *Education for critical consciousness.* New York: Seabury Press.

Freire, P. (1976) A few notes on conscientization. In R. Dale (Ed.), *Schooling and capitalism.* London: Routledge.

Gould, R. (1978). *Transformations: Growth and change in adult life.* New York: Simon and Schuster.

hooks, b. (1994). *Teaching to transgress: Education as the practice of freedom*. London: Routledge.

Horton, M. (1990). *The long haul*. New York: Doubleday.

Johnson-Bailey, L., & Alfred, M. (2006). Transformational teaching and the practices of Black women adult educators. In E. W. Taylor (Ed.), *Teaching for change: Fostering transformative learning in the classroom. New Directions for Adult and Continuing Education, 109*(Spring). 49–58. San Francisco: Jossey-Bass.

Kasl, E. (2006). Reflections on the sixth International Transformative Learning Conference. *Journal of Transformative Education, 4*(2).

Kasl, E., & Yorks, L. (2002). An extended epistemology for transformative learning theory and its application through collaborative inquiry. *TCRecord.org*. Retrieved January 28, 2002, from http://www.tcrecord.org.

Kegan, R. (2000). What form transforms? A constructive-developmental approach to transformative learning. In J. Mezirow (Ed.), *Learning as transformation: Critical perspectives on a theory in progress,* pp. 35–70. San Francisco: Jossey-Bass.

King, P., & Kitchener, K. S. (1994). *Developing reflective judgment: Understanding and promoting intellectual growth and critical thinking in adolescents and adults*. San Francisco: Jossey-Bass.

Markos, L., & McWhinney, W. (2003). Transformative education: Across the threshold. *Journal of Transformative Education, 1*(1).

Mezirow, J. (1978). Perspective transformation. *Adult Education Quarterly*, 27, 100–110.

Mezirow, J. (1991). *Transformative dimensions of adult learning*. San Francisco: Jossey-Bass.

Mezirow, J., & Associates. (1990). *Fostering critical reflection in adulthood: A guide to transformative and emancipatory learning*. San Francisco: Jossey-Bass.

Mezirow, J., & Associates. (2000). *Learning as transformation: Critical perspectives on a theory in progress*. San Francisco: Jossey-Bass.

Morrow, R., & Torres, C. A. (2002). *Reading Freire and Habermas: Critical pedagogy and transformative social change*. New York: Teachers College Press.

Newman, M. (1994). *Defining the enemy: Adult education in social action*. Sydney Australia: Victor Stewart.

O'Sullivan, E. V. (1999). *Transformative learning: Educational vision for the 21st century*. London: Zed Books.

O'Sullivan, E. V., Morrell, A., & O'Connor, M. A. (Eds.). (2002). *Expanding the boundaries of transformative learning*. New York: Palgrave.

Schugurensky, D. (2002). Transformative learning and transformative politics: The pedagogical dimension of participatory democracy and social action. In

O'Sullivan, E. V. et al. (Eds.) *Expanding the boundaries of transformative learning.* New York: Palgrave.

Sheared, V. (1994). Giving voice: An inclusive model of instruction—A womanist perspective. In E. Hayes & S. A. J. Colin III (Eds.). *Confronting racism and sexism in adult education,* New directions for continuing education, No. 61. San Francisco: Jossey-Bass.

Taylor, E. W. (1998). The theory and practice of transformative learning: A critical review. Information Series No. 374. Columbus, OH: ERIC Clearinghouse on Adult, Vocational and Continuing Education.

Taylor, E. W. (2005). Making meaning of the varied and contested perspectives of transformative learning theory. In D. Vlosak, G. Kilebaso, & J. Radford (Eds.), *The Proceedings of the Sixth International Conference on Transformative Learning.* Michigan State University and Grand Rapids Community College.

Tisdell, E. (2003). *Exploring spirituality and culture in adult and higher education.* San Francisco: Jossey-Bass.

Yorks, L. & Kasl, E. (2006). I know more than I can say: A taxonomy for using expressive ways of knowing to foster transformative learning. *Journal of Transformative Education, 4*(1), 43–64.

# Section 1

## Creating Space for Transformative Learning

# Chapter 2

## Learning in the Space Between Us

*Martin J. Leahy and M. Sue Gilly*

*Transformation,* as our editors define it, refers to deep and lasting change. Imagine the complete metamorphosis from caterpillar to butterfly. For people, a similarly drastic change occurs with a developmental shift, change in order of consciousness, or a radical revision of the ways they make sense of things. It could be that the stories and myths that once gave meaning to life no longer satisfy or alternately that their beliefs and assumptions come under scrutiny, do not survive careful examination, and require change. Persons on the other side of transformation have more choices and greater freedom of action. For societies, reflection on and questioning of the existing order can lead to revolutionary change where transformation is tangible, for example, in revised social structures that advance equality.

*Transformative learning,* again from our editors' point of view, is most aptly used to describe the intrapsychic and/or behavioral process of a learner involved in a transformative experience. It is about what the learner does, feels, and experiences, such as feeling disoriented, critically reflecting on assumptions and frames of reference, engaging in dialogue, or integrating images from our subconscious. Transformative learning as conceptualized in this way can and does occur through life experience itself as well as through formal or informal educational programs.

Most of the research and writing on transformative learning examines what occurs with individual persons with a focus on cognitive and behavioral change and more recently on transformation in body and soul. Some research and writing also examines social and cultural change. So, there is significant work at the individual level, and some at the social or group level, but little in the domain of relationship between particular persons—in the space between us—where particular individuals, the group as a whole, and the space between are all transformed.

That interhuman domain is the locus of interest for this chapter. We will explore a community of three doctoral students who set out to study high-end collaboration and created a space between them that fostered *collaborative transformative learning* (CTL). What was the process of their learning? What did they experience, do, and feel that resulted in transformation at the levels of individual, group, and space between?

## How It Happened

We, the authors, along with Donna Wyatt were doctoral students at Fielding Graduate University who discovered that we had a shared fascination with collaboration. Each of us had different interests in the topic, yet they seemed to overlap in intriguing ways. We also had diverse disciplinary backgrounds and a variety of experiences with collaboration. We saw the potential for developing a rich understanding if we worked together.

We began by exploring how we might study others' experiences of collaboration but soon realized that studying others' experiences would not allow us to know collaboration from the inside, nor could we be assured of understanding high-end collaboration. When we described this dilemma to a faculty member, she suggested that we collaborate to study collaboration. We then saw that we wanted to study our own experience of collaboration as it developed over time; we became our own learning laboratory.

Because we came together informally in the "corridors" of our self-directed, distance learning program, we had to create our own work, structure, and ways of working together. We tried to find ways to do work we sensed was important even if there were few models for collaboration within our program. We made a commitment to stay together until we learned about high-end collaboration and could pass that on to others through our research, writing, and example.

The three of us worked together for over two years. Since we lived in various parts of the United States, we met quarterly for three- to five-day retreats, held a two-hour conference call nearly every Sunday, and communicated via e-mail between calls. Our intent remained throughout to create and sustain a space that cherished us—each person, all parts of ourselves—and made the most of our diversity. This broad standard of inclusion brought about much of our transformative learning.

Over time, we changed. Some transformative learning occurred through disorienting dilemmas that individually caused us to doubt our beliefs, values, or actions. Sometimes this was Descartes' cool methodical doubt, which led to cognitive reshuffling. More often, it felt like we were, as Nietzsche said, "philosophizing a hammer," managing paradoxical feelings of exhilaration and terror. By reflecting on our collaboration, we also called into question the group's beliefs, values, and actions in ways that ranged from curiosity-driven experiments with other ways of doing things to uninvited disputes that sparked collective bewilderment and sometimes painful feelings of isolation. We also experienced more gradual transformation over time, both as individuals and as a group. We came to know more fully the experience of really learning together. Even if minds and words failed us in conveying the experience, our bodies knew the meaning of terms such as true collaboration, breakthrough, stuck, unprecedented support, fearless commitment, despair, and love. We have come to call our experience *collaborative transformative learning*.

## "I and Thou Here and Now"

It is difficult to reflect on a living practice, a way of life, that we have not had the opportunity to live together with you, the reader. As we recall and reflect on experiences, we invite you to reflect with us and yet know that our inquiry is limited since we do not share those same experiences. We are now standing not in the same time and space talking about an experience we shared; we are in different places at separate times, us talking and you listening about an experience we did not share. You are being asked to trust that we are faithfully representing what happened and depicting it with words to transport you back in time to witness for yourself. As we *back away* from the experience, we lose the knowing that inevitably comes with standing together in the same time and space. As we speak to you on this page, we cannot see enthusiasm in your eyes, hear disagreement in your voice, or be elated, frightened, touched, or puzzled as happens in the give and take of a dialogue. Since we do not know those questions that might be your abiding concerns in your life, we speak in generalities, hoping to touch on something that matters to you. And we worry that the printed page connotes knowledge that is orthodox instead of knowing that is held lightly and open to your questioning. And since we do not know *you*, we cannot address you by name. It feels one way and as if ideas were more important than you and us.

We will endeavor to bridge this divide, at least in spirit, by addressing you and speaking ourselves in the first person. We, as authors, want you to know that our intention is to be with you in a way that gestalt therapy describes as "I and Thou Here and Now."

## Four Commitments

As we reflected on our experience, we concluded that our collaborative group had at its heart four commitments or ways of being: (1) being intentional about creating the time and space hospitable for both persons and transformative learning; (2) being willing to struggle, to step into the space between us and stay there without rushing prematurely to answers; (3) being determined to do this together, that is, meeting, including, and connecting with others and all aspects of ourselves; and (4) being in inquiry around questions that matter. At the center of all four of these commitments was relationship.

By commitment we mean a pledge, vow, or covenant between persons. These are promises freely taken; there is no obligation, no binding contract, nothing based on right action or word of honor. I hold myself accountable; you hold me accountable, and we hold one another accountable. The particular commitments develop from the work and values of the specific individuals involved. The ones here are ours, refined over time.

The development of commitments and practices is important work that needs to be done by each group. Through this process they develop collaborative skills and move from individuals to a functioning group. This work also has the power to transform both the individuals and the group itself. People in groups given guidelines and a monitor do not have the same possibilities for transformation as those in groups that create their own ways of being with one another and who grow to accept full responsibility for the functioning of the group. We invite you to experiment with the commitments that follow and to question, change, or create wholly new ones for your group.

Next we discuss each commitment and offer stories from our own group experience, as well as from groups with whom we have worked, to show how these commitments can be put into practice. Each commitment is discussed separately yet it is important to state that they comprise a wholeness that is indeed greater than the sum of the parts.

## Creating the Time and Space

### Step Back

CTL requires a certain kind of time and space, a special space, separate from the normal routine of daily lives. Step back from daily affairs, withdraw, detach, or retreat. This could be for days, hours, or minutes. If possible, leave your usual locale; find space that welcomes dialogue and then make that space your own by moving furniture, bringing in whatever you might need for conversation. Flipcharts, tables, and chairs might fit production work but rocking chairs and casual seating in a circle foster inquiry. Set position aside and operate as peers, without one leading and with all responsible for creating and sustaining this different time and space.

## Take Time

If it is not possible to leave the usual locale, take 10 minutes for everyone to be silent and look within yourselves to see how you are feeling; experiment with ways to change space to make it possible to step back from what is going on and engage in inquiry and dialogue. It is important to make time for conversations to unfold and have a life of their own with no interruption or premature closure. Hold agendas lightly; put outcomes in the background; pay attention to what is happening between and among you "here and now."

## Be Fully Present

Do whatever it takes so everyone is fully present. We found it important to check in with one another at the start of a meeting, to take time to hear what was going on in each of our lives and anything that might keep us back from being present. Commitments, obligations, and problems with things outside the group's work are put on hold. Change physical space whenever task requires it or when energy fades. Business groups with whom we have worked began creating this special time and space by having a relaxing dinner together. Groups are accustomed to paying attention to the tangible aspects of being together, getting a meeting room, and creating an agenda, exchanging documents but rarely consider what is needed for everyone to be comfortable and fully present.

It is easier to step back, make time, and be fully present as time goes on; familiarity creates comfort and safety. It helps to stay connected between meetings with e-mails and teleconferences. This constancy creates a history for the group. Rituals develop that connect people.

Creating the right time and space can be challenging. A Vice President of Human Resources asked us to facilitate a retreat for his team to explore individual worldviews for "organization." We found a homelike bed and breakfast on a large farm with spectacular gardens. The plan included the team preparing and eating dinner together, socializing and staying overnight, and working a full day with time to enjoy the gardens and one another's company. At the last minute, the Finance Department insisted on a preferred vendor—a national chain hotel right on congested Route 1 in the Northeast Corridor. Even if we did not hear horns blaring, we could count on being stuck in generic, institutional rooms with no character and likely no windows. We had done our best work in places that support stepping out of the day-to-day such as retreat houses over-looking the Pacific, lodges in Pennsylvania's Pocono Mountains, and a centu-ries-old home just outside the walls of Vatican City. It is easy to fall into the trap of habit, to assume that a certain kind of place is essential; we needed to find a different way of creating time and space.

For the retreat we decided to have dinner together in a private room of a Chinese restaurant with good food. Twelve of us sat around one large table and took turns giving appreciation to each other. Speakers did not characterize the person making him or her a thing, albeit a good thing, rather they spoke from their experience of that person, offering positive regard (Kegan & Lahey, 2001) for the person as well as his or her work.

The following morning, we asked people to deposit their electronic devices on a side table, had a 15–20-minute conversation about creating space and time for important conversations. We introduced and invited them to experiment with three commitments: to struggle, be together, and ask questions that mat-tered to them. We contrasted these practices with the rush to resolution, self-interest, and worship of answers present in the typical workday. The dinner and the brief opening conversation created a space that was tremendously hospita-ble to transformative learning.

## Willingness to Struggle

With this next commitment, we would like to convey what living this was like for us. We can provide you with descriptions of incidents that were significant for us, but stepping into the between is not always significant or memorable. It is like trying to describe sunsets to someone. The ones that come to mind are the brilliantly colored ones or the ones that occurred in a special place or with someone special but describing does not convey the full range of what sunsets are like.

In addition, if you describe a memorable sunset, sharing how brilliant the reds, oranges, and yellows were streaked across the sky, the way the colors changed so quickly, how you felt connected with something larger, you still would not have done more than a satisfactory job. Because a sunset is not any one of those things mentioned, and it is not all those things added together, nor is it the same as a depiction such as a photograph. It is something that happens to your whole self, something that you know from being there. There is some sort of emergence that makes it so much more than anything that can be con-veyed to someone else.

*Step into the between.* That said, a willingness to struggle involves stepping into the between. One time the three of us were together, staying at one of our homes in order to get some face-to-face work done. We took a break, sat around the kitchen table, and discussed our graduate program. Martin gave his perspective and Sue voiced hers. Donna silently listened as Martin and Sue went back and forth explaining how they saw things. The conversation heated up and moved toward an argument. Sue felt that her perspective was important and expressed frustration; Martin was either not listening or she was unable to communicate in a way she would be heard. Martin felt angry that he and Sue did not value the same things and wondered if they could continue to work together. After many months together with time spent learning how to see from all perspectives without jumping to conclusions, Sue managed to figuratively step back from the situation, remember how much she respected Martin, and tell herself that he must have had a valid perspective. She saw that the conversation was stuck in gridlock; both were repeating the same points without any progress toward common meaning. That was the source of the frustration, the either/or nature of the discussion.

Sue shared this realization with Martin and Donna. As they discussed what had happened, they realized that Martin was pointing out how the program should be run while Sue was stating how it was actually being run—the ideal and the real respectively. Once they were all able to hold both perspectives at the same time, they understood that both were concerned with how the program could be improved and that any effort to change needs to consider both the current state and the future vision. They had moved from either/or to *both/and.*

This example of stepping into the space between us shows that it is not about winning, or compromising, or giving up. We can be more powerful together when we engage in and stay with the struggle of knowing and not knowing: knowing your own perspective, at the same time experiencing not knowing the other's perspective and being open to how they might fit together. Levoy (1997) captures the essence of this experience:

> It takes tremendous courage and hard work . . . not to take sides when we experience conflict but to stretch the soul wide enough to encompass *both* sides, stretch the imagination almost to the bursting point and understand that two utterly contrary stories can coexist even within the same person. (p. 58)

Buber's dialogue (1985) suggests standing your own ground while moving to the other side, and hearing what it would be like to speak for it, alternate positions, and then hold both. Our colleague Donna Wyatt (2002) described this as a *dynamic balance* where persons connect with all perspectives and stay in the tension until ultimately surrendering to allow a union to emerge.

Stepping into the space between us was also powerful for us when the outcomes were not as favorable, when we could not achieve a union of perspectives. Stepping into the between when there is strong disagreement is difficult. Sometimes it felt like it was impossible to withstand the tension of knowing and not knowing that felt like it would rip us and/or the relationship apart (Palmer, 1993).

Inclusion seemed to be an impossible ideal, but making a commitment to the willingness to struggle meant finding ways to practice this even when outcomes were disappointing. We learned to be willing to give the struggle some space and come back to it at another time if it was important. Sometimes the only option was to agree to our differences while retaining our respect for each other no matter the outcome.

A client of Martin's was unwilling to struggle. He had founded a church-based volunteer group where each year 150 people went on a one-week trip to Latin America and worked among people who worked hard to find the next meal. They brought medical, dental, and eye care, built cisterns and homes for people living in tents, funded construction for a church, and started a school.

Problems cropped up. Local leaders asked the visiting Americans to stop providing extravagant gifts to children, to consult them before making promises to build anything, and to reduce the number of people coming since it disrupted their small village. The founder could see only his good intentions to provide life-saving resources to people in need and to transform the lives of affluent Americans so that they would continue funding the work. He was unable to step into the between and fully appreciate the locals' concerns. This became not only his dilemma but the church group's as well; he refused to talk about it. Virtually everyone in the group knew that strategic conversations were needed but not had; an unwillingness to struggle together kept the dilemma in place.

These incidents describe individuals who found themselves in a situation where there were differences. A certain kind of time and space could then be created for them to step willingly into the space of simultaneous knowing and not knowing and possibly come to a greater understanding together.

### Stay with the Tension

Beware of the pull toward either/or choices, easy answers, stopping the tension. Be willing to become aware of and question your beliefs and to ask others to do the same. Stay in the heat of the interaction. Over time, the "muscles" to stay in the tension of differences are developed. Try to keep the dialogue open throughout. Be willing to learn from one another. Find your own voice, speak without withholding, really listen, say what needs to be said, and stay connected to one another and to the process.

Our descriptions of the willingness to struggle might bring to mind the literature on *connected knowing* (Belenky et al., 1986); we agree there is much similarity. Belenky and Stanton (2000) say: "Groups that place Connected Knowing at the center of their practice can achieve an unusually high degree of creativity and solid intellectual work. . . . People work hard to understand each other" (p. 88). We believe there is more to understand about mutual connected knowing.

## Together

We told you a story about feelings of exasperation when we were at a stand off. We used this to illustrate living a commitment to struggle. Yet, what we were relaying was far more than intellectual disagreement, a willingness to stay in the heat, and the power of perspective taking. It was our commitment to "together" that oddly enough was both source of and solution for the tension. It was not an option to win the argument by dismissing the other. Ultimately, even when exasperated, we each chose to honor not only the commitment to struggle but also the commitment to "together." We were committed to producing things; our conversations were not intellectual speculation, however, getting something done never trumped "struggle" and "together."

### Set Position and Rank Aside

Together involves operating as equals; engaging in mutually accountable relationships. You might need a facilitator, when a group is inexperienced in this kind of meeting; facilitation should be light and always temporary. In organizational meetings, the boss needs to communicate that, for the duration of the conversation, the boss is, at most, a first among equals. Participants might be asked directly: "what would allow you to operate with the others as equals?" Respect the degree to which subordinates are willing to risk treating superiors as peers.

We worked once with a tough Chief Information Officer client (CIO) who was so combative that he once asked a subordinate: "Do you want to take this outside?" During a retreat, when the CIO made a claim, we asked him to consider other possible interpretations. He was certain about his conclusion and almost screamed at us about how wrong we were. It was not easy to continue to invite him to question his conclusion, especially as his direct reports watched a consultant stand in a very familiar space with the boss. Hours later, he acknowledged that this exchange revealed to him just how difficult it must be for others to operate with him as peer and how his certainty shut down conversations. He wanted his people to rely more on one another but came to see how his some-times dogmatic stance had the unintended consequence of others coming to him for the right answer.

## Bring All of Yourself

When we speak about the together aspect of creating time and space for "col-laborative transformative learning," we are talking about making room for par-ticular persons. We are talking about a place where respect and relationship allow the persons to bring all of themselves to the situation and to really meet one another. Donna, our fellow collaborator, expressed surprise at being able to talk to us about personal concerns that prevented her, at times, from being fully present with us since she could not speak that way at work; she could not bring all of herself to work. Commitment to "together" means that persons are wel-come to bring body, mind, heart, and soul; their skills, ideas, and learning styles; and both endearing and maddening idiosyncrasies.

Try building and maintaining a safe, nurturing space where the group culti-vates accepting, nonjudgmental, and respectful ways of being with others; makes it safe to fail, look silly, and be wrong; creates a climate that welcomes persons and promotes growth. Cultivate the intent to include as if to say to others: do not withhold yourself; allow us to come to know you; engage with your whole self; let us value and use our diversity.

Once while working with an international group, we asked participants to draw a lifeline, to create some graphic representation of their personal history and then share that with everyone. A young Japanese woman presented a beau-tifully detailed yet very simple image of a bonsai refusing to be contained by its pot. She talked about her whole life as growing and breaking free of familial and cultural constraints. For this woman a safe space was created where she could share previously unknown aspects of herself with her coworkers.

## Keep Persons and Relationship as Consummate Purpose

Hold the person as central. The space is created for and literally constituted by particular people meeting at this particular moment: I and Thou here and now together. This commitment to "together" does not concern humanity, or any-thing general or abstract, but the people with the names and faces in front of you confirmed for who they are not and for their instrumental value. Nothing is cherished more than "making life possible for the other, if only for a moment" (Buber, 1985).

This is a space for community, not contractual relationships. Social contract theory, described by Rousseau (1991), assumes that we are separate, unattached units with no natural ties to each other. Since we are concerned primarily with our own independence and fulfillment, relationships are contractual, motivation is egocentric, and associations are functional, temporary, and abstract. In contrast community is "a many turned into a one without ceasing to be many" (p. 3); community is a real psychological or interior reality.

## Foster Connection

Connection is another way to think about *together*. The invitation here is to turn the world upside down and to see human development in terms of relationship rather than separation. It is also an invitation beyond Freudian drive theory or object relations theory where "the basic human motive [is] . . . better understood as the motive to participate in connection with others, rather than the need to be gratified by others" (Baker Miller & Pierce Stiver, 1997, p. 47).

So, the development of the capacities for relationship becomes important to cultivate competencies such as informed, mutual empathy (Kaplan, 1988; Surrey, 1988). These capacities do facilitate learning together but they also do so much more. Josselson (1996) said relationships are how we "overcome this psychological and physical space" (p. 5) that exists between us. She also said adult relatedness is "what gives meaning and vitality to life" (p. x). Ask people to share a story of a great teaming experience and you will have ample evidence for Josselson's claim.

We once worked with a company president who faced impossible odds in turning around a failing business. His family was in Europe and he was in the United States working in a toxic environment where paranoia was prudent. A colleague insisted it was critical for him to succeed in the turnaround. She wanted him to succeed.

We saw the toll being taken on this person and asked if he had considered walking away from the situation. He responded as if someone had given him a great gift in acknowledging that he and his family were far more important than any business conquest. Since we stood on the outside, we could create a space for him to consider what was unthinkable in a world of contractual relationships.

## Strive to Truly Meet One Another

The work of Martin Buber (1985) on dialogue informs what we mean by together. Buber's approach to dialogue is summed up this way: "In the beginning, is relation." Dialogue, for Buber, was extraordinarily simple and unusually complex—two or more particular human beings truly meeting, I and Thou. This involves true turning to the Other in a present and particular situation where you bring your whole self to the meeting and intend to create a living, mutual relation.

Ethel, a relative of Martin's, is in hospice care as we write this chapter. Sally, a former co-worker and friend, visits Ethel on a semi-regular basis. Ethel does not seem to enjoy the visits and, in fact, avoids taking her phone calls. Janet, Ethel's next door neighbor, also visits. She too has known the dying woman for decades. Even though Ethel is near death, she lights up when Janet comes in twice a day. They talk about how the day is going for each of them, share news, laugh, and sometimes sit in silence. When asked why these situations are so different, Ethel says that Sally, a very religious woman, visits everybody who is sick since that is important in her faith: "I don't want someone to come to see me so that they can rack up points in God's book; I want someone to come to see *me*." Ethel experiences true meeting with Janet.

Genuine dialogue is the means to establish a living and mutual relation. Dialogue occurs in the realm of the between. The between is neither an idea nor a metaphor but a real place that Buber said has been studied too little because it is a place accessible only to persons in dialogue, something that "has its being between them, and transcends both. . . . A genuine third alternative [to the psychological or sociological] . . . the knowledge of which will help to bring about the genuine person again and to establish genuine community" (Buber, 1985). It is also difficult to communicate after the experience. Art or poetry is best for evoking the experience. Yet even when conveyed, what is being offered is communication about the experience of dialogue and not dialogue.

Andersen, Cissna, and Arnett (1994), in the tradition of Buber, say that "dialogue emerges as an issue concerning the quality of relationship between or among two or more people and of the communicative acts that create and sustain that relationship" (p. 15). We might say that dialogue requires both *listening* and *speaking*, *reflecting* and *acting*, *knowing* and *inquiring*, *differing* and *connecting* (Leahy, 2001), but it is the latter, the capacity to differ and connect, that is in the foreground of stepping into the space between us. When a person feels connected and supported while simultaneously experiencing the reality of being separate and the honesty present in genuine challenge, the space created for transformation is breathtaking.

## Create Covenants

Together might also be thought of as a covenant between knower and known. Here both agree to fully participate in the experience of striving toward more fully knowing each other as well as whatever they are studying (Palmer, 1993). Palmer (1987) believed that community needs to become the central concept in our forms of teaching and learning. To him, community is the inward capacity for relatedness, not just to other people but also to history, to nature, to ideas, and to things of the spirit. Palmer said knowing in this way "is a bond of community between us and that which we know" (p. 24). He went on to say, "The act of knowing itself is a way of building and rebuilding community" (p. 24). The communal acts of knowing and learning "require a continual cycle of discussion, disagreement, and consensus" (p. 25). Palmer said, after all, "there is no knowing without conflict" (p. 25). A community grows through its capacity to engage in creative conflict where individuals are "protected by the compassionate fabric of human caring itself" (p. 25). Most leaders in organizations would give anything to make that happen. Few have made the link between a group's capacity for contention and disagreement and its ability to care.

So when we talk about being committed to "together." we envision participating as peers, people bringing all of themselves, relationship as the reason for being, people truly meeting one another, connections, community, and covenant. We suggest these images and hope they convey how central relationship is to CTL.

## Inquiring into Questions That Matter

The kernel of this commitment or way of being was very much there from the beginning of our long-term CTL experience. As we explained previously, we shared a desire to better understand high-end collaboration. This common interest, as well as our desire to become a high-functioning group researching our own collaborative experience naturally developed into our practice of inquiring into all sorts of questions about collaboration. After many months of developing our own inquiry process, we discovered Heron's book (1996) on cooperative inquiry. We found much there that validated what we had been doing, gave us another language to talk about our work together, and added some techniques to our growing inquiry repertoire.

*Inquire in a systematic way.* Our experience resonated strongly with Heron's *cooperative inquiry*, which

> involves two or more people researching a topic through their own experience of it, using a series of cycles in which they move between this experience and reflecting together on it. Each person is co-subject in the experience phases and co-researcher in the reflection phases. (1996, p. 1)

While this might sound similar to *action research* or *experiential learning*, Heron (1996) explains that cooperative inquiry differs in its origins, epistemological framework, scope of application, vision, and domain: "It is a vision of persons in reciprocal relation using the full range of their sensibilities to inquire together into any aspect of the human condition with which the transparent body-mind can engage" (p. 1).

After reading reports of our practice, Dr. Heron agreed that we were a bootstrap cooperative inquiry group, one "that chooses to be entirely self-initiating, and pull itself up by its own bootstrap into the practice of co-operative inquiry" (Heron, 1996, p. 40).

Heron's work on cooperative inquiry has been brought to the field of trans-formative learning by Kasl and Yorks's *collaborative inquiry* which they describe as a "facilitative structure for adult learning." This facilitative, systematic structure has components each of which was central to our practice: (a) starting with questions that mattered deeply to us, (b) sparked by our own experience of daily living, (c) questions often related to our professional practices; (d) organizing ourselves (e) in a democratic way, (f) using free and open discourse, (g) to sup-port learning (h) that resulted in transformation; evident in our (i) constructing new meaning, (j) changing, healing, and/or emancipating ourselves as persons and group, (k) collaborating of the high-end kind, and (l) sustaining meaningful connections with each other (Kasl & Yorks, 2002a; Kasl & Yorks, 2002b; Yorks & Kasl, 2002a; Yorks & Kasl, 2002b).

Kasl and Yorks, like Heron, and consistent with our experience, suggest the import of cycling between action and reflection, practicing validity via critical subjectivity, and expanding epistemology to multiple ways of knowing (including presentational or intuitive knowing). There is much to learn about CTL from the work of Yorks and Kasl, so we will not repeat here their accounts of this particular form of inquiry since we, testing their work against our own lived experience, found their depictions to be both eloquent and compelling.

## Start with Real Concerns

We find that it is important for groups to focus on their real concerns, or the possibilities they wish to bring to reality, or the dilemmas that bother them. Collaborative inquiry that facilitates transformative learning seems to require that all participants care about the group's work, that it feels like the work af-fects some aspect of their lives or is something they care about. Both of us have tried to encourage college students to work together using a collaborative in-quiry process. Usually our efforts resulted more in feelings of disappointment than in a sense of success. We have found it difficult for students to find a topic they were all committed to, that truly affected their lives; the drift was toward individual work and requirements for a grade.

Our efforts to invite groups to engage in inquiry have met with more suc-cess in business organizations. "Leading by Values: An Inquiry" was the title for a leadership development program we created for top-level executives. We helped them engage in a year-long inquiry about leadership wherein they used reflection on their real work to create their own way of leading.

Their commitment was to inquire together with questions that mattered to them: How do we lead in this time, at this place, with these people, facing these challenges, and, most important of all, given our values and who we are as people? This was a big contrast from what they were used to: being expected to consume someone else's answers about leadership—answers that are taken to be universally applicable. In the Leading by Values program, about a third of the executives participated in a polite manner since the boss was requiring this; another third found the experience to be interesting and somewhat valuable, and a final third said things such as: "I changed in ways that I would never have imagined."

## Reflect on Both Concerns and Process

Because we were inquiring into our own development as a group, we discovered the importance of using both the content of our inquiry, in our case collaboration, as well as our immediate experience of our group process as important subjects for reflection. The space between us was both the context for and the content of reflection and learning. When groups are willing to have their relationships and their process be co-content with the topic of their inquiry, learning results. Bateson (1972) called this *metalogue*—a conversation about the conversation. The group needs to let go of problem solving and step into inquiry and adopt an interested curiosity when inquiring into the functioning of the group itself.

Inquiring into the group's functioning involves looking at the assumptions, beliefs, values, and common practices of the individuals and the group. Certainty and comfort will be disturbed; create a safe space for people to stay in that disturbed place long enough for learning to occur. Inquiry here involves engaging in both critical reflection and connected knowing—"suspend judgment and struggle to understand others' points of view from their perspective" (about Belenky & Stanton's work in Cranton, 2006, p. 42).

## Use Full Range of Sensibilities

From the beginning we started using what felt like unconventional activities to explore the topic of collaboration. This was primarily due to the activities Donna enticed us into trying. Sue once talked about her work on an interdisciplinary research team. Part of the reason her team had received a grant was that the National Science Foundation wanted them to report on the research team's collaboration. However, the researchers did not seem to want to explore their own collaboration. Sue shared her frustration with this lack of interest. When Sue finished talking, Donna jumped up from the kitchen table and went to the cupboards. She began pulling out measuring cups to represent the psychologists, mugs with tropical birds to represent the anthropologists, and plain gray mugs to represent the business professors. Donna then sat down in the middle of the kitchen floor and began making a pyramid out of the cups and mugs. Placing the measuring cup on top of the pyramid, she said, "Right now the psychologists are the leaders, but what would happen if the anthropologists were the leaders?" Curious, Sue and Martin joined her on the floor and began discussing different collaborative possibilities while they enacted them with the cups and mugs.

We engaged in a variety of unconventional learning activities. We told stories to one another; acted out scenes together, like being interviewed on Oprah, to figure out the overlap of our interests; and played with ideas by mind mapping standing together over a large sheet of paper. Heron (1996) suggests that each co-inquirer "uses the full range of her or his sensibilities as a composite instrument of inquiry" (p. 37). In fact, participative inquiry methodologies, in general, suggest using different activities to stimulate creativity and tap into the tacit knowledge of the participants (Heron, 1996; Park, 2001; Reason, 1994). Heron has a holistic model of knowing that explains the need for such activities.

## A Way of Life

The four commitments we offered here are not a formula for CTL. The transformation that they produced was that we as individuals and as a group changed our ways of being. The four commitments represent a way of life—living the good life practiced as per ancient philosophy. Hadot (1995), historian and philosopher, tells us that ancient Greek philosophy was the quest for virtue or the principles that can support individuals and a community in the practice of a virtuous life. Hadot also says, "Ancient philosophy was always . . . practiced in a group" (p. 274) and was discovered through conversation where dialogue "forms people and transforms souls" (p. 20). The goal was to adopt practices for living a good life and for the knowledge that warranted those practices, the *why* behind the *how*.

For Hadot, at the heart of ancient philosophy were *spiritual practices* for sustaining a communal way of life. The spiritual nature of this quest has been echoed today by philosopher of education Parker Palmer (1993) for whom learning is about creating communal space: "knowing becomes a reunion of separated beings whose primary bond is not of logic but of love" (p. 32).

Hadot was reluctant to use the term "spiritual" but could find no better word. We believe CTL can be a spiritual practice in its best form; although we feel reluctance to use the term "spiritual," that is what we experienced together over time. We believe CTL is more about the community and relationships that are formed, the skills and shifts in consciousness that are essential for full development, than it is about the subject that brings the individuals together. Spiritual, for Hadot, means replacing my perspective with the perspective of the Whole, which results in a transformation of my vision of the world and my personality, and moving to an authentic way of living with others.

We view CTL as a way of life that is much like ancient philosophy: engaging in practices with others to examine perceptions and ways of being in the world and developing skills for being with one another in ways that support human flourishing. We have suggested commitments that facilitate engaging in conversation so that communities may develop their own good life together, a life that transforms.

## Conclusion

Through our learning together we experienced a more "holistic" form of education than we had ever before encountered. Our experience of CTL was a journey of self-development that included the psychological, the cognitive, and so much more. It also involved our relational and communal development. We find we are now better partners to each other, to other people with whom we work, and better group and community members. We have come to a new way of being, a new philosophy if you will. We now live, learn, and create more with our whole selves: our hearts, minds, bodies, and souls.

We have shared with you the background of our CTL experience, stories of our practices, as well as experiences from groups with which we have worked. We hope we have given you a sense of some practical skills we have gained from our experiences and been able to encourage in other groups. We find many of the norms and practices of our culture and our institutions push us away from the communal and back to the solitary or to the collective. It is our hope that others will discover the value of community through CTL. Rousseau points out that "we are linked ontologically and existentially to all other humans through our common humanity" (p. 15) and that we strive to overcome our human limitations by transcending our individuality by connecting with others. CTL, for us, was an experience of connecting with others that allowed us to become one with another without ceasing to be ourselves.

It is our belief that the growth that comes from CTL, most specifically what we are calling *a willingness to struggle together in the space between us,* has important implications for our society. When speaking about the dividedness of the world today, Levoy offered the following insights from Gene Knudsen Hoffman (who worked for the Fellowship of Reconciliation, the oldest interfaith pacifist organization in the world). She had these thoughts about the importance of learning to manage differences:

If you can hold paradox . . . you can hold tremendous energy within you and be a force for mediation in the world. Equanimity is an ability that naturally mitigates against tyranny both within and among people. Furthermore, by not subjugating parts of yourself and parts of others, you *belong* to more of yourself and the world, and the world belongs more to you. You're not "fighting it" all the time. (Hoffman in Levoy, 1997, p. 58)

# References

Anderson, R., Cissna, K. N., & Arnett, R. C. (Eds.) (1994). *The reach of dialogue: Confirmation, voice, and community.* Cresskill, NJ: Hampton Press.

Baker Miller, J., & Pierce Stiver, I. (1997). *The healing connection: How women form relationships in therapy and life.* Boston: Beacon Press.

Bateson, G. (1972). *Steps to an ecology of mind.* New York: Ballantine Books.

Belenky, M. F., Clinchy, B. M., Goldberger, N. R., & Tarule, J. M. (1986). *Women's ways of knowing: The development of self, voice, and mind.* New York: Basic Books.

Belenky, M. F., & Stanton, A. V. (2000). Inequality, development, and connected knowing. In J. Mezirow (Ed.), *Learning as transformation: Critical perspectives on a theory in progress,* pp. 71–102. San Francisco: Jossey-Bass.

Buber, M. (1985). *Between man and man.* New York: Collier Books.

Cranton, P. (2006). *Understanding and promoting transformative learning,* 2nd edition. San Francisco: Jossey-Bass.

Gilly, M. S. (2003). *The heart of adult peer group learning: Living the learning together.* Ph.D. dissertation, Fielding Graduate Institute, CA. Retrieved January 8, 2008, from ProQuest Digital Dissertations database. (Publication No. AAT 3080223).

Hadot, P. (1995). *Philosophy as a way of life: Spiritual exercises from Socrates to Foucault* (M. Chase, Trans.). Cambridge, MA: Blackwell.

Heron, J. (1996). *Co-operative inquiry: Research into the human condition.* London: Sage.

Josselson, R. (1996). *The space between us: Exploring the dimensions of human relationships.* Thousand Oaks, CA: Sage.

Kaplan, A. G. (1988, March 2). *Empathy and its vicissitudes.* Paper presented at the Stone Center Colloquium, Wellesley College.

Kasl, E., & Yorks, L. (2002a). Collaborative inquiry for adult learning. *New Directions for Adult and Continuing Education, 94*(Summer), 3–11.

Kasl, E., & Yorks, L. (2002b). An extended epistemology for transformative learning theory and its application through collaborative inquiry. Retrieved February 21, 2003, from http://www.tcrecord.org

Kegan, R., & Lahey, L. (2001). *How the way we talk can change the way we work: Seven languages for transformation.* San Francisco: Jossey-Bass.

Leahy, M. (2001). *The heart of dialogue.* Ph.D. dissertation, Fielding Graduate Institute, United States—California. Retrieved January 8, 2008, from ProQuest Digital Dissertations database (Publication No. AAT 3022121).

Levoy, G. (1997). *Callings: Finding and following an authentic life.* New York: Three Rivers Press.

Palmer, P. J. (1987). Community, conflict, and ways of knowing. *Change, 19*(5), 20–25.

Palmer, P. J. (1993). *To know as we are known: Education as a spiritual journey.* San Francisco: Harper Collins Publishers.

Park, P. (2001). Knowledge and participatory research. In H. Bradbury (Ed.), *Handbook of action research,* pp. 81–90. London: Sage.

Reason, P. (1994). Three approaches to participative inquiry. In Y. S. Lincoln (Ed.), *Handbook of qualitative research,* pp. 324–339. Thousand Oaks, CA: Sage.

Rousseau, M. F. (1991). *Community: The tie that binds.* Lanham, MD: University Press of America.

Surrey, J. L. (1988, March 2). *Empathy: Evolving theoretical perspectives.* Paper presented at the Stone Center Colloquium, Wellesley College.

Wyatt, D. (2002). *Living in the between: From "either/or" to "both/and."* Ph.D. dissertation, Fielding Graduate Institute, United States—California. Retrieved January 8, 2008, from ProQuest Digital Dissertations database. (Publication No. AAT 3046359).

Yorks, L., & Kasl, E. (2002a). Learning from inquiries: Lessons for using collaborative inquiry as an adult learning strategy. *New Directions for Adult and Continuing Education, 94*(Summer), 93–104.

Yorks, L., & Kasl, E. (2002b). Toward a theory and practice for whole-person learning: Reconceptualizing experience and the role of affect. *Adult Education Quarterly, 52*(3), 176–192.

# Chapter 3

## Learning Space/Work Space: Can We Make Room for Transformative Learning in Organizations?

*Pamela Meyer*

*The class has just completed their final improvised scenes of the quarter. Two and a half months earlier, most of the adults walked into the classroom the first night uneasy about a course that had both "creativity" and "improvisation" in the title. Yet, each week they encouraged each other, shared their discomfort, insights, and progress as they studied creativity theory, read about the concepts of improvisation in the arts and business, and had many opportunities to experiment with these ideas using improvisational games and eventually fully improvised scenes. As we sat in a circle this last night of class, reflecting on the experience over the entire quarter, I was struck by the number of times the participants acknowledged and appreciated each other. They thanked their colleagues for taking risks, revealing their vulnerabilities, and supporting them during their improvisations. More than one person attributed a personal transformation to the level of safety they felt and the trust they had in the group.*

Over the course of several weeks, these adults, with diverse professional and cultural backgrounds, co-created a space for transformative learning in a university classroom. Those who felt few inhibitions alternately inspired and intimidated those who were uncomfortable, while those who ventured beyond their comfort zone received encouragement, acknowledgment, and acceptance. All shared responsibility for making room for the learning and transformation that unfolded in the space (Meyer, 2006, p. 106).

As a practitioner in both educational and organizational settings, I have long grappled with the question of whether or not, and how, we can make such room for transformation in organizations. The challenge is rooted in the diverging purposes of education and organization. Education's primary purpose is the development of individual capacity, while the word "organization" itself extends from the Greek word "organon," or tool, for the purpose of executing and accomplishing tasks, missions, and strategies (Daft, 2001).

Already, there is conflict. Organizations are not designed for education, and few executives and managers see themselves as educators; they are accountable to the organizations' mission and goals and to the interests of a wide range of stakeholders. Given these diverging purposes, before we can answer the question of whether or not we can make room for transformative learning in organizations, we must ask if and why we should take on such an endeavor. "Why," organizational practitioners are right to ask, "should I care about transformative learning?"

The answer is relevant for everyone accountable to organizational success. Even, and especially, in organizations whose core concerns are grounded in the modernist values of efficiency, productivity, and profitability, there is a strong case for the need to make room for transformative learning. In such organizations, learning is often delivered via formal, structured training programs that emphasize job-related skills and technical training, or what Nowlen (1988) refers to as the "update model" of education, in which learning is limited to recent updates and advancements related to professional role.

Organizations should care about making room for transformative learning not only because such technical training accounts for only a portion of individual effectiveness in organizations, but also because such learning often has a transformational dimension. Individuals learning new skills and acquiring new knowledge often need the space to question and revise their self-beliefs and core assumptions as they develop competence in new areas. Alternatively, upon gaining new practical capacities, they may discover new dimensions of themselves and begin to question their prior assumptions about their limitations and possibilities. For example, learning to drive a car or to operate a computer appears to be primarily a technical, skill-based form of learning. However, adults acquiring these skills will soon find new worlds opening up to them, where freedom, autonomy, and new perspectives might well challenge their earlier belief systems. Many individuals may need to surface and question their fears and orientation to such practical learning before they can even begin to engage in it.

Organizations that want to ensure their ability to respond to changes in the marketplace, their competition, and their workforce have an even more compelling reason to care about making room for transformative learning: Many of the same capacities that allow individuals to reflect on their own experiences, question their frames of reference, and expand their ways of being are also those necessary to question organizational norms, operating assumptions, and strategic platforms.

Agreeing that there is value in making room for transformative learning in organizations leads to the question at the heart of this chapter: *Can* we make room for it in our organizations?

## The Paradox of Transformative and Organizational Learning

Although many of the capacities and dimensions that make room for transformative learning are also associated with organizational learning and even with the less narrowly defined learning in organizations, their diverging purposes create a paradox for practitioners, organizations, and their participants.

Both transformative learning and organizational learning include awareness of and critical reflection on preferred mindsets, perspectives, and ways of being. The process, content, and premise reflection at the center of Mezirow's theory of transformation, echo Argyris and Schon's double-loop learning and Senge's conception of the learning organization:

> At the heart of the learning organization is a shift of mind from seeing ourselves as separate from the world to connected to the world, from seeing problems as caused by someone or something "out there" to seeing how our own actions create the problems we experience. . . . A learning organization is a place where people are continually discovering how they create their reality . . . and how they can change it. (Senge, 1990, pp. 12–13)

Senge (1990) further describes learning not as "acquiring more information, but expanding the ability to produce the results we truly want in life. It is life-long generative learning. And learning organizations are not possible unless they have people at every level who practice it" (p. 142). While the link between individual and organizational capacity is so clear as to be pre-given, my practice-based experiences with organizations have taught me that the case still needs to be made.

Most agree that reflection, questioning, and reframing, whether catalyzed by rational or whole-person experiences, are central to personal and organizational transformation. As practitioners, we reason that organizations that wish to actively engage in organizational learning will enthusiastically create space for such work. For a number of reasons, this enthusiasm does not manifest as often as we would hope for. Some believe it is because, similar to the diverging purposes of education and organization, the underlying agendas of transformative learning and organizational learning are at odds.

Yorks and Marsick (2000) describe the goals of organizational transformation as "allowing the organization to more effectively realize its performance objectives" while individual transformational learning "emancipates individual learners through making them aware of how psychological-socioeconomic-cultural forces may have limited personal choice or have been the source for dysfunctionally constructed habits of mind" (p. 254). Organizational learning is concerned with learning in the service of organizational effectiveness, while transformative learning is concerned with learning for human development and liberation (Fenwick, 1998). In a generative organizational space, there is no conflict between human development and emancipation and organizational effectiveness. In organizations that are open to questioning some operating norms and assumptions but not others, the space for transformative learning is often constrained.

In my own practice, the challenge surfaces in another way: clients often begin their conversations with me by acknowledging the need for transformation—a shift in mindset. They tell me that they need their people to work more collaboratively, to communicate effectively, learn to take risks, and innovate; they want people to feel empowered, take ownership, and be leaders. As the conversation progresses, it becomes clear that they would like to achieve these transformational outcomes in a half-day training session, or better yet, in a series of brown-bag lunches. They cannot afford to have their people "off-line" for very long, and there is only so much money in the budget for development.

When decision makers do commit to investing in more integrated approaches, practitioners understand that they are still accountable to the bottom line. In advance of a recent meeting with the director of a division at a large organization, I was advised, "Our director has little patience for abstraction and conceptual thinking. She is only going to be interested in the outcomes of your work." Our challenge in working with organizational stakeholders who seem singularly focused on outcomes is to expand the conversation to include a complementary valuation of the process, as well as the space for the unexpected and unpredictable aspects of transformative learning to emerge.

Expanding the client conversation often involves facilitating a perspective shift to help stakeholders appreciate the transformative dimensions of their organizational goals. While there is a skill and knowledge component to many of the most pressing organizational issues (just visit the websites of any of the national training companies and you will find off-the-shelf seminars on communication, leadership, and innovation to name a few), making room only for the technical dimension of such issues will not affect the mindset, self-concept, and relational dynamic at the core of transformation. As practitioners, we must pay attention to the organizational constraints of time and money. At the same time, we cannot promise transformation when there is little possibility of creating the space for it to occur.

Given the constraints embedded in many organizations, practitioners may question the value of even attempting to make room for transformative learning. Kovan and Dirkx (2003) found that long-time environmental activists sustained themselves by finding ways to negotiate between the poles of hope and despair. This challenge resonates with practitioners in many fields and certainly with those charged with affecting transformation within the constraints of organizational settings. In the pages that follow, I offer an alternative, nondualistic response to the challenge and propose that rather than riding the pendulum between hope and despair, we should seize the opportunity that lies in learning to live and learn within the paradox of transformative and organizational learning by shifting our relationship to the learning space in organizational settings.

Many of the dimensions of learning space that led to my own shift emerged from my study of adults' experiences of learning improvisation, and the space they co-created as they made room for their own and others' transformative learning. While the setting for these experiences was a university classroom, and the co-researchers[4] were adult students enrolled in an undergraduate program, the study findings extend to both formal and informal learning settings in organizations. Findings from adults' experiences of learning improvisation are particularly suited for extension into organizational settings as improvisation is a core capacity valued in organizations today and includes creativity, spontaneity, collaboration, communication, and discovery.

## Learning Space in Organizations

Argyris (1992) found that even for those apparently committed to challenging their mental models and those who are willing to transform, there is little guarantee that transformative learning will occur in organizations. Summarizing a study of various graduate and professional groups who had been well trained in organizational learning and systems thinking and who were then asked to work together to surface and challenge their own theories-in-use (frames of reference), Argyris reported

All individuals who have become aware of their Model I theories-in-use [assumptions upon which their decisions and strategies were based], who have

---

[4] I use the term "co-researcher" where I might otherwise refer to "study participants." I use this term any time I refer to the adults who participated in the learning experience, even though it may at times seem more natural or appropriate to use the word "students" in a given context. My goal is to be consistent throughout, and I feel it is appropriate terminology as each of the adults, as part of their learning experience, was asked to take a researcher's perspective as they documented and shared their experiences.

learned about learning, who have chosen to learn according to it, and who try to do so under supportive condition, *are unable to do so when left to their own devices.* (p. 28, italics mine)

While disheartening, it is significant that Argyris's study did not describe the learning space within which the participants attempted to engage in personal and organizational reflection, nor did participants consciously create a space conducive to such practice. The findings do support the claim that fluency in the process and skills of reflection alone is not enough to support transformation.

This delivers us to the center of the paradox: To sustain themselves in changing conditions, organizations must continuously question their operating assumptions and norms, yet their cultural, political, and structural barriers often limit the space for transformation. New perspectives and organizational behaviors cannot emerge without a learning space in which they can develop (Voronov & Yorks, 2005). Resolving this paradox points not to alternative models or more skills, but to the learning space itself.

While terms such as "environment" and "setting" are often used to describe the learning context, I alternately use the terms "space" and "room" as they include the actual physical setting as well as the psychological, emotional, and embodied conception of space as freedom and opportunity. The conception of learning space as I use it here is not new. Others have described similar constructs that allow for both the physical and the emancipatory dimensions of learning space. One of the oldest descriptions of learning space can be found in the Japanese concept of "*ba*," described by Nonaka and Konno (1998) as "a shared space for emerging relationships . . . [that] provides a platform for advancing individual and/or collective knowledge. . . . To participate in a *ba* means to get involved and transcend one's own limited perspective or boundary" (pp. 40–41). Nonaka describes good *ba* as "superior relational situations where everyone brings energy to the others, enhancing creativity and supporting dynamic positive exchanges" (Nonaka & Konno, 1998). *Ba* shifts the focus from individual learning and transformation to the shared relational experience.

More recently Kolb and Kolb (2005) have called attention to learning space in experiential learning theory (ELT). The learning space of ELT "emphasizes that learning is not one universal process but a map of learning territories, a frame of reference within which many different ways of learning can flourish and interrelate" (p. 200). Kolb and others cited above provide strong support for the relationship between adults' whole-person experience and their ability to learn and make meaning of those experiences. In this latest extension of their work, Kolb and Kolb allow for many ways of knowing and the multifaceted ways of experiencing the learning space and learning itself.

Adults learning improvisation are invited to explore many ways of knowing and to become attuned to their embodied experiences of themselves, their surroundings, and fellow "players" to a greater degree than adults in most learning spaces. This attunement amplifies many dimensions of learning space that might otherwise be muted in less overtly embodied relational settings. Viola Spolin (1963/1983), the originator of many of the modern practices of improvisational theatre in education and the arts, describes a symbiotic relationship between the individual and the environment—one that has the potential for significant learning if the learning space "permits" it:

> If the environment permits it, anyone can learn whatever he chooses to learn; and if the individual permits it, the environment will teach him everything it has to teach. (p. 3)

Scholar-practitioners in educational and organizational settings agree that the learning space and adults' experiences of it and of themselves are central to the types and quality of learning that are "permitted" there. This was amplified in adults' experiences of learning improvisation, though I do not believe it is exclusive to this context.

Before I describe these dimensions, I must admit some ambivalence. My practice and research have led me to another paradox—a practitioner paradox. Much of the theoretical and research focus in adult learning has, either tacitly or explicitly, not been holistic. By focusing on learning outcomes, the research belies an underlying bias toward control. The underlying assumption of the emphasis on rationality in transformative learning is that understanding leads to control, and that perspective shifts help us have control over our lives via increased empowerment. The similar theoretical and research focus on educator roles and the environment is understandable as most of it is directed at adult educators, who are interested in the factors they can affect, support, and/or control.

The irony is that most of the dynamics in the learning environment are largely outside of the educators' control, such as the adults' self-beliefs, prior learning experiences, reflective capacity, the diversity of adults' experiences and backgrounds, and many aspects of the physical setting. This does not mean that we, as practitioners, have no role at all; it does mean that we have an opportunity to reconceive our relationship to the learning space. As I discuss dimensions of the learning space that my own and others' research suggests are key to transformative learning space, I propose that as practitioners we are not responsible *for* the learning space, but *to* it. As practitioners, we must carefully walk down the middle of this paradox—taking responsibility to co-create the learning space, while understanding that a successful learning space makes room for everyone to share in its co-creation.

Trust, safety, democracy, and mediation of power and authority are some of the most often cited characteristics of learning space that create room for transformation. These are supported by my own research and are based on my findings; I add *relational learning* and *time* to these dimensions. Although practitioners cannot ensure the realization of these qualities, we can be attuned to them as we share responsibility *to* the learning space.

While I believe there is great value in attuning to and describing the ways these dimensions manifest in some settings, I am wary of prescribing how to create these dimensions. The "improvisation lessons" that conclude each section describe lessons learned from my research and practice; my hope is that you will read them in that spirit and be inspired to question and to discover if and how these qualities resonate with your own practice.

## Trust and Safety

Trust and safety are essential qualities of learning space for without them individual's risk of exposure far outweighs the rewards, especially in organizational settings. In a special *Academy of Management Review* (1998) issue on trust, Rousseau et al. propose that trust is "a psychological state comprising the intention to accept vulnerability based upon positive expectations of the intentions or behavior of another" (p. 395). From the practitioner-centric view, in both educational and organizational settings, we are responsible *to* a space where it is safe to "accept vulnerability" and seems reasonable to have "positive expectations of the intentions or behavior of another."

For many adults, learning environments—especially those that are intended to create space for transformation where sharing personal experiences and questioning perspectives are encouraged—are the most vulnerable places in which they could find themselves. For adults in organizational settings where personal sharing and revelation can affect perception of competence and even job security, vulnerability is further heightened. The pioneers of organizational learning theory confirm that its challenge is that, as it moves into double-loop learning (where perspectives are surfaced and questioned), it becomes increasingly personal. Like transformative learning, double-loop learning represents a shift from acknowledging external reasons for unrealized goals to personal reasons. Senge (2003), reflecting on Argyris and Schon's single-loop, error correction, and detection learning, wrote, "To detect an error is to acknowledge incompetence. Doing so publicly in a work setting is often seen as 'career limiting,' discouragement enough even if it wasn't personally threatening" (p. 47).

It is hard to imagine a context in which organizational participants would feel free to surface and question their own behavior and assumptions, without trusting that the learning space is a safe place to engage in such risky behavior.

### Improvisation Lesson 1: Acknowledge Fears and Expectations

One of the ways adults learning improvisation co-created their learning space for transformation was to acknowledge their fears about registering for a class that included both the words "creativity" and "improvisation" in its title. During the first class meeting, we begin this sharing in less risky pairs, then open it up for large group sharing. Here people discover they are not alone in their fears of "looking stupid," "having to be funny," or "put on the spot," or their fear of discovering in a very public setting that they simply "aren't creative." There is also room for people to share if they did not have any fears or to name their positive expectations of the class. It is important not to highlight fears over positive anticipation but to make room for all. I share my own fears and anticipations that echo many of theirs, and I also use this disclosure to describe the overall flow of the class and to assure people that they will not be evaluated on any of their improvisations, simply on their willingness to participate.

In organizational settings stakes are higher, or at least different, than in the university classroom. In organizations, practitioners can be mindful of the psychological and emotional risks they are asking people to take as they enter into new learning, creative, and collaborative opportunities. If it is not appropriate to invite self-disclosure, managers, facilitators, and experienced colleagues can acknowledge the risks and ideally share their own fears and how they have negotiated them in similar circumstances. Much relief comes when we discover that our vulnerabilities are shared and that, as a recent organizational participant declared, "we are all in this together."

### Improvisation Lesson 2: Share Responsibility for the Learning Space

Soon after we share our fears and expectations, I briefly describe the role of fear in the creative process and the natural response to entering into the unknown. The outcomes of creativity and improvisation, of course, cannot be known in advance and often provoke fear. Artists, educators, and learners in all settings do not need to problematize fear but acknowledge it and learn to negotiate their experience of it as they practice. This discussion is particularly relevant to adults who have negotiated just such fear of the unknown to get themselves to the classroom in the first place.

By normalizing expectations, fear, and discomfort in learning, we begin to co-create a space where many of these fears, especially the fear of being judged, are unlikely to be realized. We agree to practice the Rogerian conception of "unconditional positive regard" that

> involves as much feeling of acceptance for the client's expression of negative, "bad," painful, fearful, and abnormal feelings as for his expression of "good," positive, mature, confident and social feelings. It involves an acceptance of and a caring for the client as a separate person, with permission for him to have his own feelings and experiences, and to find his own meanings in them. To the degree that the therapist can provide this safety-creating climate of unconditional positive regard, significant learning is likely to take place. (Rogers, 1961, pp. 283–284)

While Rogers was describing an essential dimension of humanistic psychology, he was also describing the essence of learning space for transformation. No practitioner can promise a learning space free from discomfort, nor would we want to, as experiences that emerge on the boundaries of comfort are often the richest learning opportunities. We can collaborate to create a space that is, as scholar-practitioner Charlie Seashore encourages, "safe enough."

It is equally important to make space to discuss fears in organizational settings, to understand the boundaries within which it is safe to share, and to be explicit about areas that the group agrees are "undiscussable." This kind of boundary setting is very different from the tacit avoidance embedded in Argyris and Schon's (1978) "undiscussables" and the "defensive routines" people engage in to reinforce them (p. 85). By agreeing as a group, or in individual collaboration, that certain topics are too fraught (e.g., compensation plan, rumors of a merger), individuals claim their own power and freedom, rather than fall victim to existing power dynamics.

In formal learning settings in organizations—as well as less in formal constructs such as meetings and coaching conversations—establishing ground rules, boundaries, or guidelines can also free everyone for optimum learning within the space. Depending on the construct and purpose of the setting or conversation, groups might agree not to judge others' ideas, not to discuss people who are not present, and to begin each response with a positive acknowledgment of what has just been shared.

Improvisers regularly practice the concept of "yes, and . . ." in which they agree to accept and build on whatever idea has been offered to them in the playing space. As this practice becomes second nature, everyone knows they can trust their colleagues to support them and make them look good, even in the most outlandish situations. This trust soon flows into other aspects of the workspace/learning space, creating room for each individual to experience him- or herself performing beyond their previously known capacities. The lived experience then becomes the catalyst for transformative learning as individuals begin to reframe their self-beliefs as they reflect on their emerging capacities.

*Improvisation Lesson 3: Hold the Learning Space until Everyone Can Hold It for Themselves*

My friend and long-time colleague Allison Morgan first noticed that this may be my (and all practitioners') key role in facilitating learning. Holding the space is not a position of power or control, but of custodianship, not unlike holding a friend's movie seat for them until they arrive. Some adults arrive sooner than others, needing greater or lesser degrees of encouragement.

I learned years ago as a theatre director that the biggest indicator of my success was, by opening night, everyone involved in the production—from the costume designer, to the stage crew, to the actors—was referring to the show as "my show." If this occurred, I knew that I had gotten out of the way in time for them to own the generative creative process of the show for the performance weeks ahead. In the improvisation classroom, this ownership was reflected in a shift in focus from my responses and comments on the exercises and scenes to an equal valuation of their colleagues' responses. Although I could model appreciative behavior, it was not until others shared the responsibility for the learning space that they felt they had the full permission to push beyond their comfort zones to discover previously unknown capacities and their capacity for transformation. While it is important to explicitly discuss trust and safety and agree to share responsibility for it, this dimension can grow only over time as each participant enacts appreciative and generative behavior and honors the boundaries the group has established for their learning space/workspace.

## Democracy and Power in the Learning Space

Freirean and Habermasian ideals of emancipatory learning and communication are regularly associated with transformation. Collaborative inquiry (Yorks & Kasl, 2002b) and action research (Greenwood & Levin, 1998; Lewin, 1946; Park, 1997) are two models that aspire to realize these ideals in practice. The theory and practice are well integrated, and there is a growing body of research supporting the learning space for transformation created through their practice.

At the same time, formal learning environments, such as universities, and organizations often have contextual constraints for truly democratic practice. In his analysis of the limits of organizational democracy, Kerr (2004) identifies an obvious, though often overlooked obstacle: "As appealing as democracy may be as a political and intellectual construct, organizations are not societies in the political sense, and managements are not elected governments" (p. 82).

Students in formal educational settings also know that, no matter how collaborative the learning environment, the educator has the power to evaluate the student's performance. In organizations, a similar dynamic exists between managers and their direct reports, and even between peers, regardless of the level of collegiality. Cranton (2006) proposes a number of strategies for mediating the potentially negative effects of power and authority in the classroom, such as not positioning oneself as an all-knowing expert, developing collaborative assessment practices, involving students in controlling the learning environment, being open and explicit about learning strategies, and developing authentic connections with students, many of which translate to organizational settings (pp. 122–126).

Organizational issues of power and authority can be more complex to meditate than those in traditional educational settings, as they also include cultural, political, and structural constraints and the consequences of challenging those in power can be significant. Some organizational structures may lend themselves more easily to collaboration and power sharing than others; those in a horizontal or networked organization may be more empowered for decision-making than those in a hierarchy, for example. At the same time, improvisers have learned to work within the givens of almost any scenario and find a generative space for exploration there.

### Improvisation Lesson 4: Name the Givens

Early in their introduction to concepts of improvisation, adults learn that, contrary to prevailing thought, creativity and improvisation often flow best within agreed-upon boundaries or "givens." These non-negotiable dimensions such as "who" (the players' roles), "what" (the main event or context of the scene), and "where" (the physical setting of the scene) do not limit but facilitate their improvisations. Challenges occur when there is either confusion or lack of agreement about the givens.

In both educational and organizational settings, a similar frustration can arise if roles (especially those with power and authority) are left undiscussed. For those in roles of power such as instructors, assessors, and managers, who are also committed to making room for transformation, it is essential to name the givens, the scope of the power, as well as its contradictions. I could hardly encourage adults to step out of their comfort zone if they felt that their behavior was being evaluated at every step. While I assured them that I was accountable to the university to assess the agreed-upon learning outcomes (demonstrated by their willingness to participate, their learning journal entries and class essays), I emphasized that I would not evaluate their improvisations. They would receive coaching and teaching points as they arose, and we all agreed that if there are no mistakes in improvisation, it was not fair to evaluate their content.

Organizational practitioners can similarly make room for transformation as they make explicit the givens of their roles and accountabilities, as well as their inherent contradictions. Managers may be both a champion of their team's success, innovation, and resource sharing, *and* accountable to deliver on their sales goal or profit projections. While this role includes responsibility for both positive and negative feedback, with consistent, shared cultivation of a generative learning space, power is mediated via clarity and enacted trust.

Some organizations discourage relationships that might heighten role contradictions or that appear to foster conflicts of interest. Recent research supports an opposite effect: people who report having a friendship with their manager are 2.5 times more likely to be satisfied with their job and are more likely to stay with the organization and be more productive and engaged with customers (Rath, 2006, p. 62). Knowing that their managers and colleagues genuinely care about them as people and want to see them succeed appears to be the strongest mitigating factor for the negative implications of power and authority.

## Relational Learning: Shifting from *Self-Consciousness* to *Self and Other Awareness*

In a whole-person framework for transformative learning, individual experience of the world is inextricable from the intersubjective and relational experience "because we experience the world with and through others. Whatever meaning we create has its roots in human actions, and the totality of social artifacts and cultural objects is grounded in human activity" (Wilson, 2002, p. 3). The most significant finding to emerge from my research was that as adults became more comfortable in and took greater responsibility for the learning space, their attentions began to shift from *self-consciousness* to *self and other awareness*. This shift was central to adults' descriptions of transformative learning.

Much of the literature on adult and experiential learning places the individual at the center. As I studied adults' experiences of learning improvisation, the relational, intersubjective nature of the learning soon eclipsed individual experiences to the point that it was impossible to isolate the individual experience of transformation from the group dynamic. Co-researchers learned *through* others as they observed and situated them within the learning space. They learned *in relation to* and *with* others as they directly experienced each other in improvised games and scenes, and as they connected outside of the classroom while sharing rides home, having after-class drinks, and performing outside activities. Co-researchers learned over time in ways that allowed them to witness each other's growing comfort, share in each other's good humor, and support each other when they felt frustrated and vulnerable. As they became more aware, accepting and appreciative of each other, they also began to privilege the meaning they made of their experiences in relation to each other over their relationships and experiences beyond their shared learning space that had initially influenced their meaning making and self-beliefs.

One of the unique aspects of the experience of learning improvisation is that the feedback is often immediate and public. Many co-researchers described breakthroughs or memorable experiences when they heard their classmates laughing or applauding in appreciation of their improvisation. As a group of improvisers returned to their seats, I often observed encouraging pats on the back and continued shared giggles or commentary. These experiences seemed to build as co-researchers became more attuned to each other's experiences and less concerned with judgment. As participants became more comfortable in the shared learning space, they moved from an almost exclusive focus on their own success or failure to an interest and appreciation in the group's success.

This shift was particularly facilitative for some adults. Starshine—who rarely spoke in class the first several weeks and had described herself as "shy" and declared, "I get nervous in front of people"—had a transformative experience improvising a scene halfway into the course. She reflected in her journal,

> Improvisation was great! I have never done this sort of show before. I was pretty amazed how I completely came out of my shell for once. I was physically and mentally open for anything to come my way. I have to say I was pretty astonished with myself. The class enjoyed it and I felt that I wasn't judged by them at all. In my honest opinion, I believe that this night was a defining night for me. I felt it as I was leaving the class. It was a feeling of sureness, freedom, and being optimistic about me.

Starshine's description highlights another dimension of relational learning; when co-researchers first became aware of what they were experiencing or expressing and then realized they were not being judged for those experiences or expressions, they appeared to accept and appreciate themselves more fully while embracing the experiences and expressions of their colleagues. This relational experience of awareness and acceptance appeared to be essential for those who described transformation.

The relational and public nature of improvisation experiences was not so much a dimension of the learning experience as it was *how* people learned. Individuals did not develop their improvisation skills, conceptual understanding, comfort, and confidence or have transformative experiences *separately* from their co-researchers, but they did so "with and through" them (Wilson, 2002, p. 3). Cook and Yanow (1993) centralize relational learning in their description of organizational learning as "the acquiring, sustaining, or changing of intersubjective meanings through the artifactual vehicles of their expression and transmission and the collective actions of the group" (p. 384).

While the embodied relational dynamic is heightened in the more overtly physical, interactive, and public practice of improvisation, it helps shine light on aspects to which we can be more attuned in formal and informal learning in all educational and organizational settings.

### Improvisation Lesson 5: Attune to the Embodied Relational Experience

Inviting adults to attune to the group process and their experience *within* the group supports an inclusive, embodied relational approach. Yorks and Kasl (2002a) have begun theorizing intersubjectivity in adult learning with their conception of "learning-within-relationship, a process in which persons strive to become engaged with both their own whole-person knowing and the whole-person knowing of their fellow learners" (p. 185). I would extend this conception to Kolb and Kolb's (2005) description of learning space and suggest that it is not only a "map of learning territories, a frame of reference within which many different ways of learning can flourish and interrelate" (p. 200) but also a fundamentally relational and intersubjective space in which adults engage each other and co-construct their experiences and meanings. The intersubjective nature of the learning space is inclusive of and symbiotically related to the transformation individuals describe experiencing there.

Extending this dimension of transformative learning to organizations has some constraints. While most are familiar with the ubiquitous phrase "there is no I in team," they are equally aware that their ultimate evaluation is based on their individual performance. Adults learning improvisation learned within similar contradictory constraints; they knew they would receive an individual grade, yet within their co-created learning space, they were also safe to explore beyond their comfort zones. As mindful executives, managers and other organizational participants hold and allow others to hold the learning space; a similar dynamic emerges in workplace collaborations. The shared energy and success of the collaboration eclipses individual self-consciousness, -interest, and -centeredness. Inviting attunement to the "whatness" of the experience is a key dimension of the shift from self-consciousness to self-and-other awareness.

### Time

Perhaps the most important factor for adults learning improvisation and for those who described transformative shifts was time. Each of the dimensions of learning space described above cannot emerge within tight time constraints. While it is possible to see glimpses of generative learning space within the first few class sessions, or during a single training day, the seasoning and ripening of transformation happen over time, as participants learn that they can trust each other, as they take increasing responsibility for co-creating the learning space and grow in comfort and confidence with their newly discovered capacities and frameworks. Adults also need the horizon of time to reflect on their experiences, to experiment with new approaches, ways of thinking, and relating to themselves and each other and, for some, to emerge from the shadows of their former self-concepts.

Practitioners who choose, in the interest of saving time and money, to decouple competence development from such transformative shifts will likely be disappointed in the impact of training-based strategies for transformation. To eliminate all but superficial reflection and meaning-making from experience would also eliminate many of the behavioral changes adults learning improvisation described. For adults learning improvisation, their descriptions of transformation were rooted in shifts in self-beliefs and an increasing awareness of their embodied relational experiences. For some, increasing awareness of *what* they were experiencing in a playful relational context challenged former self-beliefs as well as previously unconscious habits of being. Without the space for new embodied relational experiences and attunement to the *whatness* of the experience, transformation is unlikely to occur. In other words, an individual is unlikely to increase his or her participation in organizational creativity and collaboration initiatives if her self-belief remains "I don't consider myself that creative."

Making room for such experiences and encouraging attunement to them is a significant shift for most practitioners. Both experiential learning and much of transformative learning theory and practice, in their emphasis on the cognitive dimensions of experience, often position experience as a stepping stone to the learning, not central to it. If we believe that experience is useful only for the meaning we make of it, rather than the actual embodied experience itself, we may miss the epicenter to the transformative opportunity. Adults who begin experiencing themselves differently are already living into new capacities and competencies. They may articulate it on reflection, and the transformation is rooted in the embodied experience. Parker Palmer (1980) pointed learners in this direction when he counseled, "Do not think your way into a new kind of living, but live your way into a new kind of thinking."

## Learning to "Love the Question"

Returning to this chapter's question, "can we make room for transformative learning in organizations?" I take guidance from Rilke (1934) who counseled the young poet to

> have patience with everything unresolved in your heart and to try to love the questions themselves as if they were locked rooms or books written in a very foreign language. Don't search for the answers, which could not be given to you now, because you would not be able to live them. And the point is to live everything. Live the questions now. Perhaps then, someday far in the future, you will gradually, without even noticing it, live your way into the answer. (p. 34)

Rilke foreshadowed Kovan and Dirkx's (2003) findings in their study of long-time environmental activists, many of whom described a capacity to "listen to what is not known" and a continued openness to new learning and questioning as sustaining them in challenging times. For practitioners, "listening to what is not known" means not settling for simplistic answers to complex questions, or not considering the competing and contradictory values embedded in both our educational and organizational learning spaces. There is, of course, no one prescription for making room for transformative learning in organizations, as prescriptions assume the possibility of controlling much that cannot and should not be controlled.

Some of us despair that the barriers to transformative learning in organizations are insurmountable, especially if the responsibility for overcoming them is given to a handful of practitioners and not shared and actively supported by leaders, stakeholders, and participants throughout the organization. In these contexts, the most ethical response is to reflect the constraints back to the stakeholders and suggest responsible alternatives to ambitious transformation. Many of us are finding hope in organizations where there is room to begin making space for transformation—where there are practitioners, executives, managers, facilitators, and participants situated throughout their organizations who understand both their responsibility to the learning space and the need to make room for others to hold it for themselves when they are ready.

*Driving home the last night of another class in which adults learned improvisation, I reflect on the closing circle of shared appreciation, and the small groupings of adults exchanging contact information and good wishes for the coming spring break. An odd feeling creeps in. I notice I missed the occasional hyperbolic expressions of gratitude for my facilitation of the experience. This quarter, no small group of adults was patiently waiting to share a final private comment or hug. This quarter, while the adults connected and bid farewell to each other, I quietly orga-*

*nized their papers, packed my bag, and then slipped out with a silent wave to the last pair still engaged in conversation. I sat with this odd feeling all the way home and as I turned down my street, I realized the irony; successfully co-creating a generative social space for learning, a space where the learners truly have room to hold the space for themselves, had rendered me irrelevant. It dawns on me that, while less gratifying to my ego, this "withering away of the teacher" (Shor, 1996, p. 60) was a sign of success, just as were each actor's and stage crew member's references to "my show" by opening night. I smiled as I parked the car.*

# References

Argyris, C. (1992). *On organizational learning.* Cambridge, MA: Blackwell.

Argyris, C., & Schon, D. A. (1978). *Organizational learning: A theory of action perspective.* Reading, MA: Addison-Wesley.

Cook, S. D. N., & Yanow, D. (1993). Culture and organizational learning. *Journal of Management Inquiry, 2*(4), 373–390.

Cranton, P. (2006). *Understanding and promoting transformative learning: A guide for educators of adults,* 2nd edition. San Francisco: Jossey-Bass.

Daft, R. L. (2001). *Organization theory and design,* 7th edition. Cincinnati: South-Western College Publishing.

Fenwick, T. (1998). Questioning the concept of the learning organization. In S. M. Scott, B. Spencer, & A. M. Thomas (Eds.), *Learning for life: Canadian readings in adult education,* pp. 140–152. Toronto: Thompson Educational.

Greenwood, D. D., & Levin, M. (1998). *Introduction to action research.* Thousand Oaks, CA: Sage.

Johnston, R., & Usher, R. (1997). Re-theorizing experience: Adult learning in contemporary social practices. *Studies in the Education of Adults, 29*(2), 137–153.

Kegan, R. (2000). What "form" transforms? A constructive-developmental approach to transformative learning. In J. Mezirow (Ed.), *Learning as transformation.* San Francisco: Jossey-Bass.

Kerr, J. L. (2004). The limits of organizational democracy. *Academy of Management Executive, 18*(3), 81–95.

Kolb, A., & Kolb, D. (2005). Learning styles and learning spaces: Learning in higher education. *Academy of Management Learning and Education, 4*(2), 193–212.

Kovan, J. T., & Dirkx, J. M. (2003). "Being called awake": The role of transformative learning in the lives of environmental activists. *Adult Education Quarterly, 53*(2), 99–118.

Lewin, K. (1946). Action research and minority problems. *Journal of Social Issues, 2,* 34–46.

Meyer, P. (2006). *Learning space and space for learning: Adults' intersubjective experiences of improvisation.* Unpublished doctoral dissertation. Santa Barbara, CA: Fielding Graduate University.

Mezirow, J., & Associates (Eds.). (1990). *Fostering critical reflection in adulthood: A guide to transformative and emancipatory learning.* San Francisco: Jossey-Bass.

Nonaka, I., & Konno, N. (1998). The concept of *ba:* Building for knowledge creation. *California Management Review, 40*(3), 40–54.

Nowlen, P. M. (1988). *A new approach to continuing education for business and the professions: The performance model.* Old Tappan, NJ: Macmillan.

Palmer, P. J. (1980). *The promise of paradox: A celebration of contradictions in the Christian life.* Notre Dame, IN: Ave Maria Press.

Park, P. (1997). *Types of action-oriented research.* Unpublished manuscript. Fielding Graduate University, Santa Barbara, CA.

Rath, T. (2006). *Vital friends.* New York: Gallup Press.

Rilke, R. M. (1934). *Letters to a young poet.* (M. D. Herter Norton, Trans.). New York: W. W. Norton.

Rogers, C. R. (1961). *On becoming a person: A therapist's view of psychotherapy.* Boston: Houghton Mifflin.

Rousseau, D. M., Sitkin, S. B., Burt, R. S., & Camerer, C. (1998). Not so different after all: A cross-discipline view of trust. *Academy of Management Review, 23*(3), 393–404.

Senge, P. M. (1990). *The fifth discipline: The art and practice of the learning organization* (First Currency Paperback, 1994 edition). New York: Doubleday.

Senge, P. M. (2003). Taking personal change seriously: The impact of organizational learning on management practice. *The Academy of Management Executive, 17*(2), 47–50.

Shor, I. (1996). *When students have power: Negotiating authority in a critical pedagogy.* Chicago: University of Chicago Press.

Spolin, V. (1963/1983). *Improvisation for the theater.* Evanston, IL: Northwestern University Press.

Taylor, E. W. (1998). The theory and practice of transformative learning: A critical review, *Information Series No. 374.* Columbus, OH: ERIC Clearing House on Adult, Career, and Vocational Education.

Taylor, E. W. (2000). Fostering Mezirow's transformative learning theory in the adult education classroom: A critical review. *The Canadian Journal for the Study of Adult Education, 14*(2), 1–28.

Taylor, E. W. (2001). Adult education quarterly from 1989 to 1999: A content analysis of all submissions. *Adult Education Quarterly, 51*(4), 322–340.

Taylor, E. W. (2006). *A critical review of the empirical research of transformative learning (1999–2005).* Paper presented at the Adult Education Research Conference, Minneapolis, MN.

Voronov, M., & Yorks, L. (2005). Taking power seriously in strategic organizational learning. *The Learning Organization, 12*(1), 9–25.

Wilson, T. D. (2002). Alfred Schütz: Phenomenology and research methodology for information behavior research, *Fourth International Conference on Information Seeking in Context (ISIC4).* Universidade Lusiada, Lisbon, Portugal.

Yorks, L., & Kasl, E. (2002a). Toward a theory and practice for whole-person learning: Reconceptualizing experience and the role of activity. *Adult Education Quarterly, 52*(3), 176–192.

Yorks, L., & Kasl, E. (Eds.) (2002b). *Collaborative inquiry as a strategy for adult learning,* Vol. 94. San Francisco: Jossey-Bass.

Yorks, L., & Marsick, V. J. (2000). Organizational learning and transformation. In J. a. A. Mezirow (Ed.), *Learning as transformation,* pp. 253–281. San Francisco: Jossey-Bass.

# Chapter 4

---

## Transformative Learning in Participative Processes That Reframe Self-Identity

*Beth Fisher-Yoshida*

## Introduction

Some of us may intentionally participate in activities that are designed to change our self-images and identities, while at other times our self-images and identities may be changed as an unintended consequence of something that has taken place. This chapter discusses the personal identity transformations that took place in participants from an organization called Second Chance (a pseudonym of a nonprofit organization) while they engaged in a participatory action research (PAR) process (as part of a grant) that we as external consultants facilitated. The chapter will cover the following topics: a description of PAR including its philosophy and methodology; a description of the nonprofit organization Second Chance; the background of what led up to this initiative; the outcomes of the PAR experience; highlights of points of transformation.

## Background

I would like to refer to the organization as *Second Chance* because that is what they give their clients, a second chance at life. It is a nonprofit organization whose mission is to rehabilitate those with criminal justice histories.[5] They have been interested in improving the quality of and expanding on the services they offer their clients, enhancing the internal operations of their organization and

---

[5] A criminal justice history refers to whether someone has ever been arrested and convicted of a crime and may have served time in prison as a result of the conviction.

developing the capacity of their staff. This organization has many years of un-tapped data that is waiting to be analyzed and written up for publication.

The executive director is a dynamic and tenacious person with great com-passion. One unique aspect about Second Chance is that 70–80% of their staff are former clients. While the organization does a wonderful job at rehabilitating their clients, the reality is that their employment opportunities are constrained because of their criminal history. Another phenomenon is that many clients want to stay and work with the organization because this is where they feel comfortable and safe and can succeed. They don't feel that sense of confidence and success in the outside world, and this has been an area the organization has been trying to address. There are a fixed number of clients the organization can support and maintain as staff. So capacity building of their staff, which may include a transformation in how they see themselves as being capable and suc-cessful, and improved services to clients are critical factors for future success (Mezirow, 2000; Daloz, 1999).

Second Chance has a policy of zero tolerance for violence that they have been able to maintain with clients who either have violent backgrounds or have been in very violent environments. Somehow these clients are able to adhere to this policy, and it is important to learn from them how they are able to achieve this in the hope that this knowledge can be transferred to address school vio-lence. If there is not an effective intervention in the schools, the students could take the path in life that will lead them to be future clients of Second Chance. Second Chance staff can make a significant contribution because they can more readily identify with these youth and will be able to identify what it was they would have benefited from so that they could have taken a different path in their lives and apply those interventions with these youth. And there is a grow-ing faction within Second Chance that wants to target youth at risk.

## Theoretical Foundations

This chapter will focus on how we have been attempting to create the space in which transformative learning can take place at Second Chance. The conceptual framework from which this collaboration is built is a blending of what we have coined appreciative participatory action research (A-PAR), which is applying an appreciative approach to more traditional participatory action research proc-esses; Coordinated Management of Meaning (CMM), which is a practical theory that allows for people to tell their stories and coordinate their meanings for mutual understanding; and transformative learning, which recognizes and pro-vides processes for people to be able to shift their mindsets to have altered views of how they see themselves and their relationships. These will be discussed later in the chapter, highlighting why they were selected, identifying how they link together, and exemplifying the impact and outcomes derived (Fisher-Yoshida, 2003; Mezirow, 2000; Park, 2001; Pearce, 2004; Smith, Willms, & Johnson, 1997).

## Gaining Buy-in

There was potentially so much to cover in terms of how we worked together, we realized it was important to frame the scope of the project to manage expectations. We framed it as making recommendations on how Second Chance can improve their internal operations including capacity building and external services to their clients, while at the same time learning from Second Chance ways in which to lessen school violence, especially with youth at risk. We knew that although top management approved of this process, we needed to establish credibility with the staff. In order to do this, we believed strongly that in whatever we do we need to model the skills and processes that we are promoting. Therefore, in order to take an ecological approach in which representation of the system is involved, we limited the initial participation to the subsystem of the organization itself. We were being mindful of the manageability aspect in terms of the size of the working group and the divergence of interests, so we collectively decided not to include clients, funders, and others who were a part of the larger system of which Second Chance was a part. We depended on the chief of staff to recommend people from different areas of the organization with different levels represented. The group ended up being about 15 highly committed participants. They know their charge is to have all voices heard and they have been taking that very seriously in how they have been working and the actions they have been planning to take. The group consists of both those who have criminal justice histories and those who do not.

## Why Transformative Learning?

The population we are working with has deeply ingrained identities, both on an individual level and as part of a collective. Some of this they developed individually and is due to the life experiences and choices they have made in taking the paths they did. In other ways, the community and society have also labeled them and identified them as being of a particular group with all the attributions placed on this group. Self-image is critical in influencing what we believe we are able to accomplish. The staff with criminal justice histories needed to transform their self-image if they were to create and act on new opportunities and new ways of being in the world (Fisher, 2006; Daloz, 1999).

For the staff without criminal justice histories, transformative learning can provide opportunity to reframe how they view their clients and the possibilities for them and the organization. This will lead to them reinforcing the new attitudes, beliefs, and perceptions of their clients. We believe it will positively impact the quality of the interpersonal relationships amongst the staff and between staff and clients.

One of the organization's expressed goals is to develop capacity to expand skill sets and abilities of the staff and that in turn may also transfer to expanding the possibilities of what they believe their clients can do. We believe that for any intervention to be effective, the mindsets of the people involved have to be open to the possibility of this potential expansion. They need to identify the assumptions they have about themselves and their capabilities and the reception of society, so that they will be able to take in new information and skills and build on what they already know. The organization cannot sustain a change unless the staff believes that this change can really happen. The principles of transformative learning lend themselves to creating this dynamic so that real change can take place (Brookfield, 2005; Cranton, 2006; Mezirow, 2000).

This is why we believe the process in which we work together is so critical. It is much more meaningful to live the process and principles than to write them and espouse them without experiencing how they are actually enacted. Living what we are trying to create and struggling through how it happens and its impact is capacity building in itself. The planning focus group has been struggling with so many broad and detailed issues they have had opportunities to work through, that they have been developing the skills of being able to create an environment amongst themselves in which it is safe to show dissent from popular views and to challenge the assumptions they are each bringing and how this is impacting them all. It is allowing them to discern what works well and what is not working well, so that when they collect opinions from the rest of the organization they will be better prepared to manage opposition and challenges in a more constructive way. They will be speaking from a place of knowing through experience than only a cognitive understanding they are espousing. This will enhance their credibility, which in turn will enhance their own self-esteem in being able to be effective in a way they may not have previously been (Argyris, 1993; Deutsch, 1973; Schon, 1983).

## Creating the Space for Transformation

There are processes that need to be put in place that will facilitate having all voices heard in ways they want to be heard. There is an implication that this is built on collaboration and, therefore, a collaborative process is needed. Collaborative processes will lead to collaborative outcomes. This will ensure that the participants are satisfied and that there is a higher chance of the initiatives decided upon being successfully implemented and sets the tone for future collaboration (Deutsch, 1973).

There are many unknowns, such as the client team's previous relationships and their feelings and experiences with change in the organization. We heard about some of this in the dialogues that took place. I use the word *dialogue* intentionally because the characteristics of how they engaged in creating a shared understanding allowed for turn taking so all could be heard, opening a space for different opinions, questioning assumptions, clarifying points of view, and showing mutual respect even if there wasn't agreement (Buber, 1955; Pearce & Pearce, 2003).

Several participants in the group felt skeptical because they had been with the agency long enough to have experienced different change efforts that didn't work, or there were changes imposed with which they may not have agreed. Our ears perked up because we didn't want this to be perceived as just another "flavor of the month" change, nor did we want the participants to feel that changes are being imposed on them. This would go against the principle of PAR, which clearly emphasizes that PAR is a bottom-up approach (Smith, Willms, & Johnson, 1997).

Some of the feelings about change were centered on participants' feelings about their relationship with top management and their tenure with the agency. There were clear distinctions in terms of tenure with the organization: those having longer tenures of nine to sixteen years felt they could access top management whenever they wanted to and speak openly. Some of the newer members with tenures of less than three years did not feel as comfortable as they did not have enough of a rapport with the top management team. Until this point in the process, there was not a representative of top management on the team. This was done deliberately because we wanted to create an atmosphere in which all members were comfortable speaking openly. We felt that having a member of top management may silence some members. Through the course of conversation, the group decided they wanted and needed a representative of top management to be a part of their group, and they wanted to decide who that person would be. The chosen person gladly joined and has added a very positive, action-oriented dynamic to the group.

The newer members were initially more enthusiastic about change, believing they can make positive changes, and were willing to put the extra effort into doing so. The more senior members were more cautious because they have been through other change efforts before and realized the amount of work and commitment it takes to make them successful. The past change efforts weren't reflected in the results achieved. All agreed this would be an additional commitment.

We felt positively about group processes providing guidance so that efforts weren't wasted. This created a need for maintaining a delicate balance, providing time and space for the group members to fully discuss ideas and uncover assumptions while at the same time feeling that they had been productive at that session. Some members of the group waited their turn to speak and exercised restraint in how much they contributed. Others did not. One member frequently looked at the facilitators with pleading eyes to do something. He wanted a much more highly structured group process and didn't always see the value in the depth of the conversations others were having. He deferred to what he perceived as our authority and chose to not take it upon himself to say something to shorten the length of the conversations. Eventually, when we asked for feedback he mentioned he was happy results were being achieved.

## Managing Decision-Making Tension

In order to address this tension between dialogues with breadth and depth and productivity, we collectively decided goals for each session. This way there was agreement at every session about the purpose, goals, actions, steps, and tangible outcomes. It allowed for free discussion and redirection of the conversation as needed. It provided security for those who wanted a more structured, linear process.

We introduced other guidelines that we thought were integral to a participative process in which there would be ample opportunities for transformation to take place. This included uncovering what they knew and needed to know about the process. In doing this, we wanted to arouse curiosity, model openness, and disclosure and identify gaps for understanding the scope of the project and their roles in it. At the next session, we explored our frames of reference, where they come from, and how others have different and equally valid frames of reference from which they operate. We linked the assumptions we hold to our frames of reference and considered how this could lead to variations on the meaning each person derived from a particular conversation. This was done to allow for the presence and acceptance of difference. An assumption that is sometimes made about marginalized populations is that they have a greater capacity for acceptance of difference since they are outside of the mainstream. This is not necessarily the case. The marginalized population also has an identity and specific experiences from which their frames of reference and assumptions are drawn, and this creates the same type of boundary from acceptance of difference that may be characteristic of the dominant population (Mezirow, 2000).

## Appreciative Participatory Action Research

The A-PAR process is structured loosely because it is also an emergent process. In PAR interventions, the process and results are participant driven as they determine what needs to be addressed and how they will address it. As facilitators, we were there to introduce this concept and support them. We created a draft timeline at the beginning and, after a few months, were able to collectively modify it accordingly. Our role was to support the group by keeping the process going between sessions (Smith, Willms, & Johnson, 1997).

We explored the phenomenon of some not being active between sessions, especially because in previous conversations there had been concern about the survey to be distributed to the agency staff and sensitivity shown about how people liked to communicate. There were many in the agency not at ease with e-mail or writing, so they thought about checklists and hard copies instead of open-ended responses. We wondered if expecting the participants in the focus planning group to send e-mails was getting in the way of group members contributing, so we raised that concern and offered voice mail as an alternative. The group decided you needed to choose one or more media to communicate between sessions to stay an active member of the group. A note to highlight here is that this is one example of how the group took ownership of their process, which ensured buy-in and accountability.

The members of the planning focus group knew each other to differing degrees before this project. Since they all worked in different sections of the organization in five different locations and since they all had varying tenures with the agency, most did not know each other well. The group went through Tuckman's stages of group formation (forming, storming, norming, and performing) and for the most part was very vocal in expressing their satisfaction or dissatisfaction with what was being said and how they were managing their process. For the less vocal members of the group, they had to wait for openings to voice their opinions and the group eventually became more sensitive to making that space for those participants. The group has reached the performing stage. The creation of the survey, project name, and logo and the strategy for rolling it out across the agency really shifted them into this stage. Seeing the tangible results of their efforts allowed them to smooth out their norming processes and allow for more tolerance of difference and how they each contributed to the group (Kreitner & Kinicki, 2006).

Many of the members began discussing this project with other colleagues and built up excitement and expectations. We brought it to their attention that since expectations were being raised, they needed to pay attention to how they were going to deliver so their efforts wouldn't be labeled as one more failed change effort. They expressed awareness of this and are taking seriously how to follow through with deliverables that will engage and satisfy their colleagues. Staying focused on the process and not jumping ahead to solutions has been a challenge. If they want to stay open to the process and open to hearing all voices, they need to stay open to what actions will be taken because at this stage it is still an unknown. The presentation at the full staff meeting aroused curiosity and enthusiasm amongst the staff. Engaging all staff members in the process makes everyone responsible and is causing a notable change in the organization.

When we embarked on this journey, we were interested in conducting a PAR process with Second Chance. PAR is also known as popular education in which education is for the purpose of social change. An integral part of the PAR process is that it is for personal and social transformation for the liberation of oppressed people with a firm basis in inquiry (Reason & Bradbury, 2001). Each PAR experience is different yet they are all based on the following set of principles:

> *Intend liberation* characterized by justice, freedom, and ecological balance.
>
> *Develop a compassionate culture* as stories, values, and experiences converge to strengthen commitment to a shared struggle.
>
> *Participate in dynamic processes of action-reflection* (praxis), which are interactive and unique to each group.
>
> *Value what people know, believe, and feel* and start with where they are situated, which honors these as legitimate forms of knowing.
>
> *Investigate and act collectively* as a group.
>
> *Produce new knowledge* as a conscious effort.
>
> (Smith, Willms, & Johnson, 1997)

## Creating Knowledge

The PAR process honors knowledge in different ways from traditional research methodologies. The participants bring with them insider information that only they can possess from being within the system. Park identifies three different types of knowledge that participants possess that should be recognized and honored. These are: (1) *representational knowledge*, which has two subtypes of *functional*, which portrays a person, thing, or event in its functionality as in "heavy rainfalls lead to flooding" and *interpretive*, which takes into account background, intentions, and feelings to bring the researcher as close to what is to be known as possible; (2) *relational knowledge*, in which someone or something is known in its human aspects, affectively; and (3) *reflective knowledge*, which has its roots in critical theory and calls for emancipation as in Freire's terms *conscientization*. It is reflective knowledge that is most closely linked with the practice of transformative learning in which certain critically reflective practices are put into place so that we question our actions in terms of their morality and values (Freire, 1970; Park, 2001).

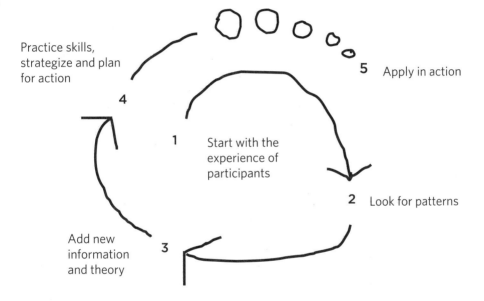

Figure 4.1: The Spiral Model (Arnold et al., 1991)

## Making Sense of Power

These PAR principles are asking for engagement in ways that people may not have typically engaged in the past. It requires a different mindset and set of skills that may be learned in the process of doing. There is also a different relationship to power that is being called forth, away from *power over* and *powerlessness* to *power within* and *power with*. The usual understanding of power is about power over—getting someone to do something s/he may not have done on her/his own—and powerlessness is a dependence on others for support. The PAR process fosters power within as the participants are feeling valued for who they are, what they know, and their contributions that they are able to bring forth with pride. The PAR process also fosters "power with" or shared power, which arises from the social relationships they are developing in the fluid and emerging interactions that take place throughout the PAR process as the participants work in praxis toward achieving their desired outcome. Park (2001) relates his three classifications of knowledge with power. Representational knowledge is linked as "the power to control objectifiable reality" (p. 87). Relational knowledge is the power of being with others in solidarity and knowing that we are not alone, while reflective knowledge builds up our moral fiber to have the confidence to engage in social change (McClelland, 1975; Starhawk, 1990; Park, 2001).

These new experiences of power have been transformative for the participants. Their life experiences to this point had them operating out of a power over and powerlessness frame of reference as they looked to authority to make the rules, make decisions, and condone or condemn their actions. Here they have honored each other through their listening and inquiry, giving recognition by having their suggestions written on the board and having their collective efforts result in a survey that has been printed and distributed agency-wide to all 200 members. We did not empower these participants but rather created a space in which empowerment could be obtained. They were rewriting their histories, their self-images (Abalos, 1998; Starhawk, 1990).

> When people struggle together to meet challenges and resolve problems, they add to their complexity as individuals, their abilities to care and be cared for, their sense of rooted connectedness, and their capacity to create social justice. Giving birth to the knowledge of hopeful dreams, people in participatory action-research processes can strengthen their commitment to a meaningful way of life. (Smith in Smith, Willms, & Johnson, 1997, p. 174)

All of the above PAR principles provide for ways the participants can gain new awareness, new skills, new relationships, and new ways of being in the world. Some of the ways PAR is described in the literature are problem or deficit focused. Groups come together to identify what is not working well, what is causing disease, and what needs to be changed. We were very conscious of capacity building, and so we modified PAR to be A-PAR, which adds in the word "appreciative" as in the process of *appreciative inquiry*, which allows for the building on past successes to create the best of what could be. The participants are being honored for their various forms of knowing as well as for what is working well in what they have been contributing to (Cooperrider & Srivastva, 1987; Reason & Bradbury, 2001).

## Modeling as a Strong Statement

In working with this group of participants in an A-PAR process that is liberating, honoring, and empowering, we as facilitators were very conscious of our behavior. This meant we needed to model the skills and behaviors that we were touting in order for us in our roles and the whole project to have any credibility. The initial success of the project rested on our shoulders. The participants were learning this new way of interacting so we had the responsibility to enable, encourage, and protect them so that they could experience the potential benefits of this process.

In creating the space for all voices to be heard, for there to be a dialogue, we had to advocate for each participant and what they needed to be able to fully engage. This meant that we had to think of respectful ways to balance voices in the conversation and to do this in a way that allowed the group to take ownership of participation. This is easier to do with those who are sensitive and self-aware of their own verbal activity. Naturally, through the course of the meetings and getting to know each other through these dialogue sessions and small working groups, the participants were able to develop trust and support of one another. This was exhibited in people opening up and sharing and in the more balanced participation.

For the project to be successful, we needed to establish trust. We heard about previous change efforts that raised expectations only to fall short on delivery. We didn't want to be guilty of being all talk and no action. The group members experienced change by making it happen, first with taking a stand and committing to this endeavor, then by listening to and honoring each other and coming together in connectivity to create an intervention into the agency that was inclusive.

## Locating What They Know and Need to Know: Coordinated Management of Meaning

In order to build the working atmosphere that we thought would be conducive to a productive process, we had them form small groups and collectively tell the stories of what they knew and needed to know about this project. We introduced CMM, a practical theory that provides tools that will enable people to better articulate what is known and needed to be known in order for them to act constructively together. CMM is based on the belief that this articulation will lead toward the making of better social worlds, and we collectively wanted to create a better social world within this group and organization. According to CMM, meaning emerges in the process of people relating to each other and we try to make sense of our fluid interactions with the exchange of our thoughts, feelings, and actions. We, therefore, co-create the meaning we are making, and social constructionism postulates that there can be multiple narratives coexisting that define truth and reality. In order for effective communication to occur in which meaning is transferred, we need to pay attention to these coexisting narratives. In looking at these narratives or stories we tell, CMM shifts the focus from *what is said* to *what we are making* in this communication process (Jost & Kruglanski, 2002; Pearce, 1994).

There are three foundational principles of CMM that address what we are making in communication: *coherence, coordination,* and *mystery.* Coherence is when we strive to understand, find meaning, or make sense of what is taking place in our lives. It is something that takes place internally and yet happens through the process of relating. Coordination is when we attempt to create shared meaning with whom we are relating. Mutual understanding happens in the space between. Mystery calls forth our curiosity to want to create deeper, mutual understanding and that life and communication are so complex that there will always be more to know and in which to inquire (Cronen, Pearce, & Changsheng, 1989/90).

CMM has several tools to use and we decided to introduce the LUUUUTT model, which is a storytelling model. It is an acronym, and the visual depiction of the model shows the flow of the stories and how their flow influences other stories.

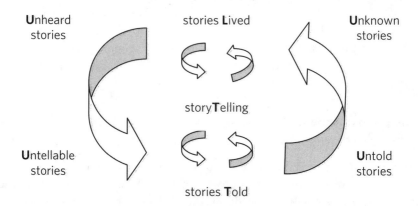

Figure 4.2: LUUUUTT Model (Pearce, 2004)

The question that was framed was: Identify what they know about this project and what they need to know. Below is a summary of what the three groups identified in response to the question.

| stories Lived | Staff's participation in focus groups, trainings, conferences, courses |
|---|---|
| | Executives running agency not present at this meeting |
| | Line staff doesn't feel comfortable challenging authority |
| | Saying hello without getting a response |
| | Everyone is willingly participating |
| | Getting along |
| | Passion and enthusiasm are evident |
| | Personal experience—sharing point of view, stories we can relate to |
| | Work we do here will indirectly affect services |
| | Promoting vision/mission of the agency via different channels |
| Untold stories | Prior research providing evidence that conflict resolution model is effective for large organizations |
| Unheard stories | How everybody feels about this so far; is everyone willing to continue? |
| | How will gaps in communication be bridged to include all levels of staff and departments? |
| | Misconception of other units' duties/responsibilities |
| Unknown stories | How this project will affect job security |
| | Real motive behind this project |
| | The outcome |
| | Why was Second Chance chosen for this project? |
| | Will the "silos" concept be decreased? |
| | Who will still be here four years from now? |
| | How heavy the commitment will be? |
| | The decision-making process in place |
| | Actual impact program has in changing clients' lives |
| | The level of participation if schools are involved |
| | Will Second Chance get paid as consultants if involved with the schools? |
| | How this will translate to schools? |
| Untellable stories | True feelings and opinions about working at Second Chance |
| | Funding dictates the services offered |
| | Our influence is advisory; we need executive approval for anything to be implemented |
| | Clash between administration and program; lack of understanding and appreciation between each camp |
| | True empathy/sympathy for different units |
| | What are the $ involved; what is the grant level? |
| | Do the facilitators think it will work with Second Chance based on their experience so far? |
| | True motive for Second Chance's part |

| stories **T**old | Staff is overworked and underpaid |
| | Staff does not receive verbal appreciation |
| | ICCCR is here to enhance the organization's communication and conflict resolution process |
| | All levels of agency staff are involved for transparency and empowerment |
| | Focus group is also for own personal development |
| | This is long-term, asking for commitment and consistency; long-term commitment for everyone involved |
| | Goal is to enhance/create services |
| | The outcome of this project will influence the school project |
| story**T**elling | Small group discussions at project kick off workshop |

Table 4.1: LUUUUTT Model Chart (Pearce, 2004)

These responses confirmed there were varying degrees of understanding as to the purpose of this process. There was a question raised about our role about which we thought we had been clear. Some thought that this was an intervention about school violence and not about their organization. We knew we had some points to clarify for shared understanding.

Since the majority of the staff at Second Chance had criminal justice histories, there was a dynamic that existed in how they dealt with authority. Many felt inhibited by authority and didn't trust them. They also didn't feel they had voice or power with authority, and this influenced how effective they thought their initiative could be.

## Being Inclusive

One of the main principles of PAR is that it is a bottom-up movement and needs to be inclusive of the system. We knew it made sense to work with a representative sample of the organization's population, and yet we didn't want this group to be perceived as being elitist and exclusionary. We emphasized inclusiveness up front, and the group embraced that notion and suggested developing a survey.

In this development, several unexpected conversations took place. I say unexpected because on these occasions many of the members present, if not all of them, were surprised at the beliefs of others in the room. One such topic that comes to mind is the relationship between the individual and the criminal justice system: to be more specific, whether the person had been arrested/convicted or has possibly served time in prison as compared to those who have never been arrested. Those who have never been arrested, which is the minority of the staff, believed that the organization favors those who have criminal justice histories. This is so pervasive among this portion of the staff that there is even a joke that goes around saying that if one of them went out and robbed a store they would get a promotion. When one of the members shared this joke with the rest of the group, those who have criminal justice histories were really surprised because it was the opposite of how they believed the organization viewed the staff. According to this portion of the staff, they believed the organization favored those without criminal justice histories, which is most evident in the composition of the top management team (the majority of whom are Caucasian and those without criminal justice histories). This is not consistent with being representative of the majority of the constituency of the organization.

This was a breakthrough moment and there was a pause in the conversation. The group was amazed that there were such extreme views held by the members of the same organization, each portion convinced that the way they were seeing the situation is the way it is. Each group attributed their career development and those of the same category to their criminal justice status, when in actuality there were competing stories being held as truth. It caused them to take a step back and examine the assumptions they were holding, the stories they were telling. They were so moved they felt it imperative to include these questions on the survey to understand how the rest of the staff felt about this. Trying to get the wording to be precise enough to capture what they wanted to know while trying to be politically correct and thorough was a challenge. Then they came up with the term "criminal justice history," which is the expression I have been using in this write-up (Jost & Kruglanski, 2002). As a reminder, a criminal justice history refers to whether one has ever been convicted of a crime independent of whether they were incarcerated.

## Identifying Frames and Assumptions

The group knew there was a lot at stake in terms of them establishing credibility with their colleagues. They did this by exploring through dialogue what it was they really wanted to know in the survey to make a difference in the organization. At times some members held onto their ideas and were not open to different ideas. They explored the assumptions they held about the organization, the survey, and the type of intervention they were trying to create. It allowed them to better craft the questions they were asking and to engage various perspectives the recipients of the survey might hold, as they were not privy to these exploratory conversations. Unearthing their assumptions also showed their biases based on their experiences in the organization and how those biases influenced the wording they selected (Brookfield, 2005; Mezirow, 2000).

There were varying degrees of flexibility in being able to hear other points of view. When the group was in their early forming stage, there were many parallel monologues taking place. They formed smaller groups and as the participants began to query each other with curiosity to explore the assumptions behind each suggestion, there were more cooperative processes taking place. They really listened to each other and were able to take core concepts and develop them to be representative of the group's ideas. There was openness to feedback as the group became more comfortable.

## Building a Broader Level of Inclusiveness

They wanted to have a name to refer to this effort that would distinguish it from others. Someone suggested the "Light the Way" project, and a large majority of the members liked that name and wanted to use it. A member of the group who is an IT specialist volunteered to design a logo, and there was great appreciation shown from other members to her for volunteering to do this. Ideas were floated and this coincided with the agency redoing its Web site and logo.

The naming of the project and the selection of the logo generated a great deal of excitement. There was a new level of camaraderie and appreciation emerging amongst the participants as a result of selecting a name. The group was bonding and this was a motivating factor for them. They were also relieved and pleased that they produced a tangible outcome after weeks of what seemed to some "just talking."

The balance between relationship building and task completion has been an interesting journey. In order to have an inclusive process, there need to be collaborative processes in place for all to be heard. To create an atmosphere that is safe enough for all to give voice takes time in relationship building. For those with a relationship orientation, this was a deeply gratifying process. For those with a need for task completion this was a frustrating process because they wanted more results. To respond to this, we defined outcomes for each session with a timeline, understanding that this is an emergent process. There were small gains along the way that kept the task-oriented people involved.

Now they had the charge of deciding how to roll this initiative out to the rest of their colleagues in the organization. They wanted to be inclusive and they knew it was critical to frame the project in a way that their colleagues could understand in the way they wanted it to be understood. They decided to introduce the project at a full staff meeting.

Anonymity came up as being critical to the success of the survey. Stories were relayed about how some supervisors would review surveys to identify handwriting and this was a concern to them. They requested that we, the facilitators, be present at each of the five locations when the survey was being presented and completed to ensure anonymity. Of course, we agreed.

There would be a combination of a survey consisting of a checklist and space for comments and possibly interviews with some as a follow-up. They would let their colleagues know that action steps would be forthcoming.

## Conducting Research

The organization was building capacity in their staff while working on this project by creating the survey, analyzing the results, writing up a report, and making recommendations based on the survey and interview outcomes. Now they were more prepared to analyze and write for publication about the data the agency had been collecting in their database. Developing research skills in some of the staff was one way of being able to satisfy both goals. Through the process of doing, they were learning by experience about research.

One of the action steps will be to create a task force to receive further training and practice in research. This will be useful to them as they appeal to potential funders and donors for more financial support of their programs and to influence policymakers around prison reform.

There is a lived experience that the participants can draw upon as a reference instead of learning about research conceptually. When they work with the data from the organization's database, the research will have additional meaning as it is about their organization and will benefit them either directly or indirectly. This will be a second round of research, with meaningful data adding to the reinforcement of their newly acquired research skills.

## Next Steps

The members of the planning focus group have been able to engage with each other in new ways and that has led to transformed perspectives in how they see themselves, each other, and the organization. They have learned through direct experience that they can make a difference and be valued for doing so. They have learned new ways to trust and collaborate with colleagues and how to create synergy, resulting in so much more than what they gained through their individual efforts.

There will be other interventions as a result of the survey and interviews. There is momentum in the agency, with many more people at all levels taking on a "can do" attitude. When decisions and action steps need to be taken, the participants of this planning focus group will take leadership in facilitating dialogue sessions and PAR processes to spread the learning more thoroughly throughout the organization.

## Summary

There were several points of transformative moments the participants in the planning focus group experienced to varying degrees. These were:

*Modified self-images and new personal identities* that evolved from them feeling recognized and appreciated as valued contributors to a process that has led to significant change in the organization, in their relationships, and in how they view themselves.

*Redefinition of their relationship to top management* as the varied points of view were explored. Some had been experiencing good rapport with top management and can continue, while others can now engage in this relationship.

*Examination of career development* in the organization in relation to whether they have criminal justice histories and the attitudes and beliefs they carried about this status. They had an opportunity to explore the assumptions they made about their own career development. They will have a chance to reexamine their attitudes, maybe modify their behavior, and see how their career options change.

## Creating Transformation

The ways in which space for transformation was created in this A-PAR process were:

*Creating an atmosphere where dialogue can take place* separate from the normal routine and where there will be no repercussions for people to speak their minds.

*Honoring contributions made by participants* by responding to them and showing interest by asking open questions to understand further what they have to say.

*Identifying frames of reference* of the participants and perhaps of the organization as well to better understand why we take the positions we do.

*Uncovering the assumptions* that are underneath the comments and action steps the participants suggest to highlight how our communication is influenced by what we assume to be true.

*Using tools for storytelling,* such as CMM, to enable participants to tell the stories that are meaningful to them and thus share parts of themselves with others.

*Creating tangible outcomes* as a result of the group's efforts to encourage more dialogue and participation and to change their image of discussions and meetings from leading nowhere to being a productive use of time.

## Epilogue

We entered into phase two after the survey was completed and results were shared. This phase is focusing on action steps, such as developing protocols for them to use in the organization and assessing the current state of learning and development in the organization. Some members of the team have changed and that posed two interesting challenges. The first and most obvious is reforming into a new and productive team. The second is that since the newer members were not members of the project at its inception, they do not have the same understanding and acknowledgment of how far the group has come. It is not derailing the process but bringing new points of inquiry to address and turn into strengths.

## References

Abalos, D. T. (1998). *La communidad Latina in the United States: Personal and political strategies for transforming culture.* Westport, CT: Praeger.

Argyris, C. (1993). *Knowledge for action: A guide to overcoming barriers to organizational change.* San Francisco: Jossey-Bass.

Arnold, R., Burke, B., James, C., Martin, D., & Thomas, B. (1991). *Educating for a change.* Ontario, Canada: Between the Lines.

Brookfield, S. D. (2005). *The power of critical theory: Liberating adult learning and teaching.* San Francisco: Jossey-Bass.

Buber, M. (1955). *Between man and man.* Boston: Beacon Press.

Cooperrider, D. L., Srivastva, S. (1987). Appreciative inquiry in organizational life. In Pasmore, W., Woodman, R. (Eds.), *Research in organization change and development*, Vol. 1. Greenwich, CT: JAI Press.

Cranton, P. (2006). *Understanding and promoting transformative learning: A guide for adult educators*, 2nd edition. San Francisco: Jossey-Bass.

Cronen, V. E., Pearce, W. B., & Changsheng, X. (1989/90). The meaning of "meaning" in the CMM analysis of communication: A comparison of two traditions. In *Research on Language and Social Interaction*, Vol. 23, 1989/90, 1–40.

Daloz, L. A. (1999). *Mentor: Guiding the journey of adult learners.* San Francisco: Jossey-Bass.

Deutsch, M. (1973). *The resolution of conflict.* New Haven, CT: Yale University Press.

Fisher, R. J. (2006). Intergroup conflict. In Deutsch, M., Coleman, P. T., & Marcus, E. (Eds.) *The handbook of conflict resolution: Theory to practice.* San Francisco: Jossey-Bass.

Fisher-Yoshida, B. (2003). Self-awareness and the co-construction of conflict. *Human Systems: The Journal of Systemic Consultation and Management, 14*(4).

Freire, P. (1970). *Pedagogy of the oppressed.* New York: Continuum.

Jost, J. T., & Kruglanski, A. W. (2002). The estrangement of social constructionism and the experimental social psychology: History of the rift and prospects for reconciliation. *Personality and Social Psychology Review, 6*(3), 168–187.

Kreitner, R., & Kinicki, A. (2006). *Organizational behavior*, 7th edition. New York: McGraw-Hill.

McClelland, D. C. (1975). *Power: The inner experience.* New York: Irvington.

Mezirow, J. (2000). Learning to think like an adult: Core concepts of transformation theory. In Mezirow, J., & Associates (Eds.). *Learning as transformation: Critical perspectives on a theory in progress.* San Francisco: Jossey-Bass.

Park, P. (2001). Knowledge and participatory research. In Reason, P., & Bradbury, H. (Eds.), *Handbook of action research: Participative inquiry & practice*. Thousand Oaks, CA: Sage.

Pearce, W. B. (1994). *Interpersonal communication: Making social worlds*. New York: Harper Collins College Publishers.

Pearce, W. B. (2004). The coordinated management of meaning (CMM). In Gudykunst, W. (Ed.), *Theorizing about communication and culture*. Thousand Oaks, CA: Sage.

Pearce, W. B., & Pearce, K. A. (2003). Taking a communication perspective toward dialogue. In R. Anderson, L. A. Baxter & K. N. Cissna (Eds.), *Dialogue: Theorizing difference in communication studies,* pp. 39–56. Thousand Oaks, CA: Sage.

Reason, P., & Bradbury, H. (2001). Introduction: Inquiry and participation in search of a world worthy of human aspiration. In Reason, P., & Bradbury, H. (Eds.) *Handbook of action research: Participative inquiry & practice*. Thousand Oaks, CA: Sage.

Schon, D. (1983). *The reflective practitioner: How professionals think in action*. New York: Basic Books.

Smith, S. E., Willms, D. G., & Johnson, N. A. (1997). *Nurtured by knowledge: Learning to do participatory action-research*. New York: Apex Press.

Starhawk. (1990). *Truth or dare: Encounters with power, authority, and mystery*. San Francisco: Harper.

# Chapter 5

A Crucible for Transformation:
The Alchemy of Student-Centered
Education for Adults at Midlife

*Steven A. Schapiro*

## Introduction: "This Experience Changed My Life"

During my over 20 years of experience as a faculty member in student-centered low-residency degree programs for adult learners, countless times I have heard students talk of how they were transformed by the experience. Their testimonials at graduations, in which each student addresses the audience, so often include impassioned speeches about how the program "changed my life." I have often wondered and speculated on the question: "What is it about such programs that catalyzes such transformations?"

This chapter begins to answer that question by bringing together insights gleaned from three sources: (1) the initial findings of a research project on adult development and transformative learning through student-centered graduate education, (2) my experience and practice in progressive education programs for adults at Fielding Graduate University and at Goddard College, and (3) the broad literature on transformative education. From these sources, I distill a set of principles and practices for a model of transformative graduate education for adult learners. This model supplements the considerable literature on classroom-based transformative learning with guidelines for how we can foster transformation through individualized, mentor-guided study in combination with brief face-to-face group learning experiences and online learning communities.

In presenting this model, I relate it to the four major and sometimes overlapping strands of transformative learning theory: (1) the *cognitive rational* approach to changes in meaning perspectives through critical reflection; (2) the *depth psychology* approach to Jungian individuation and spiritual development through dialogue with the subconscious; (3) *the structural developmental* approach to epistemological change through the life-span; and (4) the *social emancipatory* approach to education for critical consciousness and social change.

To provide a framework for the forms of transformative education that can support such learning, I draw on Kegan's (1982) notion of the key qualities or functions of a holding environment or the culture of embeddedness that supports development, growth, and transformation: *confirmation, contradiction,* and *continuity*. To those three functions, I add a fourth, *creation*, to explain the support we need to change ourselves instead of retreating backward in the face of contradiction and disequilibrium. In developing an understanding of the elements needed to provide such holding environments for adult learners, we turn first to two innovative programs that have helped to set the standard for student-centered adult education.

## Contexts: Goddard College and Fielding Graduate University

My understanding of the possibilities for transformative learning in adult degree programs has been shaped and informed by my experiences in two groundbreaking institutions: Goddard College, which was founded in 1938 to put into practice at the postsecondary level the principles of progressive education as articulated by John Dewey; and Fielding Graduate University, which was founded 40 years later to provide midcareer adults an opportunity to pursue advanced degrees through individualized self-directed learning under the guidance of faculty mentors.

For its first few decades, Goddard became widely known for its resident undergraduate program, a radical experiment in democratic education, in which faculty served as facilitators of learning rather than as dispensers of knowledge, and grades were replaced by narrative evaluations written by both students and faculty. In 1963, Goddard began an experiment in education for adult learners, initiating a study format that eventually spread nationwide. In this adult degree program, students attended a 1–2 week on-campus residency, participating in short courses and developing study plans for an individualized semester of study that they carried out at home (or anywhere in the world), periodically submitting their work to their faculty supervisors who responded with feedback, thus engaging in a semester-long dialogue. This basic format, which continues today at Goddard, makes it possible to apply the progressive education principles of student-centered, problem-focused, experiential learning to the needs of adult learners who integrate their learning with their lives.

The Fielding Graduate University's Ph.D. program in Human and Organization Development (HOD[6]), which was founded in 1978, built its original learning model on the principles of andragogy as articulated by Malcolm Knowles (1980), who was among the program's founding faculty members. It also drew on theories of humanistic psychology and education (Rogers, 1969) and peer counseling (Jackins, 1972), all of which put the individual learner, as a whole person, at the center of the educational experience. As such, it was one of a handful of innovative institutions to base a program of formal graduate study on such progressive and andragogical principles as self-directed learning (sdl) and the integration of life and learning that are more commonly used in nonformal and community-based learning programs. In more recent years, the program has been evolving into a more collaborative and critical model of education. This evolution has come in response to: a growing recognition of the limitations of andragogy and self-directed learning; new understandings and theories about adult learning, including feminist, critical, and multicultural approaches; and new modes of interaction made possible by the Internet.

The Fielding program, like Goddard's, is structured as a distributed learning model combining brief academic residencies and seminars, with one-to-one faculty mentoring at a distance (via e-mail and phone), along with group learning experiences in regional meetings in person or online. Students develop individualized learning plans and negotiate learning contracts through which they work one-to-one with faculty mentors and engage in intensive collaborative learning experiences. Learning at Fielding, like at Goddard, begins with learners' questions and interests, not with faculty syllabi and predetermined curricula. Unlike Goddard, its program is not based on a traditional semester system, and its students move through their studies at their own pace and make their own choices about which residential learning experiences to attend.

## The Learners: Adults at Midlife

Returning to school at midlife and midcareer brings with it significant implications for where people are on their journey of adult development and how that educational experience and their development may impact each other. On the one hand, one's level of cognitive and ego development, for example, can impact what sort of learning and transformation are possible or likely. On the other hand, the process and content of our learning experiences can help to catalyze movement and growth from one developmental stage or place to another.

---

[6] Henceforth, I will be referring to this program by the widely used acronym, HOD.

In terms of Robert Kegan's constructive-developmental stage model, most adult students will be somewhere between what he calls the 3rd to the 5th orders of consciousness. Many will be at the "socialized mind" and the "culture of mutuality" of the 3rd (interpersonal) order of consciousness, potentially moving to the "self-authoring mind" and the "culture of identity" of the 4th (institutional) order. This shift involves the development of a greater sense of agency and autonomy and the development of a more internal locus of evaluation. Those already at that 4th order are potentially moving to the "self-transforming mind" and the "culture of intimacy" of the 5th (interinstitutional) level. That shift, which very few people appear to make, involves the development of dialectical thinking and the capacity to see interconnecting systems of thought and behavior, to understand the interpenetration of the self and others and to embrace ambiguity and paradox. In Kegan's view, movement from one order to another takes years, and so most of us at any time are in transition from one to another, as we seek what he terms a new balance between our needs for connection and autonomy. Where students are on this developmental journey can have important implications for how they may grow as a result of a student-centered educational experience. As Kegan explains in *In over Our Heads* (1994), self-directed learning calls for the self-authoring mind of the 4th order of consciousness, and asking for such behavior may help people to move in that direction. And while only a small percentage of the population are at the 5th order, the content of the Fielding HOD curriculum, for example—with its strong social constructionist bent—may catalyze movement to that next self-transforming mind characteristic of the postmodern perspective.

In terms of Jung's theory of individuation, midlife is also a time with great potential for growth, as we move to integrate the neglected or repressed parts of ourselves. For example, at this time of life, in Jung's schema, many women find their voice as they integrate their more agentic and "masculine" side (or animus), and many men develop their more relational, affective, and "feminine" side (or anima) as they become more attuned to the needs of others. From this perspective, as both men and women go through this "middle passage" from their first adulthood to a second one, they often engage in a search for more meaning and more wholeness (Hollis, 2005; Stein, 1983). And as Cranton and Roy (2003) explain, this process of individuation, although partly an unconscious one, can be described as very similar to Mezirow's transformative learning process, as both involve a shedding or reassessment of our socialized self (or persona in Jungian terms) to integrate and express a more consciously chosen and in that sense more authentic self-definition.

In terms of Paulo Freire's stages of magical, naïve, and critical consciousness (1973), most adults in our society are at the naïve stage—blaming individuals (as either victims or perpetrators) for social problems—potentially developing a more critical understanding of the systemic or underlying socioeconomic causes of those problems. Adults at midlife and midcareer bring to their education the resource of their experiences in the workplace, in relationships, and in life in general. They are often returning to school as a result of frustrations and limitations in their work and in their lives. Many are looking for ways to think more broadly and systemically. They may be experiencing a sense of alienation and looking for new, more satisfying ways of living, working, and being. Feeling stuck, they are confronting the limits of their own ways of understanding, the constraints and limits of their organizational contexts, as well as the limits imposed by systems of oppression based on race, gender, and class. In turning these limits and problems into inquiries about how to resolve them (what Freire calls problem-posing), the educator can support the development of a more critical consciousness and recognize the necessary links between personal and social transformation.

## Findings from a Research Study

While theory and anecdotal evidence have long supported the transformative potential of programs such as those of Fielding and Goddard, very little empirical research has been done to support those claims. A recent study has begun to fill that gap. Schapiro, McClintock, and Stevens-Long explored the relationship between adult development and nontraditional doctoral education. In that study, a self-selected sample of 59 Fielding HOD graduates (about 15% of the total alumni group) was asked to describe intellectual, personal, and behavioral developments that they attributed to their graduate school experience, to give examples of each, and to specify aspects of their experience at Fielding they believed to have affected the changes they described (McClintock & Stevens-Long, 2002; Schapiro, Stevens-Long, & McClintock, 2005a).

Findings indicated a wide array of changes in all areas, which are summarized with the major themes that were identified through open coding: *cognitive development*—more perceptive, think in complex ways, see multiple perspectives, better able to appreciate research and theory; *personal (ego and emotional) development*—more tolerant, more confident, experience expanded consciousness, experience positive emotions; *behavioral development*—continuous learners, communicative, in flow, and resilient.

In a subsequent paper, Schapiro et al. (2005b) analyzed the data further in order to explore the relationship among the reported outcomes, the academic and contextual influences to which students attributed those outcomes, and the four major strands models of transformative learning noted above: cognitive-rational, individuating, social emancipatory, constructive-developmental.

Many of these outcomes resonate strongly with Mezirow's notion of perspective transformation, including such themes and subthemes as "more perceptive, reflective/critical thinking, seeing more multiple perspectives, questioning assumptions, and examining one's own and others' perspectives. Evidence of Jungian individuation can be found in such outcomes as "experiencing expanded consciousness, greater awareness and integration, changes in spiritual life, and being in flow." It appears that for many of these respondents, a rational process of perspective transformation was accompanied by a more personal process of growth and integration.

We can also see some evidence of movement from one of Kegan's stages to the next. Although such stage movements involve deep changes in a fundamental way of knowing and can take a long time to occur, the average five years of doctoral study provide sufficient time. For instance, in changes such as the "development of critical thinking, ability to suspend judgments, becoming more tolerant of self and others, thinking systemically, seeing the perspective of self and others, and becoming more empowered and autonomous," we see much evidence of movement from Kegan's interpersonal (3rd) to the institutional (4th) order. Since very few people ever reach the 5th order, there is not as much evidence of that movement, although changes such as "more tolerance of complexity, seeing complex and ambiguous patterns, appreciating diversity, and perceiving social construction" point in that direction.

While the data analysis as summarized above does speak directly to a process of conscientization as defined by Freire, the raw data and the words of the respondents provide many examples of a heightened consciousness in regard to issues of gender and race-based oppression and economic inequality, along with a commitment to act on that awareness. In the cognitive realm, these changes are reflected in such themes as "thinking systemically" and "perceiving social construction" in the personal realm in changes such as becoming "more confident of self, own voice, ideas" and "empowered/autonomous," and in behavioral changes such as "takes reflective action." Indeed, taken together, these outcomes sound much like conscientization itself.

This summary analysis clearly suggests that respondents may have experienced all four kinds of transformation, to varying degrees. They reported that the following aspects of their graduate educational experience led to these changes: a *learning process* that was self-reflective, self-directed, interactive/collaborative, and experiential; *interpersonal* relationships (faculty-student and student-student) characterized by equality, support, acceptance, and inclusion of diverse people and perspectives; *curricular content* that often leads to a transformation in perspectives and worldviews (e.g., systems thinking, theories of human development and consciousness, social constructionism, critical theory, use of self as an instrument of change); an *organizational structure* that provides for student involvement in governance and in organizing the learning experience itself.

These experiences are clearly consistent with what Mezirow and others (E. Taylor, 2000; Cranton, 2006) have described as key elements in the transformative learning process. The first phase of that process, the creation of disorienting dilemmas, may be brought on, in this context, by the paradigm-challenging content of the curriculum along with the requirement for application of theory to practice, for self-reflection, and for critical reflection on one's own and others' assumptions, all of which are included in the outcomes summarized above and described at some length by the respondents.

It is also important to note that the relatively unstructured and student-directed nature of the Fielding learning experience, in which students design their own studies in consultation with their faculty mentors, may in itself be a disorienting dilemma as those in authority are not telling students what to do but inviting them to decide for themselves. As that dilemma often requires students to change their perspective on the nature of knowledge and of the teaching-learning process and their role in it, the Fielding learning process as a whole may be a significant transformative learning experience in itself. As Brookfield (1984) points out, self-directed learning may also help learners to develop a greater sense of agency in regard to their social and political environment, as well as to their individual learning process.

The challenges of self-directed learning may also be what can lead students onto "the threshold" and into what McWhinney and Markos (2003) call the "liminal space"—the transitional space between who we were and who we will become—a first step on the journey of transformation, as we let go of some of our certainties and begin to move through uncharted waters to the other side. The initial step into that liminal space often occurs in the week-long residential orientation session, in which students are asked, in effect, "who are you and where are you going?" Taking such existential questions to heart can lead to the sort of reflection that can open one to change.

Discourse/dialogue, the other key factor identified by Mezirow as central to transformative learning, is clearly included in the "interactive and collaborative" nature of the learning experience, a major theme identified by the respondents. These findings also lend support to the importance of close faculty-student relationships, a factor not highlighted by Mezirow but identified by others such as Robertson (1996), E. Taylor (2000), Kasl and Elias (2000), Barlas (2001), and the philosopher Martin Buber (1970), who argued for an I-thou teacher-student relationship: "He must know him not as a mere sum of qualities, aspiration, and inhibitions; he must apprehend him and affirm him, as a whole" (p. 178).

What is unique about these findings as compared to other empirical studies of transformative learning within adult graduate education is that the Fielding learning experiences are not primarily classroom based but occur in the context of faculty-student mentoring relationships, such as those described by Daloz (1999), self-organized study groups, conference-like gatherings of the full student-faculty learning community, and online seminars and forums. It may be that the close relationships and interactive learning process described by many of the respondents provide a supportive context in which students can experience both the challenge and the disorientation brought on by new experiences and new perspectives and the dialogue and discourse through which new meaning can be created.

The learning processes that support individuation have been less well identified in the literature, but it would seem that the need for self-reflection, the study of human development and consciousness as a required part of the curriculum, the emphasis on affective as well as the cognitive dimensions of learning and on the artistic as well as the intellectual ways of knowing, the self-directed nature of the learning process, and the mentoring relationship to which the student can bring his or her whole self, all provide a context in which the expansion of consciousness and psychological integration characteristic of individuation can occur. Constructive-developmental transformation through an educational process, according to Kegan, Daloz, and Parks, requires a combination of affirmation, challenge, and vision, all of which are evidenced in the elements described above—the mentoring relationship, the cohort experience, the curriculum, and the challenges of being self-directed. While experiences such as dialogue, experiential learning, self-reflection, and the study of critical theory could all support a Freirean process of conscientization, respondents did not identify praxis, the social action/reflection cycle, as one of the main themes in their experience. There is much anecdotal information indicating that many students do indeed engage in such a process, but that did not come to light in this research. In the next phase of this project, other questions may need to be asked in order to get a better understanding of this aspect of students' experiences.

## Transformative Graduate Education: Key Principles and Practices

Bringing together the findings from this study, lessons learned in my experience at Goddard and Fielding, and insights from the literature, I suggest below some key principles and practices for student-centered transformative education for adults. The structure of this model draws on and integrates two frameworks for transformation, those of Robert Kegan and Kurt Lewin. Kegan's constructive-developmental model suggests a three-phase formulation of how developmental change is experienced and can be facilitated. That process involves a movement through phases of *defending*, during which people feel embedded in a present equilibrium and try to fend off or deny stimuli that cause disequilibrium; *surrendering*, during which one allows the contradictions to enter one's consciousness, which brings on feelings of anxiety, loss, and disequilibrium; and *reintegration*, in which a new balance is reached that is based on a new way of making meaning of one's experience (Bell and Griffin, 1997).

According to Kegan, each of these phases requires a certain kind of facilitating or "holding environment" (a concept that he adapted from Winnicott): *confirmation*, which involves "holding on" to someone, giving them the feelings of safety and validation that they can lean on as they stop defending and allow themselves to experience disequilibrium; *contradiction*, which involves "letting go" and presenting the individual with disconfirming information and experiences to which they can surrender; and *continuity*, which involves "staying put for reintegration" as it provides an ongoing, stable, and consistent set of interpersonal, group, or organizational relationships.

If we use Kegan's model as a framework to explain the elements that must be present in a transformative educational environment, Kurt Lewin's (1951) model of personal or organizational change—which describes phases of unfreezing, changing, and refreezing—can be used to organize the outcomes that learners must experience as they go through a transformative learning process.

Here is a simple schematic representation of the relationship between these facilitating environments and participant outcomes:

| *Facilitating Environment* (from Kegan's model) | *Participant Outcomes* (from Lewin's model) |
|---|---|
| confirmation | unfreezing (feeling safe, feeling anxiety) |
| contradiction | changing |
| continuity | refreezing |

Further differentiating this model in regard to the relationship between the environment and the objectives can make it even more clear and precise. Unfreezing must involve a combination of a feeling of safety and a feeling of heightened anxiety and disequilibrium. One without the other will leave one frozen in place, either afraid to change or not motivated to change. Because different kinds of environmental factors or teaching principles elicit those different categories of feelings, it will be useful to subdivide the unfreezing category into two. A confirming environment will lead to feelings of safety and confirmation, and a contradicting environment will lead to feelings of dissonance and anxiety.

Confirmation → Feelings of Safety
Contradiction → Feelings of Dissonance and Anxiety

On the other side of the equation, what is described as the contradicting environment really seems to be performing two discrete functions: creating disequilibrium and dissonance in regard to current behaviors and ways of making meaning, and offering means of resolving those contradictions and reaching a new equilibrium. That latter function can be facilitated through the creation of what I would call a *creating environment*, in which people are exposed to or themselves discover and articulate new ways of knowing, doing, and being. Once people see the inadequacy of their present system of beliefs and behaviors, they must see or develop alternatives in order to change the system instead of retreating into a defensive rigidity and shut out or deny the disconfirming information or experiences. It, therefore, seems useful to include the provision or development of such alternatives as a fourth category of facilitating environment. A more differentiated framework would look like this:

*Facilitating environment:*                    *Participant Outcomes:*

*confirmation*   (unfreezing)   ⟶   *feeling safe and affirmed*
*contradiction*  (unfreezing)   ⟶   *anxiety, disequilibrium*
*creation*       (changing)     ⟶   *changed behavior, attitudes, and consciousness*
*continuity*     (refreezing)   ⟶   *reintegration, equilibrium*

Although this model appears to be sequential and closed-ended, the change process is probably more cyclical and open-ended; all four kinds of facilitating environments exist to some extent at the same time, and change occurs all of the time. If we picture the change process as occurring within an environment that is always in some ways confirming, a schema of a more cyclical change process might look like this:

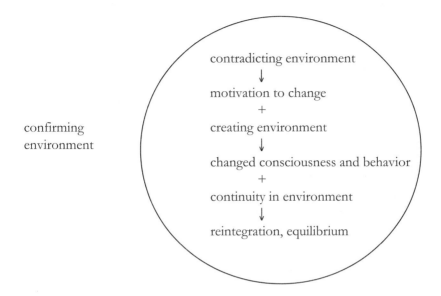

To put this schema into words within a confirming environment, which can lead to an openness to change, a contradicting environment will create the motivation to change, which, if one is aware of alternatives and options, will lead to change itself. In an environment that offers continuity, some of those changes might lead to reintegration and equilibrium, while other changes will themselves lead to new experiences and new information that might in turn lead to new contradictions and the motivation to change, which could, as the cycle continues, lead to more change. Such a cycle of action for change leading to the discovery of new contradictions, leading to more action for change, is another way of conceptualizing Freire's concept of "praxis": action—reflection—action.

We can now use this broad framework to articulate the key principles of student-centered graduate education for transformation—a crucible for transformation. This crucible serves as a container that holds learners in a safe space and provides a boundary for their learning experience; that turns up the heat and the fire, providing various forms of contradiction and disorientation that "unfreezes" people and melts their rigid frames of reference and ways of knowing, opening them to the possibility of change; adds new ingredients to the mix in the form of new paradigms, perspectives, and ways of learning; and provides continuing support as learners "cool down" to solidify a new sense of self as scholar-practitioners, reintegrate themselves into their work, community, and family contexts, and work to change those contexts.

The chart below summarizes the elements needed to produce each sort of learning environment. These elements are each explained in what follows.

**Confirming Environment**
- one-to-one mentoring relationships with faculty characterized by authenticity, affirmation, and social equality.
- small group bonding and co-learning with peers
- residential learning retreats as a part of the experience

**Contradicting Environment**
- the challenges of self-directed learning
- the paradigm-busting curriculum of areas such as systems theory, epistemology, social constructionism, human development theory, and critical theory
- the diverse and challenging viewpoints expressed in discussion and discourse

**Creating Environment**
- opportunities for ongoing reflection and meaning making
- learning by engaging with real-life problems and issues—praxis
- taking a stand and finding one's voice
- learning that includes the whole person

**Continuing Environment**
- ongoing relationships with mentors and peer learners, both during the program and after graduation
- the continuing integration of life and learning
- the inclusion of alumni in an ongoing community of learners, both in person and online

Chart 5.1

## Confirming Environment

A holding environment that provides support and affirmation, a platform from which learners can leap into the unknown, and a safety net that can catch them if they fall are some of the elements provided by a confirming environment.

*One-to-one Mentoring Relationships with Faculty Characterized by Authenticity, Affirmation, and Social Equality*

Feeling known, heard, and respected by a caring and attentive faculty mentor is an invaluable element in a confirming environment for adult learners, just as it is for an infant and her caretaker or a third-grader and his teacher. Within the safety and affirmation of such a relationship, students can open themselves to challenge and vulnerability, knowing that they have that support to fall back on. Such affirmation, which must begin with careful listening, is the first of three key functions that Daloz, in his book *Mentor* (1999), so eloquently argues that the mentor must provide. If that relationship is to encourage transformation, and not simply an affirmation of the status quo, it must also be characterized by authenticity and mutuality, as we call forth the authentic and growing self of the student. As bell hooks has said, "empowerment cannot happen if we refuse to be vulnerable while encouraging others to do so" (hooks, 1994, p. 21). And in making ourselves vulnerable, we need to take the risk that we might be changed in the process. In being willing to admit our mistakes and our doubts, we help our students to do the same to make possible truly collaborative relationships and to benefit from the powerful learning that those relationships can foster. If we can show our students that we are full of *our* questions and our own search for answers, we can model ourselves, to use Carl Rogers's phrase, "as people in the process of becoming" and thus help others to fully engage in that process as well. In helping others to grow, we grow ourselves, as we all become learners and teachers together.

*Small Group Bonding and Co-learning with Peers*

While supportive relationships with faculty are important, it is also crucial to provide opportunities for students to create close bonds and connections with one another, so that the learning experience is not just a transaction between faculty and student but a more circular transaction among a group in which everyone is learning from and with everyone else. Such opportunities can be provided by, for example, organizing students into small cohort groups for their orientation into the program, if not for the program as whole, and by making a part of these experiences a sharing of who we are as full people and not just as students and faculty. The creation of such bonding is one reason that a residential component for adult learners can be a vital part of the experience, as explained below. And even in online learning seminars, it is important to create space (a virtual lounge, for instance) for more personal interactions. Feeling like an accepted and valued member of a group provides a strong container of safety and support.

*Residential Learning Retreats as a Part of the Experience*

Critical reflection on our selves and our contexts can be deepened by taking time away from our regular lives. This sort of distance from our day-to-day responsibilities and relationships is one of the functions provided by residential retreats as part of the adult learning experience (Fleming, 1998). Without such opportunities, adult learners immersed in busy work and family lives may treat their adult learning experiences as another consumer event where they are shopping and getting something, not engaging with their full selves and not detaching enough from their regular life settings to gain more perspective on them. Immersing ourselves instead in a new community of support provides an opportunity for distance, reflection, and growth. Remote and natural settings, with only basic comforts provided, are especially conducive to this sort of re- flective experience. Living together in retreat setting, sharing meals and rooms and sometimes cooking and cleaning chores as well, can help people to connect deeply with others in ways that could take months or never happen at all if we see one another only during class time. And as faculty and students share the residential experience, their relationships can also accelerate in the same way. Whether in set cohort groups as described by Lawrence (1999), brief residential communities of learners as described by Cohen and Piper (2000), or the experi- ence in democratic living described by Spicer (1991), the impact of the residen- tial experience cannot be overestimated. The more remote and more self- contained the experience, the more powerful it can be, but even a few days in a hotel away from home can stimulate both critical reflection and interpersonal bonding in ways that cannot be duplicated online or in the commuters' class- room.

## A Contradicting Environment

Affirmation without challenge can be an empty form of support. We grow in response to challenge and contradiction, which can come both from within and without, from parts of ourselves seeking expression and fulfillment and from the demands of our environment. While we confront many challenges and dis- orienting dilemmas through the natural course of living, a transformative edu- cational environment can both hasten and heighten these contradictions and dilemmas, leading us, in concert with a confirming environment, into the sort of disequilibrium that can lead to change.

*The Challenges of Self-directed Learning*

Asking students who are used to being passive learners to take responsibility for articulating what they want to learn and how they want to learn it can be a challenging and disorienting experience. Specific elements of a self-directing learning environment can include not providing a set curriculum but asking students to work with faculty mentors to develop and negotiate their goals, resources, and learning activities. The relatively unstructured and student-directed nature of such learning experiences may in itself be a disorienting challenge. As that dilemma often requires students to change their perspective on the nature of knowledge and of the teaching-learning process and their role in it, the sdl process as a whole may be a significant transformative learning experience in itself. In terms of Kegan's model, as described above, the demands of sdl can call for and catalyze movement toward the self-authoring mind of his 4th order of consciousness. As students co-construct their own learning relationships and learning environments, and as some of them also engage in action research aimed at changing the organizations or communities in which they work and live, they also experience themselves not as objects of someone else's educational or institutional agenda but as agents and subjects, as co-constructors of their own education, their own social reality, and their own lives.

## A Paradigm-Busting Curriculum

Asking students to grapple with concepts, paradigms, and epistemologies that challenge their current ways of knowing and of conceptualizing themselves and their world is a key element in creating the sorts of contradictions and disequilibrium that can lead to transformation. For instance, the study of epistemology helps students to question how we know what we know; critical theory can lead to the capacity for critique of ideology and of our current forms of political and economic life; systems theory and social constructionism challenge our sense of how we understand our selves and our social context. In contrast, learning experiences that operate within the context of our normative and hegemonic theories and assumptions about our material or social reality tend to foster informational but not transformational learning. While Kegan suggests that the challenges of postmodern thinking may be beyond the capacity of many adult students to fully comprehend, for those already at the self-authoring mind of the 4th order, these may be just the sort of challenge and stimulus needed to begin to move toward the self-transforming mind of the 5th order.

## The Diverse and Challenging Viewpoints Expressed in Discussion

By engaging in reading, thinking, and writing by ourselves, in isolation, we can come to new insights and understandings and perhaps even transform our points of view. But often, it is through testing our ideas in conversation with others and through considering and learning from others' perspectives that we engage in the sort of reflective discourse that Mezirow sees as a key element in the transformative learning process and that Freire sees as central to the dialogical and collective construction of knowledge. It is this sort of group dialogue and discourse that independent learning lacks. While this sort of discourse is possible to some extent within the one-to-one dialogues between faculty and students, it is much more possible within a collaborative learning group, in which students can be exposed to a wider diversity of perspectives. It is through such dialogue that learners can also engage in what Belenky and Stanton (2000) have described as the "connected knowing" through which learners can transform by trying to empathize with and understand the views of others (Cranton, 2006). This is a different transformative process from "separate knowing," through which we engage in critical analysis and debate. Engaging with other group members in a collaborative search for understanding can also lead to what Yorks and Kasl (2002) have called "learning within relationship . . . a process in which persons strive to become engaged with both their whole-person knowing and the whole-person knowing of their fellow learners" (p. 183). And if the learning community includes people of diverse racial, ethnic, or other identities of difference, other opportunities for contradiction and potential transformation may arise in what Daloz (2000) calls the "constructive engagement with otherness," through which, as Parks (2000) explains, our assumptions about ourselves and others can be transformed: "Constructive encounters across any significant divide set at the soul's core an experience of knowing that every assumption may be potentially transformed by an encounter with otherness" (p. 141). Such a dialogue thus provides not only a context in which we can test out and explore our own ideas but also an opportunity to be transformed through our exposure to other peoples' thinking and ways of being.

## A Creating Environment

A contradicting environment can lead to disequilibrium and disorienting dilemmas, but unless people are able to discover or articulate new ways of knowing, doing, and being, they can often resolve their discomfort by retreating to their prior state of equilibrium. If they are to move ahead and not backward, they need a "creating environment" that can be provided by:

### Opportunities for Ongoing Reflection and Meaning Making

If students are asked to continually reflect on their experiences—both past and present—to examine their own process, to make meaning of their experience, and to articulate their learning, they can construct new knowledge and change their habits of mind and of being. This is the constructed knowing that Belenky et al. (1986) describe in *Women's Ways of Knowing*. As Dewey (1933) said many years ago, we do not learn *by* experience, we learn *from* experience as we reflect on it and reconstruct it; in the same sense, learners need an opportunity to go through all of the phases of Kolb's learning cycle including not only the abstract conceptualization of the traditional academy, but also the experimentation of more active learning (Kolb, 1984). Such reflection and meaning-making can be supported by asking students to articulate their learning from each of their learning experiences and to periodically reflect on and make meaning of their graduate experience as a whole. This process can be supported by such practices as narrative self-evaluations in which they articulate their learning, periodic reviews of portfolios of a student's work, and reflective essays on their journey through the program, articulating their intellectual and personal growth.

## Learning Through Praxis—Engagement, Action, and Reflection on Real-Life Problems

If learning can begin with a quest to understand and address issues and problems that we are facing in our own personal, family, organizational, or community lives, then it will naturally be relevant and meaningful to the learner. And if the learning process can involve not just reading, thinking, and writing, but also some form of doing—some action to address those issues, followed by reflection on that action—then the learner can be changed in the process. This is what Freire meant by praxis—the cycle of reflection, action, and reflection. We reach new insights and understandings—we transform our selves—as we try to transform the world. Such a process can be encouraged by asking students to organize their studies around their own questions and problems and by requiring an applied component to each area of study

## Taking a Stand and Finding One's Voice

By asking students not only to summarize and critique others' work but to also state their own position on the controversial issues in a field and to go on to construct and articulate their own new knowledge, we can help students to find their own authentic scholarly voices. This process is most clear in the writing of the dissertation. As students become Ph.D.s, one of the transitions they experience is to move from being consumers of knowledge to becoming producers and constructors of knowledge. Student-centered learning, like that at Fielding, is uniquely well suited to facilitate such an outcome. From the beginning of that experience, learners gradually experience a shift from seeing knowledge as something that exists outside of themselves and that faculty will impart to them, to seeing it as something that they too have the authority to construct for themselves; from thinking about their learning experience only in terms of meeting faculty expectations, to thinking about it more in terms of what they want to know and learn; from thinking of themselves as passive recipients of others' learning, to thinking of themselves as active agents in their learning and in their own lives.

### Learning That Includes the Whole Person

When we give students the opportunity to bring all of themselves to the learning process and to engage their hearts and bodies as well as their minds, we open more pathways to transformation. We also increase the likelihood that the transformations that do occur will be integrated and lasting. We are whole people, and change in one dimension of our being must eventually involve changes in other dimensions as well. As Cranton has explained (2006), using the Meyers-Briggs typology, learners' entry points to transformative learning may depend on how they experience the world; for some, change begins with reflection, for others with experience, and for still others with intuition. And as Yorks and Kasl (2006) argue, when we include expressive ways of knowing, "those ways of knowing that engage a learner's imaginal and intuitive processes" (p. 45), in the learning experience, we open the door to other routes to transformation.

Practices that can enable learners to make use of these other ways of knowing include autobiography and narrative means of expression; journals for ongoing self-reflection; making space for the expression of feelings as well as thoughts in the learning process; rituals, movement, dance, and singing as an integral part of group learning experiences; artistic and symbolic means of expression; meditation and other contemplative practices as a means to access the deeper, subconscious parts of ourselves (Hart, 2000; Lennox, 2005). Such practices can be used as a complement to the usual reading and writing of the academy, not as a substitute for them.

## A Continuing Environment

Change and transformation that come about through extraordinary learning and life experiences often do not last if we cannot integrate our new habits of mind and being into our "real lives." Many of us have experienced an awakening and a new sense of self and fresh possibilities in various learning and growth retreats, during travel in other cultures, or through psychotherapy, only to slide back into our old ways when our changed self threatens the status quo in our relationships and contexts. If these changes and transformations are to last, we need somewhere in our lives a holding environment that is there for us through our change process and does not need to change along with us but can provide us some stability and support. That "continuing" environment can be provided in graduate adult education through such means as:

## Ongoing Relationships with Mentors and Peer Learners

Having at least one close connection with a faculty mentor, from the beginning of the program to the end, can provide some of the support that we need. When such a relationship transcends the time limits of a particular course or learning experience, students have someone they can use as a sounding board to hear their developing thinking, a shoulder to cry on or lean on, and a platform to jump off from. It is important that such relationships do not always involve evaluation and grading but provide a context from which it is safe to venture out and make mistakes and then come back to lick one's wounds or celebrate one's successes. When such bonds are established during the academic experience, they can continue afterward as needed, as the connection established is between two people, not simply between a teacher and a student.

Similarly, when students can connect with one another as fellow travelers on their journey and not as competitors for a scarce resource of high grades, continuing supportive relationships becomes possible. In this way, students can serve as mentors for one another, part of the "network of belonging" that Sharon Parks (2000) identifies as a key feature of a mentoring environment. If we provide the structure and space in which relationships can develop, then students will take care of the rest on their own.

## The Continuing Integration of Life and Learning

When we base the academic learning experience on students' life experience and when their own questions drive the learning process, then students develop their capacity to be lifelong learners and the sharp distinction between learning in school and out of school disappears. The transition to postgraduate life is thus much less jarring. While one is no longer paying tuition or earning academic credit, the scholar-practitioner's integrated quest for knowledge can continue unabated.

## The Inclusion of Alumni in an Ongoing Community of Learners

If alumni can continue to feel themselves a part of a community of learners, they never need to feel that they have left that nurturing and challenging context in which they were transformed. At Fielding, for instance, alumni are invited to attend the biannual conference-like gatherings of students and faculty called national sessions, both attending and leading workshops and seminars. Continued access to internal online resources, which may include various discussion groups and forums, as well as use of the electronic library databases can provide other means through which students can stay connected. Since these national sessions and electronic networks were the primary means of being connected while enrolled, the transition to postgraduate status once again does not have to be so severe.

## Conclusion

Provision of all the components of the confirming, contradicting, creating, and continuing environments described above does not guarantee that students will experience transformation. That is up to them. Transformative learning is not something we do to other people, it is something that people do for themselves. All that we can do is to provide the opportunity and the stimulus, the container and the heat. If all of the ingredients are there, if the learner is ready to change and engages the process with his or her full self, then the alchemy of transformation will take care of the rest.

If we agree with John Dewey, as I do, that "development is the aim of education," then we can "teach with developmental intent" (K. Taylor, 2000) as we provide the sort of learning environments described above. These environments can help learners to experience transformative learning that can stimulate, support, and sometimes hasten their developmental journey through midlife—a journey toward wholeness, more open and inclusive frames of reference, a more self-authoring and self-transforming frame of mind, a more critical consciousness, and a more integrated and more satisfying way of being in the world.

During the 23 years that I have had been privileged to accompany so many adult learners on their transformative journeys, I myself have moved through my own midlife growth and transformation, in no small part due to the inspiring examples I have seen all around me. These learners—my teachers—have taught me a great deal about the courage of the human spirit and about our continuing capacity for growth and development, no matter what our age. They have inspired and challenged me to try to be and become my own best and fullest self. Like so many of them, I can say that "this experience has changed my life."

# References

Barlas, C. (2001). Learning within relationship as context and process in adult education: Impact on transformative learning and social change agency. *Proceedings of the Adult Education Research Conference.*

Belenky, M., Clinchy, B., Goldberger, N., & Tarule, J. (1986). *Women's ways of knowing.* New York: Basic Books.

Belenky, M., & Stanton, A. (2000). Inequality, development, and connected knowing. In Mezirow, J. (Ed.), *Learning as transformation.* San Francisco: Jossey-Bass.

Bell, L., & Griffin, P. (1997). Designing social justice education courses. In Adams, M., Bell, L., & Griffin, P. (Eds.). *Teaching for diversity and social justice: A sourcebook.* New York: Routledge.

Brookfield, S. D. (1984). Self-directed adult learning: A critical paradigm. *Adult Education Quarterly 35*(2), 59–71.

Buber, M. (1970). *I and Thou.* Touchstone: New York.

Cohen, J., & Piper (2000). Transformation in a residential adult learning community. In Mezirow, J. (Ed.), *Learning as transformation.* San Francisco: Jossey-Bass.

Cranton, P. (2006). *Understanding and Promoting Transformative Learning,* 2nd edition. San Francisco: Jossey-Bass.

Cranton, P., & Roy, M. (2003). When the bottom falls out of the bucket: Toward a holistic perspective on transformative learning. *Journal of Transformative Learning, 1*(2), 86–99.

Daloz. L. (1999). *Mentor: Guiding the journey of adult learners.* San Francisco: Jossey-Bass.

Daloz, L. (2000). Transformative learning for the common good. In J. Mezirow (Ed.) *Learning as transformation.* San Francisco: Jossey-Bass.

Dewey, J. (1933). *Experience and Education.* New York: Collier.

Dirkx, J. (2000). Transformative learning and the journey of individuation. *ERIC Digest No. 223.* Columbus, OH: ERIC Clearinghouse.

Fleming, J. (1998). Understanding residential learning: The power of detachment and continuity. *Adult Education Quarterly, 48*(4).

Freire, P. (1973). *Education for critical consciousness.* New York: Seabury Press.

Hart, T. (2000). *From information to transformation.* New York: Peter Lang.

Hollis, J. (2005). *Finding meaning in the second half of life.* New York: Gotham Books.

hooks, b. (1994). *Teaching to transgress: Education as the practice of freedom.* London: Routledge.

Jackins, H. (1972). *The human side of human being: The theory of re-evaluation counseling.* Seattle: Rational Island Publishers.

Kasl, E., & Elias, D. (2000). Creating new habits of mind in small groups. In Mezirow, J. (Ed.), *Learning as transformation*. San Francisco: Jossey-Bass.

Kegan, R. (1982). *The evolving self.* New York. Harper Collins.

Kegan, R. (1994). *In over our heads.* Boston: Harvard University Press.

Knowles, M. (1980). *The modern practice of adult education: From pedagogy to andragogy,* 2nd edition. New York: Cambridge Books.

Kolb. D. (1984). *Experiential Learning.* Englewood Cliffs, NJ: Prentice Hall.

Lawrence, R. (1999). Transcending boundaries: Building community through residential adult learning. *Midwest Research to Practice Conference.* St Louis.

Lennox. S. (2005). Contemplating the Self: Integrative Perspectives on Transformative Learning. Dissertation. Santa Barbara, CA: Fielding Graduate University.

Lewin, K. (1951). *Field theory in the social sciences.* New York: Harper and Row.

McClintock, C. and Stevens-Long, J. (2002). Assessing ineffable learning outcomes in graduate education. American Association of Higher Education Assessment Conference, Boston, MA.

McWhinney, W., & Markos, L. (2003). Transformative education: Across the threshold. *Journal of Transformative Education, 1*(1).

Mezirow, J. (1991). *Transformative dimensions of adult learning.* San Francisco: Jossey-Bass.

Parks, S. D. (2000). *Big questions, worthy dreams.* San Francisco: Jossey-Bass.

Robertson, D. (1996). "Facilitating transforming learning: Attending to the dynamics of the educational helping relationship. *Adult Education Quarterly*, 47, 41–53.

Rogers, C. (1969). *Freedom to learn.* Columbus, OH: Charles E. Merrill.

Schapiro, S., Stevens-Long, J., & McClintock, C. (2005a). "Passionate scholars: Reforming doctoral education, a research project on educational outcomes and processes." In R. Hill & R. Kiely (Eds.), *Proceedings of the 46th Annual Adult Education Research Conference.* Athens: University of Georgia Press.

Schapiro, S., Stevens-Long, J., & McClintock, C. (2005b). "Passionate scholars: Adult development and transformative learning in a non-traditional Ph.D. program." In D. Vlosak, G. Kielbaso, & J. Radford (Eds.) *The Proceedings of the 6th International Conference on Transformative Learning.* Lansing: Michigan State University.

Spicer, C. (1991). Folk education: Resurrecting roots of adult and experiential learning theory. *The Journal of Experiential Education, 14*(3), 13–16.

Stein, M. (1983). *In Midlife.* Dallas: Spring.

Taylor, E. (2000). Analyzing research on transformative learning theory. In J. Mezirow & Associates (Eds.) *Learning as transformation*. San Francisco: Jossey-Bass.

Taylor, K. (2000). Teaching with developmental intention. In Mezirow, J. (Ed.), *Learning as transformation*. San Francisco: Jossey-Bass.

Yorks, L., & Kasl, E. (2002). Toward a theory and practice for whole-person learning: Reconceptualizing experience and the role of affect. *Adult Education Quarterly 52*(3), 176–192.

Yorks, L., & Kasl, E. (2006). I know more than I can say: A taxonomy for using expressive ways of knowing to foster transformative learning. *Journal of Transformative Education*, 41, 43–64.

# Section 1 Summary

## Creating Space for Transformative Learning

*Steven A. Schapiro*

In the chapters in this section, we have identified the key principles and practices contributing to the creation of transformative learning spaces in four varied contexts.

These contexts include the implications for learning in organizational settings of a class on improvisation, nonformal collaborative learning among peers, a participatory action research project in a nonprofit organization serving and largely staffed by former criminal offenders, and mentor-guided student-centered educational programs for midlife adults. In describing the characteristics of these spaces, we draw from a variety of theoretical perspectives. Some of these perspectives provide an overarching concept of a learning space, including Kegan's notion of holding environments and cultures of embeddedness, Lewin's concept of life spaces as applied by Kolb to learning spaces that support experiential learning, Nonaka's and Konno's articulation of the concept of *ba* as a shared space that harbors meaning, and Palmer's paradoxes and creative tensions. Other perspectives focus on the nature of the relationships among learners (and sometimes teachers as well), including Buber's I-Thou relationship, Belenky et al.'s notion of connected knowing, and Yorks and Kasl's learning in relation. Still other perspectives focus on the nature of the discourse and inquiry process, including Heron's cooperative inquiry, Mezirow's critical discourse, Pearce's Coordinated Management of Meaning (CMM), and the principles of participatory action research and popular education.

While there is much variation across these different perspectives and experiences, there is also much that they have in common. From this rich mix of theory and practice, we can begin to distill a set of five common themes or characteristics of transformative learning spaces: (1) learning happens in *relation-*

*ships,* (2) in which there is *shared ownership* and control of the learning space, (3) room for the *whole person*—feelings as well as thoughts, body and soul, as well as mind, (4) and *sufficient time* for collaboration, action, reflection, and integration, (5) to pursue a process of *inquiry driven by* the questions, needs, and purposes of the *learners.*

## Transformative Learning Happens in Relationships

Relationships do not just provide the context or container for the learning, but it is within the dialogue, debate, and interaction of the relationship that transformation occurs. Gilly and Leahy's notion of collaborative transformative learning—*Learning in the Space Between Us*—is about the commitments needed to struggle together in dialogue and shared inquiry in support of transformation. This sort of relationship does not happen easily but takes intentionality and commitment. Meyer's *Learning Space/Workspace* also puts relationships at the center of the process. In her terms, it is within the embodied relational experience that people are able to live their way into new ways of being and thinking. In Fisher-Yoshida's *Transformative Learning in Participatory Processes That Reframe Self-Identity*, it is in the process of collaboratively naming and changing their shared reality that people are able to transform their organization and their self-images in more positive directions. And in the terms I use in my chapter, *A Crucible for Transformation*, it is relationships—between faculty and students, and among students—that provide key elements of some aspects of all the holding environments, including the support and safety of the confirming environment, the challenges and disorientation of the contradicting environment, the opportunity to explore new ways of thinking and being of the creating environment, and the ongoing support and presence of the continuing environment. Transformative learning spaces are relational spaces characterized by affirmation, challenge, and creativity. In these spaces, the learning relationship and process are primary, the content secondary.

## Shared Ownership and Control

In the transformative learning spaces described, teachers or facilitators do not unilaterally control the curriculum and learning process nor do they lead people through a carefully prestructured transformative learning experience. Rather, they design processes through which learners are able to share control over what happens, through, for instance: peer inquiry into questions of shared interest in a self-managed and evolving learning process (Gilly and Leahy); collaborative improvisation in an atmosphere of mutual support (Meyer); the shared goal-setting, action, and reflection of participatory action research

(Fisher-Yoshida); and negotiated curriculum, individualized and group learning contracts, and student involvement in program governance (Schapiro). In all of these processes, the leader (if any) must relinquish some control to the group and submerge his or her ego to make room for others'. While such processes leave open what may happen, they create a space that invites learners to bring their deep passions and concerns, and their whole selves, into the experience. Once those selves are fully engaged, transformation becomes possible. The paradox here is that we create spaces for transformative learning by setting up processes through which we let go of (at least some of) our control of those spaces.

## Inviting the Whole Person

Since transformative learning must ultimately involve our feelings as well as our thoughts, our bodies as well as our minds, the transformative learning spaces described here all invite our whole selves into the process. Recognizing as well that for different people the transformative process may begin at different points; with ideas, feelings, images, actions, and movements, these spaces allow room for people to begin where they are. In the chapters in this section, we can see the whole person invited in a variety of ways: bringing all of our selves to the dialogue with others helps us to develop the intimacy and connection through which deep collaborative learning can occur, as we are transformed through the encounter with others (Gilly and Leahy); bringing the embodied relational self fully to the improvisation process is what enables people to discover and make real new aspects of themselves (Meyer); making room for everyone's stories and experiences, in all of their dimensions, is a key element in both the process and content of the participatory action research process (Fisher-Yoshida); and a confirming environment makes it safe for us to bring up thoughts, feelings, or subconscious images that can lead to contradiction and disorientation, followed by a creative reintegration (Schapiro).

## Time—for Relationship Building, Action, Reflection, and Integration

From the perspectives and experiences that we present in all four chapters, transformative learning is not something that can necessarily happen on a schedule or within the confines of a particular structured learning experience. Developing the trust and safety that can make it possible for people to take risks—allowing the needed space for disequilibrium, exploration, and reintegration, and for action and reflection—takes time, time that can best be measured in weeks, months, or even years, and certainly not in hours or days (Gilly and Leahy, Meyer, Fisher-Yoshida). Relationships develop and learning occurs on their own due time, and we need to be careful that formal academic or organizational calendars do not push people back into their comfort zones or to premature foreclosure on a new way of thinking or being. Ideally, a transformative learning space thus needs to transcend a particular learning experience and provide some sort of ongoing container or continuing holding environment (Schapiro). In this respect, if we are to support transformative learning, we need to adapt the time dimension of our learning spaces to the needs of learners, as all of the projects described here do in different ways, and not the other way around.

## A Process of Inquiry Driven by the Questions, Needs, and Purposes of the Learners

The transformative learning spaces that we have described in these chapters all begin not with the agenda or outcomes defined by a teacher or leader, but with the deeply felt concerns, questions, and problems of the learners. We can see examples of this in the process of collaborative inquiry around a shared concern (Gilly and Leahy), the self- and group-generated process of improvisation (Meyer), the questions and goals leading to a participatory action research project (Fisher-Yoshida), and the self-directed learning process for adult learners (Schapiro). It is this engagement with questions that really matter that makes transformative learning, as differentiated from instrumental or incremental learning, possible. Once people engage in that sort of inquiry, they enter a process that does not have a clear end point in sight. If learners are given the space and support to address and potentially resolve questions and issues in their personal, community, and professional lives, then working toward those answers and solutions can lead to deep changes in their ways of knowing, doing, and being.

## Section 2

Looking Through the Lens of Culture, Difference, and Diversity

# Chapter 6

## Culture Matters: Developing Culturally Responsive Transformative Learning Experiences in Communities of Color

*Charlyn Green Fareed*

On May 15, 2005, four African American women gathered at the home of one of the group members to deeply discuss a topic not normally broached beyond the in-passing, customary advice to *stay strong* usually offered to Black women who seem to overcome despite all odds. As the women entered the *warm, inviting* environment of the spacious living room, the aroma of freshly baked cake seemed to fill all the spaces in the home. All of the women commented how good it was to be in such a comfortable setting that put them immediately at ease. One woman said it made her feel *safe* and unguarded. Although they knew each other at some level, only two were close friends. However, by the end of the three-day session, all four of the women openly shared aspects of their learned experiences of being a *strong Black woman*. What factors contributed to the women deeply sharing personal aspects of their lives as strong Black women? Perhaps it was the warm, inviting home, the cultural makeup of the group, or the nature of the topic. It may have been all of the above.

The focus of this chapter is to present a culturally responsive transformative learning (TL) model that may be of interest to community-based action researchers, nonprofit program developers, or anyone interested in designing culturally responsive transformative learning experiences at the individual or community level with people of color. The model was built into an African American women's inquiry group and contributed to the catalyzed transformative learning occurring in one of the group members.

The central elements of the model are the learning method of *collaborative inquiry* (CI) and four culturally relevant transformative learning goals that fully established the setting, culture, shared meaning, and assessment of learning. Key culturally responsive transformative learning and African concepts provide the theoretical foundation for the model. All of these components of the model are fully described in this chapter.

The chapter reviews the purpose of the inquiry group, the learning method of collaborative inquiry, culturally responsive theoretical foundations of the learning model, and a presentation of four culturally relevant transformative learning goals through the lens of the inquiry group. The chapter concludes by offering the culturally responsive learning model development process and how it can be applied to other community-based learning settings with people of color.

## Purpose of the Inquiry Group

Four women gathered to explore the relationship between the *strong Black woman* cultural ethic and their health and wellness. The strong Black woman cultural ethic is often referred to as an unconscious culturally embedded message that promotes (and often celebrates) toughness and self-sacrificial behaviors, frequently at the expense of Black women's health and wellness. These behaviors are rooted in African American culture where, from slavery to the present day, Black women often have little choice but to persevere, carry on, and sacrifice for family and others. However, this constant striving without examining the impact on their health and wellness has come at a cost. Recent health statistics report African Americans constitute 13% of American women but suffer greater illness and death rates than other women. Their chief causes of death are heart disease, cancer, CVD (stroke), HIV/AIDS, and accidental and intentional violence (AUI) (Washington, 2003, p. 25). In light of these reports as well as personal experiences related to the ethic, the women recognized the need to collaboratively learn, reflect, and change critical health and wellness perspectives and take personal and collective action.

## Learning Method—Collaborative Inquiry

The learning method of collaborative inquiry provided the *container* or setting as well as the process for which TL could occur in the strong Black women's inquiry group. Collaborative inquiry is defined by Bray, Lee, Smith, and Yorks (2000) as "a process consisting of repeated episodes of reflection and action through which a group of peers strives to answer a question of importance to them" (p. 6). It is one among many inquiry methodologies that are experience-based and action-oriented and provides a systematic structure for individual and community learning from lived experience. Individual as well as group learning occurring during the collaborative inquiry process is fostered by the process itself.

Other strategies commonly included in this group are action research, action inquiry, action learning, action science, and participatory action research. Three key collaborative inquiry concepts support the collaborative inquiry method:

*Reflection and Action on Lived Experience* is described by Heron (2000) as, "two or more people conducting human inquiry through a series of cycles in which they alternate between having experience and reflecting together on this experience" (p. 4).

*Peers as Co-inquirers* or the concept of conducting research *with* people, rather than *on* them, is the defining principle of collaborative inquiry. In the inquiry, each participant is a *co-inquirer* shaping the question, designing the inquiry process, and participating in the experience of exploring the inquiry question and making and communicating meaning.

*Recording the group's learning* ensures proper documentation for the meaning-making process in collaborative inquiry. These records provide the data in the form of narrative (storytelling, narrative journaling, poetry), presentational illustrations (video and audio tapes, drawings), or reflective observations (journaling) that are the objectified bases for making interpretative meaning (Bray et al., 2000).

The key concepts of collaborative inquiry underscore its appropriateness when designing learning environments with people of color because, as Heron (2000) notes, "certain aspects of the human experience cannot be understood by conducting experiments and collecting data from other people. Rather, one must be authentically inside the experience to properly explore and understand it" (p. 4). This was especially true for the strong Black woman inquiry group because in order to "authentically" explore the ethic, the women had to be in an environment that allowed them to be fully "inside the experience"; collaborative inquiry helped to provide this environment.

## Key Transformative Learning: African and African American Theoretical Concepts Supporting the Model

Certain aspects of the transformative learning perspectives of Brookfield and Kegan are culturally responsive and best describe the type of transformational learning that occurred in at least one of the group members. Brookfield (2000) defines his concept of critical reflection as "a process where individuals engage in some sort of power analysis of the situation or context and try to identify assumptions they hold dear that are actually destroying their sense of well-being and serving the interests of others: that is, hegemonic assumptions" (p. 126). In this aspect of Brookfield's transformative learning, emphasis is on critical reflection around power analysis and changing meaning perspectives for personal and group re-empowerment. Given the systemic health and wellness disparities of African American women as previously cited, including this aspect of Brookfield's concept offered the group members a place to examine critical health and wellness issues related to being strong Black women from both a systemic power dynamics as well as group perspective.

Applying a constructive-developmental perspective to Mezirow's frame of reference concept, Kegan (2000) suggests that "a frame of reference is a way of knowing" (p. 48). He states, constructive-developmental theory looks at the process it calls development as the gradual process by which what was "subject" in our knowing becomes "object." When a way of knowing moves from a place where we are "had by it" (captive of it) to a place where we "have it" and can be in relationship to it, the form of our knowing becomes more complex, more expansive (pp. 53–54).

Including this aspect of Kegan's transformative learning concept into the theoretical foundation of the inquiry group provided learning from a developmental view where the women examined how they were "had by"—"subject to"—the ethic or captive to seeing only the positives of being a strong Black woman and moving to a place where the ethic was "object," that is, they could be "in relationship" with the concept through the course of the collaborative inquiry discussions.

Through this developmental process, the women were better able to expand their understanding of the ethic and its relationship to their health and wellness. They began to experience the ethic as more complex, multifaceted, and dynamic.

The principle of African communalism served as both a cultural theoretical concept as well as formed the basis for the four culturally relevant transformative learning goals of the model. The principle emphasizes learning for the sake of the whole and is an important concept in the lives of many African Americans.

African communalism is defined by Kigongo (1992) as "the state of affairs whereby individuals in the society consistently pursue certain fundamental virtues on the basis of enhancing a common or social good" (p. 10). In communal societies, "people are not seen as important in their own right, each one is an integral part of the *whole;* in a communalistic social order, community welfare undergirds actions" (Moemeka, 1998, p. 124).

The principle of community welfare or the welfare of the *whole* is very evident in the day-to-day lives of many African Americans. Black women's collectives and African American traditions such as Kwanzaa demonstrate that the principle of African communalism is a central value in African American community and family life. This connection to community "reflects certain Africentric principles of the Black experience that is communal, spiritual, and holistic that recreates the simultaneous, holistic affirmation of Black individuality *and* collectivity, two opposing tendencies in the Eurocentric worldview which find harmonious expression in Black life" (King & Mitchell, 1995, pp. 3–4).

The body of literature often referred to as "Black Womanist Thought" (Collins, hooks, Jones, & Shorter-Gooden) was incorporated into the group discussions to enrich, expand, and deepen the learning from a broader cultural perspective. As a critical social theory, Black Womanist Thought aims to empower African American women within the context of social injustice sustained by intersecting oppressions (i.e., race, class, and gender) (Collins, 2000, p. 22).

References to this literature allowed the group members to have all aspects of their experiences present and were to a large extent validated by other Black women who were physically absent but *fully present* through their poignant portrayals of their lived experiences. Inclusion of this body of literature further increased the likelihood of critical TL occurring among group members because it fostered the type of learning that Brookfield described; it "emphasized critical reflection around power analysis and changing meaning perspectives for personal and group re-empowerment."

## Four Culturally Relevant Transformative Learning Goals

The following four goals were developed to increase the possibility of transformative learning occurring within the context of the strong Black woman inquiry group. They suggest, if culture is purposefully attended to when designing learning experiences with people of color at the community level, the likelihood of transformative learning occurring among group members increases. In the context of the strong Black woman group, this was accomplished through the inclusion of the key transformative learning, African, and African American concepts previously described. These concepts provided the foundation for the four culturally relevant transformative learning goals that established the optimal cultural learning environment for the women. Each of the four goals is described through the lens of learning that occurred within the strong Black woman collaborative inquiry group.

### Goal 1: Create Culturally Sensitive Learning Environments

The collaborative inquiry learning process supports transformative learning by setting the right conditions (setting) for individual and group learning to occur during a gradual process of reflection. This gradual depth of reflection is especially important for strong Black women because it allows them time to transition from busy lives focused on the needs of others, to time focused on self-reflection. Providing learning environments that help strong Black women take a break from their "pursuit of perfectionism, meeting goals, mediating family conflicts and challenging the criticisms and doubts of others," is key to their learning (California Black Women's Health Project, 2003).

These environments should be of the type Bray et al. (2000) describe as "ones where there would be a minimum of disruption in order to guarantee that the participants could be attentive to the group and not be easily distracted, and ones that are relatively secure and relaxed" (p. 59). When these types of learning environments are established, it allows Black women to stop, relax, reflect, re-flect deeply, and make changes. This was accomplished by holding the collabo-rative inquiry sessions in group members' homes; one session was held over a weekend in the country home of a member. The women emphasized the im-portance of retreat type locations, which allow one to be away from work, fam-ily, and other responsibilities in order to fully relax and focus on the discussions.

As a result of our experiences with racism, many African Americans, both men and women, view issues of safety and security as a key cultural environ-mental need. With this in mind, great care was taken to ensure that the design for the inquiry group was sensitive to this need. Evidence that this number one goal was met was in the easy flow and depth of sharing of life experiences from the beginning through to the end of the collaborative inquiry sessions. All re-marked that the comfortable, relaxed, and secure learning environments con-tributed to them feeling free to share their experiences as strong Black women.

The depth of reflection due to a relaxed and secure environment is evident in Marsha's quotes that follow—at the beginning of the inquiry she is unsure if she wants to explore her strong Black women meaning perspectives and "do all the secrets." However, in later sessions her meaning perspectives are clearly changing in relation to the notion of strong Black women being on a "tread-mill."

Marsha's *treadmill* comments at the beginning of the study:

You know it's like a skeleton's in a closet, and that type of thing; and then you're here and you want me to trust you; want me to do all the secrets. That's kind of powerful to do all of that.
*Marsha—Co-Inquirer*

Marsha's *treadmill* comments midway through the study:

Even if we find that we are on it, [treadmill] how in the hell are we supposed to get off? I mean how can we work ourselves to get off, or how can we work

our self not to see our children in these same patterns like I was telling you about my son; "Oh Mama, it ain't all that—don't worry" you know, and I'm trying to fix it and like you said, the whole environment it tells you what success is, all this stuff is set up, this whole umbrella, this is what success is, you need to work for these companies, you need to have this, this, this. So all this stuff is set up, so your environment is forcing you to be that strong Black woman.
*Marsha—Co-Inquirer*

Marsha's *treadmill* comments toward the end of the study:

I'm on the treadmill, I need to get off, I'm doing too much, I need to back off again, I need to come back to where I should be, you know be reminded. And that's what I got out of it [study] so far as being related to our health and wellness.
*Marsha—Co-Inquirer*

We all saw and commented on Marsha's shift in her ways of knowing. It was clear that she had experienced the type of transformative learning Kegan described, where she was "had by" the notion of being a strong Black woman and not wanting to "do all the secrets," to later questioning "how in the hell are we supposed to get off?" then moving to say, "I'm on the treadmill, I need to get off, I'm doing too much, I need to back off again, I need to come back to where I should be, you know, be reminded." She was no longer "had by" or captive to the ethic but was able to "have it" and be in relationship with it. The ethic "had become more complex, more expansive."

## Goal 2: Encourage Culturally Inclusive Learning Experiences

CI usually takes place during a fluid process with a variety of activities occurring during each phase. All group members were equal and active contributors to group formation, establishing guiding principles and collectively leading the group.

The creation of African Communalism guiding principles among the members clearly helped the women to move from being individual learners to a culturally inclusive learning community. The group chose to begin each session by reciting African-centered principles that served both as a culturally inclusive learning element and as group norms.

*Unity of Spirit:* The sense of unity is invisible but members are characterized as cells in a body—the group needs the individual and the individual needs the group.

*Trust:* Everyone is moved to trust all other members of the group in an inclusive way. It is further assumed that everyone is inherently well-intentioned.

*Openness:* Being open to the other members requires trust. Individual problems are taken on as community problems, so each person is open to others.

*Respect for Elders:* Elders represent the collective memory of the group and should be respected for their life experience and wisdom. They are responsible for keeping the group together and for monitoring group dynamics.

*Ancestors:* Those who have passed on are not considered dead or unavailable. The community of the spirits becomes a guide or inspiration to those living.

Inclusion of these African-centered principles helped to create a space to discuss our ancestors' enslaved experiences and our present-day lives as strong Black women as noted in this quote from Marsha.

> But I say it still stems back to health and slavery. When you even look at the whole thing, we was *fix'n* it, we was *fix'n* it, we was having the babies, we was doing it all. Continuously, continuously, continuously, continuously.
> *Marsha—Co-Inquirer*

The importance of creating culturally inclusive learning experiences via elements such as African-centered guiding principles was to make a place for the women's cultural identity to be present. Inclusion of this goal also enabled the group to deepen the conversation through an examination of systems of oppression and power that Brookfield (2000) described when the group "critically engaged in some sort of power analysis of the situation or context."

## Goal 3: Create Opportunities for Critical Reflection and Learning Through Critical Questioning on Culturally Shared Meaning

As the group further explored and reflected on the relationship between the *strong Black woman* cultural ethic and their health and wellness, goal three learning experiences were designed to create opportunities for critical reflection and learning through critical questioning on our *strong Black woman ways of knowing.*

This type of critical questioning can facilitate movement to deeper levels of reflection where, as Brookfield (2000) suggests, participants "engage in some sort of power analysis of the situation or context and try to identify assumptions they hold dear that are actually destroying their sense of well-being and serving the interests of others" (p. 126), and as Kegan (2000) notes, "we not only form meaning, and we not only change our meanings; we *change* the very form by which we are making our meaning" (pp. 52–53).

The group members were encouraged to share meanings of their strong Black woman assumptions in culturally based language that often conveys the essence of the lived experience. Many African Americans, even the well educated, often express lived experiences in *code* language that only other African Americans can fully understand. Having the choice to express thoughts, feelings, and experiences in culturally based language allows individuals to have uncensored freedom of expression. Many of the critical questions that the group explored examined both power dynamics and long-held assumptions of the ethic and the relationship to health and wellness.

- Has it been used as a strategy to survive the impacts of racism?

- How is the cultural ethic of the Strong Black Woman learned? Is the ethic passed down from mother to daughter?

- How do African American women experience being strong? Are there differences? How do these differences compare to other women who are "strong"?

- To what extent does the cultural ethic of the Strong Black Woman impact the health and wellness of African American women? What are the implications?

- What are some of the actions African American women can take as a result of increased understanding of the impact of this ethic on their health and wellness?

Creating opportunities for critical reflection on identifying, analyzing, and understanding power dynamics, long-held assumptions, and the relationship to lived experiences may have provided the key component to Marsha's catalyzed transformative learning. Her quote is an example of the type of critical reflection described by Brookfield.

> You ain't suppose to have feelings, you ain't suppose to call them [Whites] on anything, you know. So what's the big deal. I don't see why; like they just stand up there . . . well why you afraid of me? What did I do to make you feel that you should be scared of me, or something like that. So this whole thing I think when we start talking about cultural, it goes all the way back to slavery.
> *Marsha—Co-Inquirer*

## Goal 4: Assess Personal and Group Learning and Change Using Evaluation Methods That Allow Freedom of Expression

The specific learning experiences of goal four provided a space for the group members to make explicit the changes in their forms or ways of knowing. This was done by conducting post-session learning debriefings where the women assessed their levels of awareness, insights into or changes in perspectives of being a strong Black woman, and the relationship to their health and wellness.

The four authenticity criteria of Lincoln and Guba (cited in Bray et al., 2000) were in keeping with a culturally relevant design and provided a useful guide that helped the women evaluate their learning using a self-assessment that encouraged freedom of expression.

*Fairness*—do the findings demonstrate that the viewpoints of the participants have been given evenhanded representation?

*Ontological authenticity*—to what extent does the record show a growth in the perception of the participants?

*Educative authenticity*—the existence of evidence that members have gained increased appreciation for the sources of alternative positions around the question.

*Catalytic authenticity*—the accounts of the actions and decisions promoted by the inquiry process as demonstrated by the willingness of participants to be involved in change.

Post-session responses to the self-assessment from the group members indicated that in summary:

- All members felt that their individual contributions to the group theme findings were fairly represented.

- All members expressed "lots of growth" and "greatly enlarged" growth in their perception of themselves as strong Black women.

- All members expressed they gained "ultimate appreciation" and it was "very confirming" to hear the viewpoints of others.

- All members shared their individual as well as group actions that resulted from the new learning and expressed in the major learning and action findings.

These culturally relevant transformative learning goals should not be viewed as a lock-step but as a fluid process. One goal may precede another or move faster or slower than another. More important is that it calls attention to some of the culturally relevant learning experiences necessary in order for transformative learning to possibly occur for African American women and other people of color.

Central to achieving the transformative learning goals is the role of the inquiry initiator/co-inquirer/researcher. In the context of collaborative inquiry and probably for most types of participatory research, this complex role can be challenging because it requires attention to *in and out* skills.

These are specific skills that the initiator/co-inquirer/researcher used at various times to help stimulate reflection on the question but were barely noticeable to the other group members. They involve presenting thought-provoking questions, encouraging different viewpoints, and documenting differences and conflicts on the meanings of being a strong Black woman that emerged from the group.

## Culturally Responsive Transformative Learning Model Development Process

The goal of this chapter was to present a culturally responsive learning model that may be of interest to community-based action researchers, nonprofit program developers, or anyone interested in designing culturally responsive transformative learning experiences at the individual, group, or community level. The key elements of the model are the four culturally relevant transformative learning goals previously outlined that were incorporated into a collaborative inquiry group in order to increase the likelihood of transformative learning occurring for the group members.

Although other research or group process methods may be more appropriate for a particular community-based project, the collaborative inquiry process proved to work seamlessly with the four culturally relevant transformative learning goals. As stated earlier, collaborative inquiry usually takes place during a fluid four-phase process as outlined by Bray et al. (2000). In the following diagram, the development process of the four culturally relevant transformative learning goals is outlined in conjunction with the four-phase collaborative inquiry process.

As noted in the preceding diagram, each of the four culturally responsive transformative learning goals were used in conjunction with a corresponding collaborative inquiry phase. The value of designing the strong Black woman inquiry group using these two learning processes was that it supported "single-loop" learning as well as "double-loop" learning (Argyris, 1982).

Argyris and Schon (1998) describe single-loop learning as learning that fits prior experiences and existing values, which enables the learner to respond in an automatic way. In the strong Black woman inquiry group, the four culturally responsive transformative learning goals provided the women with single-loop

| CI PROCESS | CULTURALLY RELEVANT TL GOALS |
|---|---|

## Phase I: Forming a CI Group

- **Initiating a CI Group**
- Obtaining Institutional Consent
- Establishing a Physical Context
- Ensuring Diversity
- Orienting the Group
- Developing the Inquiry Project
- Framing the Inquiry Question
- Designing the Inquiry Project
- Transitioning to Collective Leadership
- Reflecting on Group Process

*Goal 1: Create Culturally Sensitive Learning Environments*
Culturally sensitive environments should be planned along with the CI initiating the group activities. Group members can give input into the types of environments that are important in order to meet their specific cultural learning needs.

## Phase II: Creating Conditions for Group Learning

- **Agreeing on Criteria that Define the Group**
- Repeating Cycles of Action
- Reflection to Generate Learning

*Goal 2: Encourage Culturally Inclusive Learning Experiences*
During the CI activity of agreeing on criteria, the inclusion of culturally inclusive elements should be encouraged.

## Phase III: Acting on the Inquiry Question

- Putting Plans and Designs into Practice
- Keeping Reflective Records
- Respecting Group Ownership of Ideas
- **Questioning Honestly**
- Practicing Dialogue and Reflection

*Goal 3: Create Opportunities for Critical Reflection and Learning Through Critical Questioning on Culturally Shared Meaning*
During the CI process of questioning honestly, incorporate questions that promote critical reflection on culturally shared meanings that are specific to the inquiry question.

## Phase IV: Making Meaning by Constructing Knowledge

- Capturing the Group's Experience
- Understanding the Experience
- Selecting a Method for Interpreting Experience
- Constructing Knowledge
- Avoiding Flawed Meaning Making
- Guarding against Groupthink
- Checking Validity
- Celebrating Meaningful Collaboration
- Communicating in the Public Arena

*Goal 4: Assess Personal and Group Learning and Change Using Evaluation Methods That Allow Freedom of Expression*
All of the areas indicated directly relate to goal four planning. Careful selection of evaluation methods allow flexibility of expression where participants assess their learning and change in culturally

Bray, Lee, Smith, & Yorks (2000)          Fareed (2006)

learning because the four goals were developed from "prior experiences and existing values."

Double-loop learning is described as learning that does not fit the learner's prior experiences or schema. In the collaborative learning group, double-loop learning occurred via the type of perspective transformation process defined by Mezirow (1975) where Transformative Learning is a process through which adults critically reflect on assumptions underlying their frames of reference and resulting beliefs, values, and perspectives; engage in a reflective rational dialogue about those assumptions; and, as a result, transform their assumptions and frames of reference to make them more inclusive, open, and better justified.

All of the co-inquirers expressed they did not have a prior, *conscious* understanding of the health and wellness impacts of being a strong Black woman before the inquiry group. It was through the process of perspective transformation that double-loop learning happened among all of the co-inquirers.

The value of designing this type of depth learning is that it provides learners with multiple "layers" or opportunities to gain critical understanding. It can be assumed that this layered learning design—that is, collaborative inquiry culturally responsive theoretical foundation and four culturally relevant transformative learning goals—created the optimal learning environment for Marsha's catalyzed transformative learning to occur.

## Application of the Culturally Responsive Transformative Learning Model in Communities of Color

The culturally responsive transformative learning model can be applied to community-based educational programs or to other group settings where a change in critical meaning perspectives among people of color is sought. The collaborative inquiry process fully supports the incorporation of culture-specific elements, such as the four culturally relevant transformative learning goals presented in this chapter. It may be useful to be aware of some guidelines for the incorporation of the four culturally relevant goals by groups in other settings.

### Goal 1: Create Culturally Sensitive Learning Environments

The group initiator/leader should be a member of the cultural or racial group and should be flexible in understanding the many facets of the culture. Having this understanding allows the initiator to ensure that the proper learning environment/setting is achieved.

### Goal 2: Encourage Culturally Inclusive Learning Experiences

The most optimal place to include cultural artifacts into the learning experience is in the Phase I, Collaborative Inquiry process wherein the group begins to form. All group members should be encouraged to develop the type of cultural artifacts that will guide the learning experience.

### Goal 3: Create Opportunities for Critical Reflection and Learning Through Critical Questioning on Culturally Shared Meaning

Group initiators/leaders should be skilled in group process and in injecting critical reflective questions at key learning points in the discussion. This skill may well provide the impetus for group members to "negotiate his or her own purposes, values, feelings, and meanings rather than simply to act on those of others" (Mezirow, 2000, p. 8).

### Goal 4: Assess Personal and Group Learning and Change Using Evaluation Methods That Allow Freedom of Expression

Group members should decide on the evaluation methods to assess group learning based on the group's cultural practices. For some groups, these could include guiding questions, narratives, or written accounts.

## Summary—Culture Matters!

This chapter presented a culturally responsive transformative learning model and key elements of the model. The incorporation of the *layered learning design*—that is, collaborative inquiry, culturally responsive theoretical foundation, and four culturally relevant transformative learning goals—created the optimal learning environment for Marsha's catalyzed transformative learning to occur and for perspective transformation among all of the group members to happen.

The model was developed in response to the cultural learning needs of a specific group of African American women: women who identify themselves as strong Black women. It highlights the importance of attending to all elements of the learning design: (1) learning method, e.g., collaborative inquiry; (2) theoretical foundation, e.g., culturally responsive transformative learning concepts; and (3) culturally relevant transformative learning goals. All of the elements of the learning model were highly culturally responsive, which is critical when designing transformative learning experiences with people of color in order to set the ideal conditions for transformation to possibly occur.

This was especially important in the strong Black woman inquiry group since a change in vital health and wellness meaning perspectives was the goal of the learning. Each of the four goals were incorporated into the collaborative inquiry process at key places from the beginning through the end of the sessions in order to set the optimal transformative learning conditions through gradual levels of critical reflection.

The activity of assessing personal and group learning, change, and action using a culturally appropriate evaluation brought the transformative learning full circle by allowing the group members to self-report and assess their learning, change, and action and those of the group.

The overall outcomes of the strong Black woman inquiry group clearly show that *culture does matter* when designing community-based learning experiences with people of color. Studies conducted by researchers such as Abalos (1998), who discussed a theory of social transformation aimed specifically at the needs of the Latino community, also support the importance of attending to specific cultural learning needs when designing community-based learning.

So what were the factors that contributed to the women openly sharing aspects of their lives as strong Black women and experiencing warmth, a sense of belonging, and a transformative learning experience? It was the cultural factors because culture *truly* does matter!

# References

Abalos, D. (1998). La *Communidad Latina in the United States*. Westport, CT: Praeger.

Argyris, C. (1982). Reasoning, learning and action: individual and organizational. San Francisco: Jossey-Bass.

Argyris, C., & Schon, D. (1998). In M. Knowles, *The adult learner*. Woburn, MA: Butterworth-Heinemann.

Bookfield, S. (2000). Transformative learning as ideology critique. In J. Mezirow (Ed.), *Learning as transformation: Critical perspectives on a theory in progress*. San Francisco: Jossey-Bass.

Bray, J., Lee, Smith, & Yorks (2000). *Collaborative inquiry in practice: Action, reflection and making meaning*. Thousand Oaks, CA: Sage.

California Black Women's Health Project (2003). http://www.womensenews.org/article.cfm/dyn/aid/1392/context/archive

Collins, P. (2000). *Black feminist thought: Knowledge, consciousness, and the politics of empowerment*. New York: Routledge.

Fareed, C. G. (2006). *Strong Black Woman: A collaborative study on understanding, experiences, and relationship to health and wellness*. Unpublished doctoral dissertation, Fielding Graduate University.

Heron in Bray et al. (2000). *Collaborative inquiry in practice: Action, reflection and making meaning*. Thousand Oaks, CA: Sage.

Kegan, R. (2000). What "form" transforms? A constructive-developmental approach to transformative learning. In J. Mezirow (Ed.), *Learning as transformation: Critical perspectives on a theory in progress*. San Francisco: Jossey-Bass.

Kigongo, J. K. (1992). The concepts of individuality and social cohesion: A perversion of two African cultural realities. In A. T. Dalfovo (Ed.), *The foundations of social life: Ugandan philosophical studies,* Vol. 2. Washington, DC: Council for Research in Values and Philosophy.

King, J., & Mitchell, C. A. (1995). *Black mothers to sons*. New York: Peter Lang.

Mezirow, J. (1975) *Education for perspective transformation: Women's re-entry programs in community colleges*. New York: Center for Adult Education, Teachers College, Columbia University.

Mezirow, J. (2000). *Learning as transformation: Critical perspectives on a theory in progress*. San Francisco: Jossey-Bass.

Moemeka, A. (1998). Communalism: A fundamental dimension of culture. *Journal of Communication, 48*(4), 118–141.

Washington, H. (2003). *The National Black Women's Health Project in Collaboration with the Congressional Black Caucus Health Brain Trust and the U.S. Senate Black Legislative Staff Caucus*: In National Colloquium on Black Women's Health. April 2003.

# Chapter 7

---

## Socially Constructing a Transformed Self-view and Worldview

*Ann Davis*

You never know a line is crooked unless you have a straight one to put next to it.

Socrates

Successful intercultural [expatriate] experiences based on my research supported transformative learning and growth related to cultural difference and disorienting dilemmas. The cultural difference and disorienting dilemmas participants engaged in, in their daily lives, allowed them to see their own cultural self clearly when compared with others. The participants' perceived changes to their self-view [identity] included becoming more than their own culture affirmed, developing a broadened worldview, and reflecting a movement toward becoming intercultural.

> It's very hard to change and so something similar to that is exposures, different traveling experiences, educational and working, it opens me up and gives me more perspectives. So when I go back to China where I grew up even though they are different, we are co-related; we are overlapped because we are all human beings.

Dr. Zhang, China, University Professor

Analysis in relation to the ways disorienting dilemmas within intercultural lived experiences related to cultural difference exposed factors and identity orientation for the co-construction of shared meaning making. The participants' responses demonstrated factors connected to one's identity that resulted in discursive interaction related to cultural difference, relationships, and transformation. Shifts in self-awareness and a broadened worldview supported a self/other orientation. The evidence of participants' transformed self-views supported dialogue activities and interplay connected to disorienting dilemmas and cultural difference to foster transformation. This chapter discusses the use of my ENRICHED Dialogue Model, which incorporates approaching communication differently to raise awareness (knowledge of self and others) and to promote and prepare people for intercultural communication and cross-cultural experiences so that growth and change may occur in classrooms and organizations.

As most participants so truly stated, experiences abroad change you. Jarrett, an instructor from South Africa, responded to my query,

> When I went back to South Africa, I was a different person. I had been in a relationship prior to going to the U.S.A., which was put on hold. Obviously when I came back from the States, I would pick up and continue. But I couldn't because I was a different person, and this relationship was no longer compatible with who I was. I had definitely changed. I think it was purely in terms of just saying I can do anything that I want to do; therefore, it kind of changed the way that I approached everything. I couldn't tell the difference, and it was only after, honestly, about 10 years that I realized how much I had changed in my overseas experiences. I think America definitely did that for me. I had an achieving outlook. If I wanted to do something all I had to do was do it.

> Jarrett, South Africa, Instructor

Jarrett expressed vividly his transformed self-view and broadened worldview, "it kind of changed the way that I approached everything." This statement exemplifies the shifts from self-view to self/other [worldview] orientation that takes in factors found for the social construction of shared meaning. The ENRICHED Dialogue Model has evolved from my research to encompass these factors. These factors related to identity perception also support the role of relationships and a need for other ways of knowing in transformative learning, which supports a holistic view of Mezirow's theory. Discursive episodes around cultural differences also encourage these factors when using the ENRICHED Dialogue Model. This connects transformative learning theory to intercultural communication theory to focus on "the communication perspective" as defined by the Coordinated Management of Meaning (CMM) theory (Pearce, 2007).

# ENRICHED Dialogue Model:
# A Self-Other Construction

The Outer Circle represents the communication perspective using a
social construction approach: (a 3-D open, adaptive, and fluid system).

The Black
represents Self
(or selves)

The two (or more)
energy spaces inside
each space represents
the co-constructed
ENRICHED Dialogue

The White represents
Other (or others)

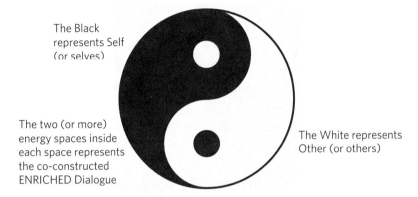

The dynamic results in transformation: a blending, "glocal" consciousness,
that evolves by one's self-view being broadened through the process.

**E**mpathy = being mindfully present to others; listening empathetically

**N**etwork of Relationships = is necessary, interconnectedness, shared

**R**eal = self-reflective, reciprocity (helpful, advantageous), equality, authenticity
(genuine, true), and again listening (to take notice, pay attention to)

**I**ntegrity = safe, trustworthy, sincere, reliable, honest, and good

**C**ollaborative = co-construct; work together to produce or achieve

**H**olistic = consider the whole (all parts), all voices; beings; together, collective,
and individual effort

**E**ngagement = attention, interactive, interest; interplay, involvement (critical
thinking and action that benefits most)

**D**iscussion = conversation, exchange, talk, argument; what we are making together?

Figure 7.1: The ENRICHED Dialogue Model, © 2006 Ann Davis

The ENRICHED Dialogue model adds to these theories rooted in communication and has the potential to transform one's self-view and worldview by looking at who we are and what we are making together. It is positive, possible, and inclusive of all perspectives. It concentrates on making and doing and looks at communication [naming, making and doing] holistically, not through it, to solve problems of everyday life episodes, situations, and events. It has the potential to make better social worlds. Mei Mei from Hong Kong exemplifies this integration of perspectives well.

Mei Mei, a teacher, told about who she had become:

The experiences I had in Canada have encouraged me to be myself or to enjoy being whoever I am. It was a wonderful experience! Every time I think back to its environment—it's very supportive, very accepting. A lot less, a lot fewer regulations, rules to follow and stuff like that. It's a funny thing because I keep being asked by others, so what do you consider yourself to be? Are you a Chinese or are you a Canadian? And nowadays I just answer, yes well I'm Canadian-Chinese or Chinese-Canadian whichever I am able to be, but yes, I am both. Because I have to be fair to Canada, all the experience I've had there. It's a country that helped me to grow up a lot in a very positive way. The whole country is more accepting whereas here it's a lot more judgmental, and we have to fit a certain form, we have to behave in a certain way. I consider myself a true east-meets-west type of creation.

Mei Mei Chan, Hong Kong, Teacher

These brief cameos are from my research that focused on an integrated, holistic understanding of transformative learning related to communication, culture, consciousness, and difference. Connecting transformative learning practices to intercultural communication provides an underpinning for the transformation of mental structures and cultures. Yet the intermingled use of practical theories such as these is necessary to understand the coordination, coherence, and mystery of dialogue and interplay within particular instances of communication to meet the challenges of our times. To bring transformative learning into action, it is necessary to communicatively join together to deconstruct, reflect, reframe, and reconstruct concepts in order to understand and perceive multiple perspectives from which to co-construct shared meanings and new directions.

Successful long-term living/work experiences and engagement within nonnative cultures facilitate participants knowing themselves more, "who I am," which leads to transformation with the deconstruction, reflection, and reframing of their self-view [identity] These cameos demonstrate how influential most relational dialogues between different cultures can be. Participants' self-view and worldview were transformed—not just their personality, but their individuality, the whole of who they are. Their points of view changed and also how they perceived the world and acted in it. As Jarrett stated so well, "not personality . . . it kind of changed the way that I approached everything." Other participants, Apple Siu from Canada and Kumar from India, each said, "Now I am a world citizen."

This cultural communication [acquired (unconscious) culture] is transformative, altering boundaries of and reframing not only one's self-view but worldview. Successful long-term living/work experiences and engagement within nonnative cultures enrich and broaden one's self-view and transform one's relational (cultural) community.[7]

The participants' involved in my study experienced the disorienting dilemmas of numerous intercultural experiences over many years. Here are some of the various ways they described their feelings to illustrate their transformed points of view:

| | |
|---|---|
| I grew out of my shell, | Increased confidence |
| Tuned into Western culture | You become more aware |
| Talked with others about it | More than one way to see the world |
| It gave me more perspectives | Taking risks is easier now |
| Mindboggling | I feel I have so many skills |
| My beliefs were all shaken | I learned so much about myself, difference(s), and different peoples |

Table 7.1: Transformed points of view

The integration of Mezirow's process of perspective transformation and Kim's intercultural transformation, as linked by this research, supports a holistic view of transformative learning from a communication perspective that can be applied to practice by using the ENRICHED Dialogue Model's social construction approach.

This study used thematic analysis of interview texts that examined, using descriptive research design, the narrative, self-reports of intercultural expatriate teachers' cross-cultural experiences. The study used an interpretive approach (to explore clustered subcategories, recurring patterns, and themes related to transformations of self-reported, individual cross-cultural lived experiences). The

---

[7] Relational (cultural) community is a community of like-minded people whose culturally, socialized self-views have been transformed by long-term living/work/travel experiences and/or engagement within other cultures.

goal of this method was to rely on the participants' views of the experiences being studied. Such an understanding describes how communication between cultural differences transforms one's self-view and worldview.

Hall (1998) verifies,

> Most of us remain lonely until we meet someone else who also knows that other people are real and not the paper cutouts that those who do not know make them out to be. This kind of loneliness is impossible to describe but is experienced as a kind of hunger—a hunger for the lost part of the self longing to be reunited. (p. 65)

Apple expressed this, "it was just a very lonely experience because I had gone through so much of my own personal, spiritual and human development. Lots of my friends hadn't changed very much. They had stayed the same. I think my mother really understood." Back in Canada from Africa, the part of Apple's self that longed to be reunited was found when she joined an international club. Everything fell into place in the relational community of that international club, and what had been a puzzle was now a door opening to a new world, as Apple explained it.

Hall (1998) makes this point affirming, "word [learned] culture and tacit-acquired [unconscious] culture are both languages and tacit-acquired culture is a language of the past, present, and the future that is part of culture and of ourselves as well" (p. 66). These differentiating aspects of consciousness: identities, relationships, and cultures are socially constructed. Looking at communication and transformation from a social construction paradigm distinguishes them "both by what it says about things and by the things about which it has something to say" (Pearce, 2006). Both transformative learning and social construction look at the action of communication, what we are making together. The practical application addresses increasing knowledge and awareness about identities, differences, relationships, communities, and cultures that relate to what this chapter is about.

## Transforming One's Self-View

One's view of oneself derives from one's socialization. Childhood is seen as a formative period of uncritical assimilation of cultural beliefs, socialization, and learning from significant interactive experiences with adult figures: parents, teachers, and mentors. These experiences "mirror the way [one's] culture and those individuals responsible for [one's] socialization happen to have defined the various situations" (Mezirow, 1991, p. 131). Combined with other similar experiences, these meaning structures become our taken-for-granted frames of reference, habits, mindsets, points of view, and ways of knowing and doing over time.

> We rely on our cultural frames of reference to diminish the chaos of our everyday world. These meaning-making structures support us by providing an explanation of the happenings in our daily lives but at the same time they are a reflection of our cultural and psychological assumptions that have been socially constructed. These assumptions constrain us, making our view of the world subjective, often distorting our thoughts and perceptions. They are the double-edged sword whereby they give meaning (validation) to our experiences, but at the same time skew our reality. (Taylor, 1993, p. 45)

These meaning-making structures rooted in communication when linked together are integral to all three of the following theoretical concepts: perspective transformation, intercultural transformation, and interpersonal/intercultural communication (Davis, 2006).

Mezirow's (2000) transformative learning theory is based in communicative learning—learning with others that may lead to transforming and retransforming of perspectives and what we do when we communicate. Kim's (2001) integrative theory places personal communication at the center of the structure of cross-cultural adaptation. It is the factor that affects and is affected by all else in the process. Pearce's (2004) CMM theory integrates culture and communication arguing that communication is a social act that permeates all we do daily in our action between the interactive cross-cultural experiences of everyday life and intercultural communication. Intercultural communication within these experiences around cultural difference permeates everything—all the senses.

A willingness to change may be expanded by learning how to approach communication differently. We can shift our understanding of communication from simply transmitting messages and naming or referring to objects to the process by which we collaboratively converse, what we are making together and the actions that result. "The self is a process that arises out of social activity and relations; it is within the continual *making* of relationships and experiences in adulthood that the self evolves" (Pearce, 2006). Within long-term successful living/work experiences and engagements within nonnative cultures, this new communicative, social environment is a conflicting and contrasting one. This transformative learning environment of relationships, difference, critical reflection, and awareness of self and others transforms one's ways of knowing and being in the world, one's self-view and worldview.

Dale from England testified to this,

> On a personal level I became a lot more confident just having to deal with all sorts of different situations and ideas. I became much more confident as a

person, but as a British person it was strange because I'd never considered myself to be British. But in going somewhere else all of a sudden you become,
British. You have to; you're almost an ambassador of Britain. And so you become more British; then you start to realize as well things that maybe you do
that you never even really noticed before that people pick up and you don't.
You just think its normal, and so you're exposed. You know people can see.
So that was quite different.

Dale Davies, England, Instructor

This awareness of one's self-view together with situations and ideas about
others' cultural views is transforming and leads to a more inclusive worldview
"as a citizen of the world" (Adler, 1998). Exposure is a choice as is change
when one goes to live and work abroad; it is something we can explore, discuss,
and practice to increase awareness and knowledge to prepare, value, and enjoy
intracultural and intercultural experiences.

The willingness to change these meaning-making structures or not is each
individual's choice. Some may not be willing or desire to change. My research
results found several factors that most participants described aided success and
resulted from their willingness to change. Factors rooted in communication
related to cultural difference, relationships, and transformation encompassed
within the cross-cultural experiences of everyday life activities were:

| | |
|---|---|
| increased self-esteem | accepting |
| confidence | creative |
| belonging | outspoken |
| a sense of community | suspension of judgment |
| growth in positive ways | increased ability to take risks |
| becoming more open | gained new perspectives, new skills were |
| respectful ` | acquired |

Table 7.2: Success factors related to cultural difference, relationships, and transformation

## Self/Other Orientation toward an Inclusive Worldview

One's self-view is formed by one's culture. Culture characterizes the human
species and also simultaneously differentiates one social group from another.
Communication underlies everything. Hall (1998) asserts,

Any culture is basically a system of creating, sending, storing and processing
information, and cultural communication is deeper and more complex than
spoken or written messages. Humans are guided by two forms of information

assessed in two different ways: type A—manifest culture—which is learned from words and numbers, and type B—tacit-acquired culture—which is not verbal but is highly situational and operates according to the rules which are not in awareness, not learned in the usual sense but acquired in the process of growing up or simply being in different environments. In humans, acquired culture is made up of hundreds and possibly thousands of micro-events comprising the corpus of the daily cycle of activity, the spaces we occupy, and the way we relate to others, in other words, the bulk of experiences of everyday life. This tacit, the taken-for-granted aspect of culture, a natural part of life is the foundation on which rests 45 years of Hall's scholarly research. (p. 54)

This acquired culture corresponds with an integral understanding of transformative learning and CMM's primary question "what are we making together." It examines the transactions [communication experiences of everyday life] at cultural interfaces (spaces we occupy). The interfaces reveal the conflicting and contrasting patterns about both types of culture, such as the interviews of participants' successful long-term living/work experiences in nonnative cultures. Another way of illustrating interactions at cultural interfaces, what we are making together, is the figure/ground (participants and their environments and/or the disorienting dilemmas within cross-cultural experiences) phenomenon that can be seen in the ambiguous drawing below first introduced by Rubin, a Danish psychologist (Kvale, 1996).

The Research Interview Seen as InterViews

The Research Interview: a conversation between the two faces on a white background or the *InterView*: what is being made, co-constructed, betweenness, link, hyphen (the intersecting white space shaped like a vase; the self/other orientation).

Let me illustrate this phenomenon in yet another way using an InterView from my research.

Dr. Lau, a business professor from China, expressed these feelings,

I am a much more open and outspoken person than I ever was. I still hold onto my values, but I also feel everyone is allowed to make new choices and deserves a good life. The strongest, conflicting transformation that I have experienced and have difficulties with still is from my kids. When I went to the USA, I was almost 30, so I had already formed a clear set of values and standards. They were exposed to a very different set of values. Being a mother in Chinese culture, we believed that children should listen to you. We believed for kids all we need to do is provide the best we can that was the Chinese traditional way before the one child policy now. It is different from the American way. Now, my son is 17 and saying that we never communicate. We never talked, and it's shocking to me! But when I think back, it's true. It started when we came back to Hong Kong when he was 11 and in middle school. Between the teenage changes, cultural differences, and conflicts of instruction, I think he also had a tough time. Already now he is in college, but I'm still, I'm trying and actually barely starting to understand him, getting on, and talking with him, so that part is actually the biggest difficult frustration, to call it, because if I had stayed in China then I probably would not have had all these problems.

Dr. Grace Lau, China, Professor

This space (co-constructed dialogue—between-ness) is the transformed interpersonal/intercultural communication frustration Dr. Lau mentions that she and her son experienced and continue to experience in their communication with each other even as it evolves along with its transformative process.

Kumar, an English professor, puts it this way when recounting his innumerable long-term experiences concerning cultural difference:

I was interested in my culture more when I lived abroad, like an eye-opener so rich, intuitive, and so much more intellectually satisfying to treasure my philosophy not in an exclusive way, but I could say I saw myself the same and yet different. It changes you and your teaching experiences, so you learn to become more adaptable and flexible. It is another learning process; one negative is one doesn't feel at home anywhere, but now I am a world citizen.

Kumar, India, Professor

The evolving of one's self-view toward an inclusive worldview fosters the process of transformative learning. We seek to communicate our identities as part of who we are, and who we are is continually evolving due to our everyday interactions and experiences. These myriad communicative experiences transform our identity and how we label them, for example, "now I am a world citizen, I'm Canadian-Chinese or Chinese-Canadian whatever, you become more British, and I have so many perspectives, more complemented, more mixed, more overlapped." The making anew of the perceptions of oneself, consciousness, relationships, and difference leads to the common within us all.

## Using the ENRICHED Dialogue Model and Others in Practice

As Pearce (2006) explains, communication is the process by which we make our social worlds. The etymological meaning of the term "communication" is "to make common, placing the emphasis on the verb, 'to make'" (p. 1). Communication comprises three things: naming, making, and doing. If we see communication as just naming, we limit it. Communication is enhanced by making and doing together with naming. Communication calls us to use all three of its parts (naming, making, and doing) holistically in relation to ourselves: those that are verbal and nonverbal, conscious and unconscious—just like learned and acquired culture. If we leave out making and doing and/or acquired culture, we lose major parts of the process. By creating space in which to use the ENRICHED Dialogue Model to open ourselves repeatedly to more than what is first seen as an entity or object and seeing it as an ongoing process of reciprocated communicative action much like the visual images in the reversible pictures below enables and promotes the possibility for change.

This process lets us look beyond the known (self) at the unknown (other). Being open to embrace dual images, as in the pictures above (one's self-view or another's is but one perspective, one perspective among many possibilities), begins the ENRICHED Dialogue Model's learning process. Seeing both the vase and two faces; both the young woman and the old woman, along with learning how to switch back and forth to be able to hold both images simultaneously changes one's perspective [worldview]. We can learn to perceive and accommodate both, which is transformative. Also when one is not focusing totally, s/he can see each picture together as part of the same picture, the mix, overlap, and co-relatedness. The young woman is part of the old woman and vice versa. This speaks to the space between us; what we are making together, which teaches us how to expand our awareness and approach communication and the meaning-making process differently. The ENRICHED Dialogue Model supports holistic communication, what we are making together.

Ever since Mezirow introduced the concept, scholars have evolved an integrated understanding of transformative learning theory that captures well the meaning-making process of adult learners. This integrated understanding has braided together multiple ways of knowing and doing across a myriad of domains. Kim's (2005) integrative communication and cross-cultural adaptation theory supports this holistic view and states that this progression of internal change and identifiable changes results in intercultural transformation (p. 139). This process is maintained as long as some form of communication, conscious or unconscious [learned and acquired culture], continues.

Communication scholars Stewart et al. (2005) declare, "Humans live in worlds of meaning, and communication is the process of collaboratively making these meanings. Culture and communication are intertwined. Cultural features always affect communication and are affected by it. All communicating involves negotiating identities or selves; the most influential communication events are conversations" (pp. 17–55). The ENRICHED Dialogue Model uses an applied communication focus that thinks about and looks at communication differently—conversations that encourage engagement and discussion. It is a communication perspective that elicits opportunities for transformation and social change within a myriad of disciplines and organizational settings. One's being comfortable with one's self-view [who I am] aids the process of critical self-reflection—assessment and evaluation of one's premises and assumptions that result in transformative learning. As I found from my research, it is important to have a real sense of "who I am" since discerning more about one's self-view [identity] clearly occurs during communicative activities amongst difference and other cultures. Educators, consultants, trainers, and stakeholders can use the ENRICHED Dialogue Model's applied communication focus to transform perspectives, do communicative activities, and engage students and clients to envision other ways to make better social worlds. The following are examples that create space [relationships, community] for the ENRICHED Dialogue Model to lay the foundation upon which to co-construct something new.

## Activity 1: Cultural Collage

The facilitator and all participants prepare a "who I am" cultural collage presentation from goals, photos, food wrappers, crafts, maps, and other visual aids and related items of their cultural selves as an introduction to "who I am" for the rest of the class/workshop. Each person needs to be prepared to explain the "who I am" cultural collage to the rest of the class/workshop. The facilitator outlines what one might choose to share for this assignment and models the activity by sharing his/her "who I am" cultural collage with the class/workshop first before the task is done in class/workshop.

This exercise creates space for other ways of knowing, a greater sense of community, and a foundation upon which to build mutual respect, trust, safety, openness, suspension of judgment, and opportunities to form closer relationships. Participants gain insight and knowledge about each individual's identity, cultural background, experiences, and life. It is a starting point from which the social construction of conversations around what we are making together can begin, evolve, and change our self/other orientation and future actions in the process.

## Activity 2: Creating Positive Solution

Another exercise follows that allows for discussion, critical thinking, and the creation of positive solutions or "nexting" in conversations that may transform perspectives, collaborations, systems, products, and diplomacy. Nexting begins the process of altering the way one perceives communicating [conversations] to be.

## Activity 3: Attribute Lists

Working individually, each participant writes one positive statement [observation/attribute] about each person in the class/workshop including the facilitator. Secondly, these statements are all turned in to the facilitator, who lists each of them for every participant on a separate sheet of paper to be passed back to that participant at a later class/workshop. Next, after each person has had a chance to look at his/her list of observations/attributes, the participants share and discuss in small groups their own list, how it made them feel, what they think, any confirmations and/or unexpected delights, and their view on the exercise as a whole; has this happened before, if so, when, where, why, and how. A participant within the group takes notes, and the chosen spokesperson in the group shares with the class the reactions of the group. At the end of sharing, the class discusses this activity as a whole, what they learned about themselves and others, and how they felt about this exercise. Possible questions to ponder and discuss are: Why does communication affect us and others? Why is how we socially construct our worlds from a communication perspective important? What does this make you think about in reference to all interpersonal/intercultural conversations? What does this exercise exemplify about perception and different perspectives? How might we apply this exercise to other relationships, episodes, situations, events, and cultures? When and/or where is it appropriate to use the communication perspective?

These activities raise participants' awareness about how others view them since we don't see ourselves as others see us and our [self-] talk is not always positive. This focuses the class on looking at the positive side of communication [conversations, negotiations, and conflicts] to reframe, resolve, and change results. Also it leads to continually building mutual respect, relationships, and a safe, trusting community environment in which participants may question, learn, reflect, discuss, and work collaboratively, listen empathetically, be open, sensitive, conscious, and aware of all voices, alternative opinions, and differences. It is an opportunity to use and build upon the ENRICHED Dialogue Model to involve everyone "rather than confront, challenge, or solve situations identified" for them; they join with and "invite others in the revolutionary process of dissolving (rather than resolving) conflicts, reauthoring stories, and acting strategically to call into being or change existing patterns of communication" (Pearce, 2006).

The above activities along with these next exercises create a favorable environment that may

> Provide options for teaching in ways to create tensions and polarizations in the classroom that:
>
> - Allow/prompt tensions[8] to emerge in messy and potentially explosive ways,
>
> - Allow the co-deconstruction of those tensions, and
>
> - Create possibilities for reframing them and chancing how we act in the world
>
> (Pearce, 2006)

### Examples

*Sample #1—Gendering Exercise*
Tension Creation: Distribute random cards assigning gender (as simple as male and female or as inclusive as masculine gay male, feminine female, masculine female, androgynous male, androgynous female, etc.). Impose unfair rules or other strictures (e.g., require hand raising to obtain permission to speak for one gender, not others, and other such rules) for a large part of the class discussion.

Co-deconstruction: Ask participants to write personal reflections in the form of freewrites on the experience of being privileged or discriminated against because of their gender. Discuss freewrites and connect to principles and "musts" from session practice group. Discuss the differences between sex

---

[8] Examples of tensions include but are not limited to: (1) race, class, and gender, (2) political orientations and power (perceived and unperceived), (3) ideological (religious, ethnic, and cultural) differences.

(ascribed) and gender (arbitrarily achieved) based upon time, place, and who's looking/who's aware of being seen.

Reframing: Based upon their experience, reflection, and discussion, co-create a social contract for social interactions that includes ways to address divergence from the social contract.

*Sample #2—Ethical and Moral Quandaries*
Tension Construction: Offer a series of neutral statements and/or questions that require participants to make ethical judgments and assign a numerical score. Examples: Is it appropriate for Michael Moore to give a campus lecture and discuss only what he sees wrong with the war in Iraq? Is it as appropriate for a grocery store to advertise its meat as 80% lean as it is to advertise it as 20% fat? All Republicans are corrupt and all Democrats are authentic, etc. Display scores.

Co-construction: Converse about ethicality. Discuss differences in scores. Consider why the classroom/workshop community has disparate opinions.

Reframing: Continuum of scores will encourage participants to think about moving "beyond dichotomies" (Davis et al., 2006).

These activities stimulate dialogue and raise awareness around a variety of issues. This develops critical self-reflection and awareness of one's own and others' alternative perspectives. This increases awareness, knowledge of cultural similarities and differences, acknowledges alternative perspectives and practices that may lead to suspension of judgment, consideration, acceptance, and integration of related facets that might not have been thought about, considered, and/or possible previously. Using my ENRICHED Dialogue Model and other scholars' communicative models to practice communication differently and do exercises such as these is a means to examine dialogue through a new lens.

If instances of communication are socially constructed, "we can create a more life-affirming reality by attending to our communicative behavior and choosing communicative acts that are more likely to improve than worsen our life situations" (Galanes, 2006, p. 2). This is the goal of many academic courses and organizational training programs and initiatives such as interpersonal and intercultural communication, diversity courses, global studies, human development, integral studies, organizational training programs on safe space, discrimination, harassment, and programs for leadership, organizational development, and organizational change. With models to guide us, varied experiential examples for investigation, and increased awareness, we can scrutinize all sides of a story or concept so that all perceptions are given voice to resolve issues and reauthor stories, become equitable, transform perspectives, and/or result in transformative learning for social justice.

A participant in my research, April, gives a simple image of how context and meaning making might be misconstrued, misinterpreted, and/or misunderstood,

> I often overheard teachers talk a lot about students and the quality of students, many of whom were immigrants and had just come from abroad. I had one of those students in my accounting class, I couldn't believe it, there was a problem about if you went to the store and bought 10 donuts and each donut cost $1.00 how much would you have to pay? He just looked at me, and I said, you don't understand what a donut is, right? And he said, no, I don't know what a donut is. Since I had just come home from Africa, I knew [donut was a foreign concept]. But when teachers here are talking about how dumb their students are, I just think maybe they don't really have the same experiences.

April, Canadian, Instructor

If we don't make assumptions but ask questions for clarification and further explanation without judgment and/or diminishing one's ability or know-how, it may further learning and understanding of alternative perspectives and lead to transformation. There is no such thing as getting too much information and asking too many questions; especially when communicating between cultures and where learning is concerned, you have to exhaust all possibilities. Sometimes the questions we might ask are not even known at first so double checking and asking in a variety of ways is a good idea. Miscommunication happens time and again even when we are speaking the same language, let alone communicating between cultures.

It is in the InterView, between-ness, connect of conversations that the *extra*ordinary is formed and where conjoint, co-created, co-related creativity resides. Where the bridges and transformations are built, the blends occur that produce newness that we wonder and marvel at—like mixing red and yellow to make orange, yellow and blue to make green, or blue and red to make purple, to say nothing of how far this "making" of different hues can go and what might be accomplished if we act on that making. We can make and relish so many hues. The world citizen of today is a blending of many hues. Today's world [global] citizen is a person who is socially and psychologically a product of the interweaving of cultures and an innovation of our transportation and technological revolution. With the overlaps within our global village, are we not challenged to take a radically different approach to communication to make better social worlds and become global citizens?

As mentioned in the book's introductory chapter, an integrated understanding or holistic view of the transformative learning process has continually evolved to practically serve organizations and institutions for implementing change. Transformative learning is correlated from a holistic perspective to one's self/other orientation. Edward Taylor (2006) has cited, "it is learning predicated on the idea that people are seriously challenged to assess their value system and worldview and are subsequently changed by the experience" (p. 1). Embracing one's self-view (being rooted in one's own culture/knowing who I am) while simultaneously assessing and evaluating it in comparison and contrast to others' points of view provides an environment for social construction conducive to transformed learning and enhancing one's self/other orientation, worldview.

A performative, social construction approach to communication to elicit transforming the coordinated and collaborative way we construct and reconstruct communication may make better social worlds. This is a way to analyze and look at texts and contexts to open up new perspectives and co-constructed ideas to reform and transform learning. The expatriates in my research study engaged in these activities daily that led to a continual, evolving transformed self-view and worldview.

Treating communication as substantive, a process that—like white water in a swiftly flowing river—has shape and energy, effects that which enters it, and uses a radical approach to coordinate the meaning-making process is holistic. This holistic view of transformative learning in practice integrates multiple ways of knowing. These multiple ways of knowing go beyond the rational and affective to include a soul-nurturing perspective, an inclusive worldview that seeks to know all reality concerned with all domains. To understand ourselves better, the similarities and differences, in a global context and to continue to develop and form a self/other orientation [individualization], we must explore and consider the multiplicity of views within all spheres of influence.

These experiences and activities provide a communicative avenue through which to examine who we are and what are we making together. That is, what kinds of identities, episodes, relationships, and cultures are being constructed by the patterns of communication put together as people interact with each other? This resonates with Cranton's (2005) research related to the necessity of establishing authentic and transforming relationships. It also speaks to individuation, a Jungian process by which we come to recognize and develop an awareness of who we are and how we relate to others, that scholars have stated is necessary for transformative learning to take place.

In Dirkx (2006) paper on emotions and transformative learning, he refers to Boyd's (1991) discussion of a Jungian perspective of transformative learning that refers to the unconscious emotional issues evoked within individual learners as psychic dilemmas, "a semi conscious discord—an unresolved conflict that the individual is generally able to acknowledge with the prodding or encouragement of opposing choices" (pp. 179–180). The experience of this dilemma is often experienced as a draining away of psychic energy, while its resolution through conscious realization and reworking is often accompanied by deeper insights into the self and a renewed sense of energy and life. This developmental process is ongoing and is composed of all positive and negative aspects of our learning. Like culture, it is an open system, constantly changing and adapting if we are willing to change and adapt. Transformative learning is stimulated by any event or experience that calls into question our habitual expectations about ourselves and the world around us. Successful work-life experiences in nonnative cultures are even more important today due to our unfolding global village. These repeated experiences and activities challenge our self-view and worldview, thus helping the development of a self/other orientation.

Cranton and Dirkx (2005) state in their article, "while some of this writing casts these different perspectives as potentially competing, we believe they are actually uncovering the fundamental nature of adult learning and deep change." Communicative learning is learning involved in understanding the meaning of what others "communicate concerning values, ideals, feelings, morals, decisions, and what others mean by such concepts as freedom, justice, love, labor, autonomy, commitment, and democracy" (Mezirow, 1990, p. 8). Transformative learning is taking place when these domains of learning involve "reflective assessment of premises [and] of movement through cognitive meaning structures by identifying and judging presuppositions" (Mezirow, 1990, p. 5). In order to foster an environment where transformative learning can occur, learning contexts, texts, teacher, learner, consultant, and clients need to be considered, involved, and participating. A social construction approach using the different communication perspective of the ENRICHED Dialogue Model is necessary.

The communication process that looks at what we are making together is socially constructed and brings into being the reality of self and other in the context of consciousness. In order to foster transformative learning in action, we must nurture multiple points of view. Global organizations and institutions spend billions of dollars to prepare and train individuals for successful work-life experiences abroad. Needless to say, most do not choose and/or desire to go abroad but are sent by their companies, so success is unpredictable. Using the ENRICHED Dialogue Model to look at what we are making together—raise awareness and knowledge of ourselves and others in the process—gives institutions and organizations the skills to prepare and train people to communicate differently in ways that can transform and alter these success rates.

## Conclusion

The formative thinkers in the field of transformative learning have been Mezirow and Boyd, who provided the watercourse from which integral streams of thought evolved to build a holistic view of how adults use the contexts and texts of their learning experiences to construct and reconstruct personal meaning. Scholars in the fields of transformative learning and intercultural communication agree adult education is a continual, evolving process of questioning, rethinking, and reformulating one's perspectives and moving toward an inclusive worldview [self/other orientation, individualization] conjointly. Transformative learning happens in the process of calling into question one's self-view and worldview.

In taking the communication perspective toward treating such things as beliefs, personalities, attitudes, power relationships, and social and economic structures as made, not found, they are seen as constituted in patterns of communicative action. We can then look at what makes a good communication process to bring about changes in our reciprocated communicative behavior and acts. "Communication is an observable practice of a relationship" (Pearce, 2007). This might then be applied across disciplines in academia and within organizations by examining the contexts of relationships. Processes, however, require participation and reciprocity along with work and a time commitment from everyone involved for growth and change. This way of thinking requires holding multiple ways of knowing, being open to conflict and contrast that spurs us on to imagine, innovate, create, and experience possibilities in the link of between-ness. Like the ambiguous drawing of the two faces, there are unknown, unheard, untold ways to make meaning that are yet to be discovered. Realizing everything that is known is a questionable form of objectivity always subject to difference and transformation. This approach to relational knowing is a "self-transforming self" (Debold, 2004) consciousness—a consciousness process of *glocal* meaning making that is rooted in who I am as an interdependent part of human life on this planet but is also open to being a part of the evolving, pluralistic, postmodern global systems within which one's conjoint *glocal* [9] consciousness is a vital part and out of which a continually changing worldview is formed.

---

[9] Glocal represents the blending of one's cultural self-view and others' cultural perspectives, a meaning-making process that is rooted in who I am as an interdependent part of

It is one's realization that multiple self-views are possible that leads to truth and reality, and one's holding that truth and reality are just as real as having one self-view. This multiplicity or glocal consciousness of twenty-first century global citizens may definitely change social worlds for the better, "expanding the boundaries of transformative learning" (O'Sullivan, Morrell, & O'Connor, 2001) and moving "learning toward an ecological consciousness" (O'Sullivan & Taylor, 2004). Research and practice that promote behavior patterns and processes of reciprocated communicative action that transform not only self-views but worldviews work toward promoting these goals.

---

human life on this planet that one chooses from all possibilities as their self/other orientation in our pluralistic, postmodern society of the twenty-first century.

# References

Adler, P. (1998). Beyond cultural identity: Reflections on multiculturalism. In M. J. Bennett (Ed.), *Basic concepts of intercultural communication, selected readings*, pp. 225–245. Yarmouth, ME: Intercultural Press.

Boyd, R. D. (Ed.) (1991). *Personal transformations in small groups: A Jungian perspective*. London: Routledge.

Cranton, P. (2005). Developing criticality and authenticity as a transformative process. In D. Vlosak, G. Kielbaso, & J. Radford (Eds.), *Appreciating the best of what is: Envisioning what could be: The Proceedings of the Sixth International Conference on Transformative Learning*, Michigan State University & Grand Rapids Community College.

Cranton, P., & Dirkx, J. M. (2005). Integrating theoretical perspectives through online dialogue. In D. Vlosak, G. Kielbaso, & J. Radford (Eds.), *Appreciating the best of what is: Envisioning what could be: The Proceedings of the Sixth International Conference on transformative learning*, pp. 91–97. East Lansing, MI: Michigan State University and Grand Rapids Community College.

Davis, A. (2006). *Cross-cultural experiences of intercultural expatriate teachers: From cultural difference within disorienting dilemmas to shared meaning*. Doctoral dissertation. Santa Barbara, CA: Fielding Graduate University.

Davis, A., MacDougall, R., Standerfer, C., & Utley, E. (2006). *"Socially constructed tensions and polarization exercises for the classroom."* Working Group paper presented at the Summer Institute Co-sponsored by NCA & Crooked Timbers Project, Albuquerque, NM: August 1–4.

Debold, E. (2004). Epistemology, fourth order consciousness, and the subject-object relationship or how the self evolves, with Robert Kegan. *What is enlightenment?* Retrieved February 13, 2005 from http://www.wie.org/j22/kegan.asp?pf=1

Drikx, J. (2006). Engaging emotions in adult learning: A Jungian perspective on emotion and transformative learning. *New Directions in Adult and Continuing Education. 109* (Spring). San Francisco: Jossey-Bass.

Galanes, G. J. (2006). "Social constructivist approaches: How they are taught in the discipline." Paper prepared for Catching Ourselves in the Act: A Collaboration Planning Session to Enrich Our Discipline through Social Constructionist Approaches. NCA Summer Institute: Albuquerque, NM

Hall, E. T. (1998). The power of hidden differences. In M. J. Bennett (Ed.), *Basic concepts of intercultural communication, selected readings*. Yarmouth, ME: Intercultural Press.

Kim, Y. Y. (2001). Becoming intercultural: An integrative theory of communication and cross-cultural adaptation. Thousand Oaks, CA: Sage.

Kim, Y. Y. (2005). Adapting to a new culture: An integrative communication theory. In W. B. Gudykunst (Ed.), *Theorizing about intercultural communication,* pp. 375–400. Thousand Oaks, CA: Sage.

Kvale, S. (1996). *InterViews: An introduction to qualitative research interviewing.* Thousand Oaks, CA: Sage.

Mezirow, J. (1990). How critical reflection triggers transformative learning. In Mezirow, J., & Associates (Eds.), *Fostering critical reflection in adulthood: A guide to transformative and emancipatory learning,* pp. 1–20. San Francisco: Jossey-Bass.

Mezirow, J. (1991). *Transformative dimensions of adult learning.* San Francisco: Jossey-Bass.

Mezirow, J. (2000). Learning to think like an adult: Core concepts of transformation theory. In J. Mezirow & Associates (Eds.), *Learning and transformation: Critical perspectives on a theory in progress,* pp. 3–34. San Francisco: Jossey-Bass.

O'Sullivan, E., Morrell, A., & O'Connor, M. A. (Eds.). (2001). Expanding the boundaries of transformative learning: Essays on theory and praxis. New York: Palgrave.

O'Sullivan, E., & Taylor, M. (Eds.) (2004). *Learning toward an ecological consciousness: Selected transformative practices.* New York: Palgrave Macmillan.

Pearce, W. B. (2004). The coordinated management of meaning. In W. B. Gudykunst (Ed.), *Theorizing about intercultural communication,* pp. 35–54. Thousand Oaks, CA: Sage.

Pearce, W. B. (2006). *On using CMM in consulting.* Paper prepared for DISPUK, second year consultants' class,*1*(2). Fielding Graduate University & Pearce Associates, Public Dialogue Consortium.

Pearce, W. B. (2007). *Interpersonal communication: Making social worlds.* East Brunswick, NJ: University Publishing Solutions.

Stewart, J., Ziediker, K. E., & Witteborn, S. (2005). *Together communicating interpersonally: A social construction approach,* 6th edition. Los Angeles, CA: Roxbury.

Taylor, E. W. (1993). *A learning model of becoming interculturally competent: A transformative process.* Unpublished doctoral dissertation, University of Georgia Press.

Taylor, E. W. (Ed.) (2006). Teaching for change: Fostering transformative learning in the classroom. In *New Directions for Adult and Continuing Education, 109* (Spring). San Francisco: Jossey-Bass.

# Chapter 8

---

## Engaging Diversity: Disorienting Dilemmas That Transform Relationships

*Ilene C. Wasserman and Placida Gallegos*

> Mitch Samuels from Optimistic, Inc. approached our consulting firm with concerns about his organization's growing diversity, citing numerous examples of conflicts among different subgroups both functional and cultural. Concerned about issues of productivity and potential legal actions, Optimistic decided to engage our consulting firm.
>
> Initially, Mitch wanted us to do some communication training and coaching. He and his leadership team believed their problems were related to a "few bad apples," employees who were not cooperative and needed coaching or disciplinary action. Some members of the leadership team were particularly disturbed and felt betrayed, as some of the targeted employees had been people they had mentored and had provided special opportunities.

## Overview

Many organizations are facing similar challenges as Optimistic Inc. While the stories might seem related, people have different ideas about how to frame their goals and to determine how to begin. This chapter focuses on the opportunity that a diverse workforce offers for challenging our everyday assumptions and reflexive responses to our social worlds. Critical reflection and engaging with those whose social world, values, or historical narratives are significantly different from our own expand our ways of construing meaning and making sense in relationships. Given the challenges of our increasingly diverse organizations, new skills and tools for making sense of our experiences are critically important. Our chapter introduces a model we have developed and found useful for helping our consulting clients manage and take strategic advantage of the differences within their workforce and the marketplace. We have created the **REAL** Model to guide the transformative reflection process using a social construction lens with an emphasis on creating work cultures that foster new forms of relating to and engaging differences in today's complex organizations.

Based on the theory of transformative learning, we view the process of reflection as a critical component in taking the perspective of another and, in so doing, see one's own meaning-making processes in a new way. In our prior work, we expanded the theory of transformative learning from the individual cognitive perspective by emphasizing the value of critical reflection *in relationship with others* (Wasserman, 2004).

Our consulting practice with a wide range of organizations based on this research has demonstrated that focused, intentional reflecting in relationships with others shifts not only habits of mind, but habits of relating as well. Transformational learning practices thus provide organizations with new and constructive ways of addressing challenges and issues previously found to be at best inhibiting and at their worst, intractable.

## Disorienting Dilemmas and Diversity

Life in organizations is so complex that we encounter disorienting dilemmas or moments of mis-meeting in our social encounters on nearly a daily basis. Cognitive dissonance (Festinger, 1957) describes the experience people have when there is an incongruity or incompatibility between aspects of what one knows and what one encounters. These moments often come from a dissonance between our self-concept or our story of ourselves and what occurs in our encounter with others (Aronson, 1969).

Many scholars see this confusion or disorientation as a potential catalyst for transformative learning. Mezirow calls the trigger that challenges one's taken-for-granted assumptions a *disorienting dilemma* (1991). Similarly, Brookfield (1986, 1991) describes a *trigger event* that is perplexing or discomforting as the first of five stages of transformational change process. Taylor (2000) describes *disconfirmation* as an awareness of a discrepancy between the learner's expectations and his or her experience followed by disorientation and discomfort. Cranton (1997) identifies confusion and withdrawal as stages in the transformational learning process. Mezirow suggests that taking the time for reflection, particularly in the presence of a disorienting dilemma, provides the opportunity to challenge our habits of mind and action, by challenging not only *what* we know but also *how* we know what we know, opening the door to novel ways of being, thinking, and engaging (2000).

Given the increase in diversity in organizations and globalization, these sorts of encounters are only on the rise. Nearly 25 years have passed since *Workforce 2000,* the highly lauded Hudson Institute Study, was published warning major employers that the workplace of the future would look very different from the one to which we were accustomed. According to this study, 85% of new workers would consist of men and women of color, White women, and people who were not born in the United States. Current demographic studies show that people of color are expected to comprise 32% of the labor force by 2010 and 36% by 2025. Women are 47% of the labor force (Bureau of Labor Statistics, 2004) and their workforce participation is expected to outpace increases in men's participation in the next decade. Workplace diversity extends to other groups as well. People with disabilities are 12% of the workforce (U.S. Census, 2000), gay men and lesbians constitute between 4 % to 17% of the workforce, and 42% of the workforce will be over the age of 45 by the year 2015. Increased immigration contributes to increasing religious diversity in the workplace, and it is projected that Islam will be the second largest religion in the United States by the year 2010 (Digh, 1998). These trends place the invitation to notice, reflect, and reconsider taken-for-granted assumptions front and center (Fullerton, 1999; Fullerton & Toossi, 2001).

Stories of self and other are often so deeply embedded that for significant shifts to occur in the dynamics of relationships, transformative learning must occur in *relationships* and the culture of organizations, rather than merely for individuals. At the point that we are confused or thrown into uncertain situations, we have a choice—do we ignore the difference and move away from the interaction or do we engage in critical reflection? If we avoid moments of mismeeting, dissonance, or disorienting dilemmas, we miss the potential opportunity to learn more about ourselves, the other, and new ways of relating. Wasserman (2004) suggests that critical reflection on these moments with those others with whom we experience dissonance opens the possibilities of creating new forms of relating that include our differences more fully.

The following example from our consulting practice demonstrates the confusing situation people often find themselves facing. When intentions do not align with impact or outcomes, people wonder what went wrong and feel confused, ineffective, and often resentful.

> Maya is a senior manager of a medical technology organization. She conveys a lot of optimism and is committed to not only her own continued growth and development, but that of others as well. After all, she is an immigrant from

China who has been afforded many opportunities along her career path. She is eager to learn about how she can understand the obstacles others feel and to learn what she can do to help them. She has been having a particularly hard time understanding the difficulties others have encountered in adjusting to this country when it has felt so easy for her.

Teresa is a supervisor in the same organization. She has great pride in having risen through the ranks of the organization, having started as a janitor. She was born in Puerto Rico and feels that her successful movement into a professional role positions her as a role model for other Latinas in the organization. She takes every opportunity to tell her story in the hopes that it will inspire others to invest in their own development. Rather than see herself as a victim, Teresa sees herself as a survivor who can help others grow by sharing her life experiences.

Maya serves as a mentor to Teresa and offers her feedback intended to advance her career. She suggests that Teresa not tell people of her humble background as it only invites negative judgments and distracts from her positive attributes.

Teresa responds defensively to Maya's advice, wondering why she should be ashamed of her progress. Maya feels misunderstood and underappreciated for her efforts to provide constructive feedback and coaching to her colleague.

In the story of Teresa and Maya, each would need the skills, and both would need to have the context that would enable them to take the time to reflect on their interaction. The opportunity for reflection would support Teresa and Maya in moving from being identified with the conflict or *being* the conflict to *looking at the conflict*. This would be characterized by a move from the first- to the third-person perspective. Using reflective tools derived from the Coordinated Management of Meaning (CMM) theory, we can map out the different rules, norms, and influences—messages if you will—that Teresa and Maya bring to their encounter (Pearce, 2006). The "daisy" diagram on the opposite page outlines some of these.

In the encounter between Teresa and Maya, Teresa learned that Maya places a high value on accommodating to the expectations of others and promoting oneself in the most positive light possible. Maya's taken-for-granted frame of reference is grounded in her Asian cultural norms that value conformity, fitting in, being part of the group, and deference to the dominant culture. Teresa shapes her story based on her Latino cultural value of remembering where you came from and honoring your roots. This dynamic of group identity norms playing out in interpersonal dynamics is a frequent source of disorienting dilemmas at the workplace. Maya and Teresa are two members of a larger organization that is a living example of workplace diversity challenges. Their CEO and senior leadership team recognized the value that strengthening communication, leadership, and management skills contributes to the organization's success (Ferdman & Gallegos, 2001; Gallegos, 1987). Disorienting dilemmas occur within organizations at the individual, interpersonal, and systemic levels. Individuals such as Maya face dilemmas related to contradictions between the person they think they are and the person others perceive them as being. Between individuals at the interpersonal level, people struggle to understand how their own perspectives and those of others can be so different.

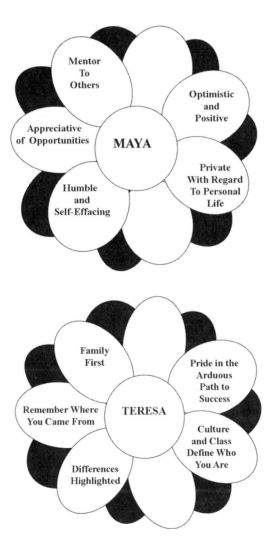

Figure 8.1: Adaptation of the Daisy Model from B. Pearce,
*Communication and the Human Condition*, 1989

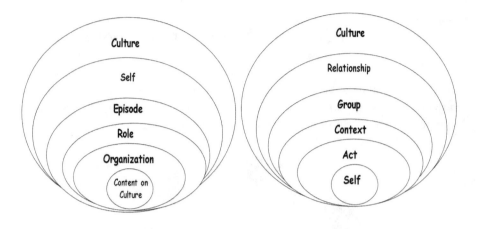

Maya's Frame of Reference          Teresa's Frame of Reference

Figure 8.2: Adaptation of Hierarchy Model from B. Pearce,
*Communication and the Human Condition*, 1989

We each make sense of the other and each other based on how we contextualize the episode we are in. Teresa places more emphasis on group identity and history, while Maya emphasizes the rules of the organization's culture as tantamount to guide her actions with her role as further refinement of what those actions might entail.

At the organizational or systemic level, leaders are charged with breathing life into cultures that allow all differences to be engaged while at the same time focusing on productivity and accomplishing their business objectives. Our clients engage us to work with them at all three of these levels to foster more inclusive cultures by strengthening policies, practices, procedures as well as forms of relating. Advancing an inclusive culture requires new skills that call for shifting habits of mind and habits of relating (Wasserman, 2004). These skills strengthen one's agility to both be in the encounter and reflect on what the multitude of dynamics between and among people are making in the encounter. This agility expands the kind of choices one makes in the next response.

We have developed a model that supports individual, interpersonal, and systemic development by fostering new ways of relating that are based on the principles of transformative learning. In the next section, we describe the model that we use with organizations to foster a more inclusive culture by expanding the dominant narratives to incorporate the multitude of experiences people bring.

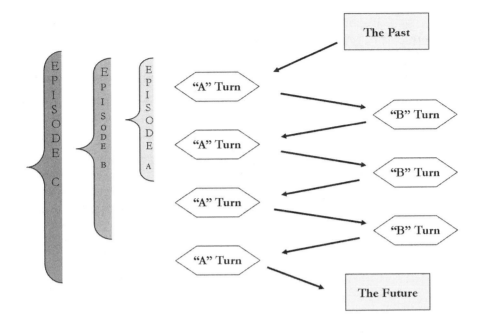

Figure 8.3: Adaptation of the Serpentine Model from B. Pearce, *Communication and the Human Condition,* 1989

## Model for REAL Dialogue and Engagement

The **REAL Model** offers a way to create traction and insure meaningful contact in relationships. REAL is an acronym that represents:

**R**: Reflecting on current relationships, assumptions, and situations

**E**: Expanding awareness across differences

**A**: Agility in behavior and ways of engaging

**L**: Learning from shared stories that transform individuals and organizations

| Reflect on Current Assumptions | Expand Awareness Across Differences | Foster Agility in Ways of Engaging | Learn from Shared Stories |
|---|---|---|---|
| We tend to believe that laws that protect equal opportunity for all people foster diversity. | We seek to expand awareness of systemic barriers to the advancement of some that are deeply rooted in structural issues and barriers to career pathing. | We give voice to stories of people who, despite being part of groups, have been historically marginalized and have risen through the ranks. We identify the enabling factors. | We seek out people who have ideas of how they would like to contribute and advance. We develop mutual mentoring relationships and broadcast success stories. |
| Good communication means being polite. Whose rules of politeness are we adhering to? (e.g., not engaging in conflict) | Good communication means connecting with each other. This may mean hearing a perspective that is unpleasant or unpopular. | Working through the complaint to discover what the shared commitment might be enhances agility and creates a more inclusive solution. | We learn to articulate shared norms and processes for engaging in constructive disagreements and expanding our rules of engagement. |
| We give people feedback when we are scheduled to or *have* to do so (e.g., annual performance reviews). | We avoid giving *some* groups of people feedback out of concern for how they will take it or fear of being accused of racism or sexism. | We enhance our agility by holding all people accountable for shared norms while encouraging freedom of expression within those boundaries. We monitor the norms for relevance and appropriateness to the job and organization. | We value learning as continuous. We give people feedback on an ongoing basis as part of supporting growth and development. We come to an agreement about how to best do so. |
| We emphasize what we have in common and are comfortable in that realm. We are careful when communicating with someone who is different from us. | We notice when we are confused or feel our intentions have been misunderstood as opportunities to explore rather than avoid. We recognize when we are using similarities to mask differences. | Staying in the dissonance with the safety net, being that we can be messy together in order to discover deeper levels of understanding. | We see confusion or misconnections as everyday and ordinary opportunities to learn and connect. |

Table 8.1: The REAL Model

## REFLECTING on Current Relationships, Assumptions, and Situations

We are taking the perspective that we are continuously constructing our social worlds in the process of communication. Communication consists of an action that makes rather than reports meaning. Thus every communication act is consequential. Since we influence and affect our social worlds in what we say or do or how we do or don't respond, we enact ethical implications and consequences with every choice we make.

Engaging with others whose life experiences have been significantly different from one's own is commonplace in today's workplace. Such experiences often create a sense of confusion or dissonance as the norms that one might take for granted may be interpreted differently by a person from a different ethnic, cultural, racial, gender, class, or geographic background. Those whose way of making sense becomes the norm of the whole organization are considered to form the "dominant culture." Typically, members of the dominant culture see their way of thinking as "normal" and may not even notice it. Those who have a different perspective based on their history and cultural norms are more likely to notice and be able to describe the norms of the dominant culture, as they have had to pay more attention to making some sense of it. Members of the dominant culture may experience a sense of dissonance when they hear the voices of those who have felt marginalized under conditions they have deemed "normal."

Wasserman (2004) studied what discursive practices foster transformative learning. She specifically studied groups that were engaged in what they deemed a dialogic process that explored social identity group differences. Moments of dissonance among group members emerged as turning points for the transformative learning process. In this study, the group reflection on these moments of dissonance expanded how people viewed both their own perspective as well as their relationships with one another. Wasserman's study extended the notion of transformative learning from the individual cognitive perspective to the context of relationships (2004).

Changing our frames of reference, particularly in relationship with others who are different from us, requires a particular set of skills and a process for engagement. Wasserman identified five skills that fostered transformative learning in group relationships:

- *Relational agility*, or the capacity to move from monological relating or *presenting* to dialogic engaging or *being with*.

- *Capacity for critical self/other reflection*, or to see one's taken-for-granted assumptions or frameworks as one of many possibilities.

- *The willingness to hold one's own perspective at risk of being changed* in relationship with those of others (Buber & Smilly, 1959; Wasserman, 2004).

- *Intentional reflection with those involved,* using storytelling and circular questions.

- Creating an empathic engagement by sharing stories.

Wasserman found that relational learning was particularly profound when people reflected collectively on encounters where there had been dissonance. Storytelling enhanced emotional connecting and empathy with another's story and objectivity in relationship with one's own story (Wasserman, 2004).

The value of taking time for reflective practice has been demonstrated in other research as well. Geller has identified six dynamics that operationalize transformative learning theory for human resource development practitioners (Geller, 2004).

- Identifying and reflecting on the key influences on one's frames of reference or worldview.

- Identifying and challenging assumptions through a critical reflection process of exploring and imagining.

- Reflecting in action, praxis, noticing what we believe taking this action will *do*, why are we *choosing* this action; what *alternatives* are there that we have yet to consider?

- Engaging in dialogue.

- Creating an understanding amongst a group through a horizontal relationship based on mutual trust and solidarity.

- Intercultural appreciation.

Given the many levels of complexity of today's workplace, the need for taking time for reflecting and confirming that we are making sense together is ever-more critical to a continuous learning process. In some more progressive organizations, attention to issues of diversity is seen to benefit the organization as a whole, as something from which to learn and increase effectiveness.

Thomas and Ely (1996) describe three paradigms of engaging diversity at the workplace: the *discrimination-and-fairness* paradigm, which focuses on addressing federal requirements; the *access-and-legitimacy* paradigm, which values diversity to better serve a wider pool of customers; and the *learning-and-effectiveness* paradigm, which recognizes the various backgrounds and experiences that create people's identities and outlooks. The third paradigm promotes learning from differences in ways that incorporate skills at the workplace and in the marketplace. Along with the presence of diversity, it is the form of discourse that engaging diversity takes that can make the difference between *managing* diversity and *leveraging* diversity.

## EXPANDING Awareness Across Differences

Having explored current relationships, assumptions, and situations, the next phase in our work with clients is focused on expanding awareness and deepening understanding of how the current situation is lived in the organization. Within every organization, there coexist multiple versions of the story of the organization, past, present, and future, as well as multiple ways of contributing and servicing the mission and contributing to its success. We support the sharing of stories and co-create the conditions for people to have deep and rich conversations across differences. These conditions include exploring what creates safety and trust, and the importance of suspending *knowing* and certainty in social encounters. Leaders play a key role in modeling and communicating permission for vulnerability.

When people come to work, they bring the stories of their lives with them. According to Bruner (1992), people organize their experiences and knowing in the form of narrative. Who I am, who you see me as, how I treat others, how I see others being treated, and who we are together are all mediated by narratives we inherit and narratives we live. Consequently, narratives create a space for the representation of diversity in organizations within which people find themselves (Phillips, 1995).

The very narratives that potentially foster connections and affiliations among people may also create walls of misunderstanding and disruptions to relating. When my narrative conflicts with yours, we find ourselves in a *relational* disorienting dilemma. My story of me and *us* is not lining up with your story of you and *us*. This moment of dissonance is a turning point. It can lead to deeper understanding if addressed, or permanent rupture if passed by.

A poignant example of this dynamic occurred in a large financial services firm where we were working with the senior leadership team. Among the six senior vice presidents, only one was an African American man, Andre. He interacted well with his White male colleagues in business settings and became an avid golfer to socialize with them outside of work as well, recognizing the important conversations that took place during these leisure activities. In one particularly candid team-building session, Andre disclosed the day-to-day challenges he faced as a Black man in a predominantly White organization, discussing his marginalization in relation to other African Americans at lower levels as well as the difficulty he encountered fitting in with his peers at the senior level. He likened his experience as having to "put on a suit of armor" every morning to face the onslaught of racism and exclusion that was to be expected daily. His colleagues on the team could not have been more shocked by his disclosure. Their story was that Andre fit in effortlessly with them and felt totally accepted. It was an extreme challenge for them to understand that his story and their story were far apart. The ability of the team to hold the contradictions and learn from them enabled the senior leaders to more fully embrace Andre as an African American man who was also their esteemed coworker.

Daily routine communication, such as reporting on each other's tasks, actions, and operations, usually takes place in the form of storytelling. Different representations of the different groups in an organization—be they cultural differences, functional differences, or other kinds of differences—are created in everyday communication. Some of these may seem harmless but in effect are offending and harassing and debilitating to the organizational atmosphere. Raising awareness of such harmful representations is often one of the central focuses in diverse organizations.

For example, a large hospital located in an ethnically diverse community is struggling to deal with the many languages spoken by employees and patients. Initial attempts to manage this linguistic diversity led to the establishment of a harsh and punitive "English Only Policy" whereby staff was not allowed to speak their native language in the workplace. Problems arose for the nursing staff when patients and medical staff addressed them in other languages and they were not allowed to respond accordingly. Eventually as a result of dialogue and reflection, they were able to arrive at a more realistic and appreciative stance on multilingual communication that was respectful of employees' cultures, patient care, and business need. They are well on their way to becoming an employer of choice for diverse nurses in their region at a time when nursing shortages are reaching critical levels in most healthcare institutions.

Given the centrality of narrative as a fundamental structure of human meaning making, the generative quality of narratives for organizational learning speaks for itself. In short, narratives foster learning since they are memorable and easily accessible experiences. In addition, narratives stimulate our empathetic orientation that provides a basis for both cognitive and emotional responses to the experiences and worldviews of other people. The participatory narrative draws on this feature of narrative. It helps people in organizations to learn to become capable of imagining not only their own position but also the position of others (Alvarez & Merchan, 1992; Rossiter, 1997).

In our consulting work, we often rely on storytelling across difference to create breakthrough experiences for coworkers. We typically find that most people carry stereotypes about others that are more or less fixed depending on the extent of real life exposure one has to other groups. These stereotypes are fostered in narratives that are influenced by one's own ethnicity, gender, class, and generational cohort. For example, the Russians were the other to be feared in the 1950s and 1960s. Since 2001, we have been bombarded with images of dark-complexioned immigrants such as Arabs or others who resemble them as the other. Absent real connections across difference, we often base our assumptions on limited data or media depictions.

## AGILITY in Behavior and Ways of Engaging

In a recent education session, a participant was overwhelmed by the vast range of differences present in the organization and exclaimed sincerely his intention to "never say anything that would offend a person of difference ever again." While his sincerity was admirable, his goal will be difficult if not impossible to achieve. None of us can expect to be perfect, to fully understand or be eloquent in all interactions. The best we can hope for is to humbly position ourselves as curious learners willing to listen and reflect on our own behavior and taken-for-granted frames of mind and habits of engaging, to explore how we make sense of our experiences with others and what other possibilities for sense-making exist.

The rapid pace of organizational life these days creates a challenge to taking the time to reflect. The rules and norms of an organization are typically set up by and designed to accommodate the needs and values of dominant groups. Such accommodations are typically unconscious and unintentional, set in place by the founders and leaders based on their own styles and preferences. The degree of intent does not mitigate the effect on subordinate groups. Ask women on male-dominated teams if they notice the modes of communicating and relating, and they will tell very different stories than those of their male colleagues. For example, women entering into previously all-male professions such as firefighting, police work, or engineering often describe the dilemmas they face in trying to fit in with their peers. If they attempt to be "one of the guys," men who see them as overly strident or masculine often rebuff them. If, however, they act according to a more feminine style of engagement, they are rejected as being too emotional or weak. Either way, it becomes clear to the outsider that the rules and norms of the organization were not made for them. They face the dilemma of either forcing themselves to fit in with the predominant methods of communicating and relating or risk being ostracized with potentially harmful and sometimes dangerous consequences.

In a diverse environment, it is easy to assume that we are all having the same experience and that the organizational culture is the same for each of us.

The data we collect in conducting organizational assessments clearly indicate that people, although working in the same building (literally or virtually), live very different narratives. People are making sense of their lives based on both individual and collective social identity group experiences. Part of the difficulty of addressing these dominant rules and making them more inclusive for all is the fact that some of the rules are visible and explicit while others are invisible and implicit. Everyday practices such as giving and receiving feedback, offering advice or mentoring, paying compliments, and building trust become fraught with the potential for misunderstanding. Increasingly these diverse worlds are encountering each other side by side—presenting opportunity for people to gain, benefit, and learn from their encounters. The first step in transforming these dilemmas into organizational learning is staying engaged with each other long enough to challenge our assumptions and form new ways and patterns of relating (Wasserman, 2004).

Telling a story about, as distinct from describing, what life is like in the organization from different perspectives helps to stimulate people's empathetic orientation, which provides a basis for connecting to the experiences and worldviews of other people. Thus, it helps people in diverse organizations to learn to become capable of imagining not only their own position but also the position of others. By combining your story and my story, we are able to co-create *our* story, which is inclusive of the dilemmas we *both* live daily. Learning in the process of shared reflection allows us to expand our frames of reference to hold the awareness of our different worlds along with the commitment to create a new, participatory narrative.

Similarly, organizational culture is created and perpetuated by communication processes. The culture defines "what kind of an organization we are" and "what kind of people the members of our organization are" through narratives and communication processes. As it relates to diversity, an inclusive culture is one in which multiple realities are acknowledged and openly explored. In establishing norms in teams and departments, leaders may need to attend to the conflicting narratives being told by various groups and support a more participatory narrative that honors the differences and yet establishes clear boundaries and expectations (Barrett & Cooperrider, 1990; Lämsä & Sintonen, 2006).

In a problem brought to us by one of our clients, a conflict revolved around the music that would be played over the loudspeakers on the plant floor. The workforce consisted of largely Hispanic and African American employees. Each group wanted only their music played and demanded that the other group's music be silenced. One solution posed was to eliminate all music. This solution would have communicated a norm of avoiding addressing diversity. Instead a committee of both Latinos and African Americans was formed and asked to create a plan for playing music that everyone could agree to. The collaborative solution told a very different story about the lived experience and culture of the organization. In the new narrative, employees are engaged as partners in addressing conflict and finding creative alternatives through elevating and including the differences.

Time is another difference that is mediated by our personal and cultural narratives. Our relationship in the present moment is mediated by our relationships (e.g., attachment, focus, etc.) with the past, our attention to the future (hope, possibilities), and the degree to which either and both bear a relationship to what is and what is possible in the present. A woman sweeps the floor of an expensive salon as she imagines owning one herself some day. A man who packs up families in a moving van believes he is doing deeply meaningful work as he eases their stress during a traumatic transition in their lives.

A president of a university, perceived as omnipotent by his staff, feels marginalized by his board of governors and hopeless about creating substantive change. It is rare to encounter leaders who recognize the organizational power they hold and how people below them in the hierarchy perceive them. They often see themselves as limited by economic factors, their board of directors, and stakeholders.

Subordinates from their perspectives see their leaders as all-powerful and able to change policies and practices with the wave of a hand. How we frame the relevant features of our environment directly impacts our individual experience as well as the way we interact with significant others. It is only when we are able to loosely hold our own perspectives and open to the differences around us that we can move toward a more constructive future that serves all of our diverse needs.

## LEARNING from Shared Stories That Transform Individuals and Organizations

There are certain episodes or events that, unfortunately, have occurred in many different organizations with which we have worked. We find that when we use these examples in a teaching venue, we see many nods that indicate, "Oh, I know that one!" One story is of an African American employee who discovers that she or he has been depicted in an e-mail by a racial epithet. In this scenario, the person who sent the e-mail claims not to have meant anything racial. Rather, the communication was an expression of frustration with the individual. In this case, the Serpentine model along with the Daisy model are two tools we might use to help us stand back and reflect on what we are making and how:

## How the Meaning of an Episode Unfolds

1. Person A sends Person B an e-mail about Person C.

2. Person D is inadvertently copied on the e-mail as she serves as administrative support for Person B.

3. Person D, a friend of Person C, outraged by the e-mail, with an untold story of distrust for her supervisor and the organization, forwards the e-mail to Person C. This act is an act that verifies her shared story of "life in the organization for *us*" with Person C.

4. Person A would describe the event as beginning with a request to Person C that was "just another example of how *she is*—demanding and rude."

- For Person A, the past was one month ago. The contextualizing of meaning was first and foremost interpersonal, contextualized by interdepartmental politics and within department pride. The intent was "to have fun with clipart."

- For person C, the incident is part of a long history of how she and her ancestors are treated unfairly. She sees this as yet another incident in a long list of injuries inflicted over the past 200 years in general and the last 5 years in particular in this organization. The meaning of the clipart on the e-mail was racist, which amplified the event to include the pattern of microinequities that she and others feel on a daily basis. This was a tipping point.

In the e-mail example described, the sender claims to be expressing judgment about an individual's behavior; the person depicted believes it is because she is African American. Usually the story is much more complex than one or the other's, but this difference can make it very challenging to resolve an issue constructively unless there is an opportunity to make sense of this together. Again, reflective tools help people to do so.

Another tool for shared sense making is Kegan and Lahey's four-column process. This process helps people recognize how the way they talk influences their relationships. The process guides the participants to identify complaints and to recognize the commitments embedded in those complaints. Naming the commitment then guides the participants to recognize what stories, rules, and desires they bring, knowingly or unknowingly, to the complaint. The process helps to shift the story from *what you are doing to me*, to *what we are creating in the back and forth process* and *what I can do in my next turn to make a different future.*

The case example introduced at the opening of this chapter is a composite of various client organizations we have worked with over the years. To protect the privacy of our clients, we have disguised identifying information but the examples we refer to are based on *real* people and situations we have encountered repeatedly throughout our consulting practice.

---

Building REAL partnerships with our clients begins from our first meeting. We see ourselves as key business partners who support our clients' learning process and leadership skills. Our appreciative stance places the focus on what they desire to foster and create, to notice where and how they have seen glimpses of that, and what and how they can do to make what they desire that is currently the exception, everyday and ordinary.

We see our role as coaches, strategists, educators, and researchers. We engage with candor and authenticity, sometimes raising difficult issues and speaking the unspeakable in service of organizational growth. In other words, we made every effort to be "real," authentic, and *real*istic in setting expectations and defining our role with the client.

We begin by gathering information about the issues by:

- listening to the story the client told,

- listening to the form of storytelling we heard from various constituents,

- identifying the untold stories, the unheard stories, the unknown stories, and unallowable stories, and

- exploring the wished for, hoped for, and desired story.

We then design and facilitate a Gathering Stories project that allows us to harvest stories from diverse perspectives: all levels, departments, ethnic and cultural groups, nationalities, sexual orientations, gender, tenure with the company, etc. Organizational members interview each other guided by questions that invite stories that articulate issues and complaints in relationship with wishes, hopes, and desires. This process accomplishes the following:

- It grounds the change efforts in the *real*-life activities of the business.

- It shifts the storytelling from complaint to possibilities.

- The process itself fosters relationships among people across differences.

The process produces a rich collection of stories that serve as the foundation for our planning sessions with formal and informal leaders. We engage the leaders in telling their own stories as well, sharing their experiences of what it has been like for them within the organization. We bring in "story partners" to meet with leaders and directly share their experiences of engaging in the process. This cross-functional diverse team is then able to use these transformative learning experiences to redefine their organizational norms and practices to more fully accommodate the changing needs of the broader organization and its diverse customers.

## How Challenges to *Taken-for-Granted Assumptions* Enhance the Workplace

We have seen many situations where issues faced by diverse individuals and groups become opportunities for organizational learning and success. Some examples from our work include:

- *Work schedules.* We are so accustomed to the expression "a 9 to 5 job." Yet as we became more attentive to the needs of families where both parents worked and as the support systems that extended families used to provide disintegrated, work-family balance became part of our vernacular. At first, flexible schedules were considered special dispensation for working mothers who needed to take care of children. Over the past 20 years, we have seen others benefit from flexible schedules and workspaces beyond the needs of mothers. The benefits clearly extend to life style, co-parenting, eldercare, as well as workload issues.

- *Who does what work* often brought to light taken-for-granted habits of mind or assumptions that did not necessarily reproduce the most efficient, safe, or smart ways of working. For example, fighter planes required men over six feet tall to fly them because they were built for those specs. When women joined the police and fire force, they compensated for differences in physical capabilities with a new way of doing things that were less physically demanding for both men and women.

- *Different abilities* shifted our attention to how the workplace could accommodate different needs and in the process improve team performance. In one instance, one of the authors was working with a leadership team of a major university. One of the members of the team was hearing impaired and read lips. She requested that, at our meetings, we pause between speakers to enable her to notice where she needed to shift her eyes. The effect of her request was to slow down the conversation, so each person listened to whoever was speaking and people did not talk over each other. In another case, women firefighters were able to teach their male counterparts alternatives to backbreaking heavy lifting.

- *Products are moving toward customization* as technology enables companies to more closely address diverse markets.

These are only a few areas in which having skills and processes for addressing differences opened the possibilities for doing work as usual in a different way, expanding our repertoire while better meeting the needs of the customer.

## Summary

Leveraging the value of diversity requires fostering a culture of inclusion to develop the skills and competencies that cannot be easily transmitted in a short training session. Advancing an inclusive culture requires new skills that call for shifting habits of mind and habits of relating. In this chapter, we stressed the importance of capturing the opportunity for disorienting dilemmas as portals for transformative learning in action. While letting things "roll off one's back" is a noble quality, too often each instance of letting it go becomes a pattern that creates divisions among people. If we wait too long, those divisions become too deep to transverse. Creating the norm in organizations, that we address moments in which we misconnect, we do not blame or criticize but rather see them as opportunities for relational learning; such a norm can be transformative for individuals, teams, and organizations as a whole.

# References

Alvarez, J. L., & C. Merchan (1992). "The role of narrative fiction in the development of imagination for action." *International Studies of Management & Organization 22*(3), 27–38.

Aronson, E. (1969). The theory of cognitive dissonance: A current perspective. In L. Berkowitz (Ed.), *Advances in Experimental Social Psychology.* New York: Academic Press.

Barrett, F. J., & D. L. Cooperrider (1990). "Generative metaphor intervention: A new approach for working with systems divided by conflict and caught in defensive perception." *The Journal of Applied Behavioral Science 26*(2), 219–239.

Boje, D. M. (1995). "Stories of the storytelling organization: A postmodern analysis of Disney as 'Tamara-Land.' " *Academy of Management Journal 38*(4), 997–1035.

Brookfield, S. (1986, 1991). *Understanding and facilitating adult learning: A comprehensive analysis of principles and effective practices.* New York: Wiley.

Bruner, J. (1992). *Acts of meaning: Four lectures on mind and culture,* Cambridge, MA: Harvard University Press.

Buber, M., & R. G. Smilly, Trans. (1959). *Between man and man.* Boston: Beacon Press.

Bureau of Labor Statistics 2004, http://www.bls.gov/data/

Cox, T. (1994). *Cultural diversity in organizations: Theory, research and practice.* San Francisco: Berrett Kohler.

Cranton, P. (1997) Transformative learning in action: Insights from practice. *New Directions for Adult and Continuing Education, 74*(Summer). San Francisco: Jossey-Bass.

Cronen, V. E., & Pearce, W. B. (Eds.) (1982). *The Coordinated Management of Meaning: A theory of communication.* New York: Harper and Row.

Digh, P. (1998). "Religion in the workplace: Make a good-faith effort to accommodate." *HR Magazine, 43*(13), 85–91.

Ferdman, B. M., & P. I. Gallegos (2001). Latinos and racial identity development in *New perspectives on racial identity development: A theoretical and practical anthology.* C. L. Wijeyesinghe & B. W. J. III. New York: New York University Press.

Festinger, L. (1957). *A theory of cognitive dissonance,* pp. 32–66. Stanford, CA: Stanford University Press.

Fullerton, F. N. J. (1999). "Labor force participation: 75 years of change, 1950–98 and 1998–2025." *Monthly Labor Review 122*(12), 3–12.

Fullerton, F. N. J., & M. Toossi (2001). "Labor force projections to 2010: Steady growth and changing composition." *Monthly Labor Review 124*(11), 21–38.

Gallegos, P. I. (1987). *Emerging leadership among Hispanic women: The role of expressive behavior and nonverbal skill.* Unpublished doctoral dissertation. Riverside, CA: University of California.

Geller, K. (2004). *A relational model of leadership development for multinational corporations in the 21st century.* Dissertation. Santa Barbara, CA: Fielding Graduate University.

Kegan, R., & L. Lahey (2001). *How the way we talk can change the way we work: Seven languages for transformation.* San Francisco: Jossey-Bass.

Lämsä, A. M., & T. Sintonen (2006). "A narrative approach for organizational learning in a diverse organization." *Journal of Workplace Learning 18*(2), 106–120.

Mezirow, J. A. (1991). *Transformative dimensions of adult learning.* San Francisco: Jossey-Bass.

Mezirow, J. A. (2000). *Learning as transformation: Critical perspectives on a theory in progress.* San Francisco: Jossey-Bass.

Olsson, S. (2002). "Gendered heroes: Male and female self-representations of executive identity." *Women in Management Review, 17*(3/4), 142–150.

Pearce, W. B. (1984). *Communication and the human condition.* Carbondale, IL: Southern Illinois University.

Pearce, W. B. (2007). *Making social worlds: A communication perspective.* San Francisco: Blackwell.

Phillips, N. (1995). "Telling organizational tales: On the role of narrative fiction in the study of organizations." *Organization Studies 16*(4), 625–649.

Ricoeur, P. (1991). Life in quest of narrative. In D. Wood (Ed.), *Narrative and interpretation.* London: Routledge.

Rossiter, M. (1997). *Possible selves and adult learning.* New York: Wiley.

Senge, P., O. Schwarmer et al. (2005). *Presence: An exploration of profound change in people, organizations, and society.* New York: Currency Doubleday.

Taylor, E. I. (2000). Analyzing research on transformative learning theory. In J. Mezirow (Ed.), *Learning as transformation.* San Francisco: Jossey-Bass.

Thomas, D., & R. Ely (1996). "Making differences matter: A new paradigm for managing diversity." *Harvard Business Review, 74*(5), 79–91.

Wasserman, I. (2004). *Discursive processes that foster dialogic moments: Transformation in the engagement of social identity group differences in dialogue.* Dissertation. Santa Barbara, CA: Fielding Graduate University.

U. S. Census 2000, http://www.census.gov/

# Chapter 9

Transformative Learning Dynamics
for Developing Relational Leaders

*Kathy D. Geller*

## Overview

The focus of twenty-first century organizations is on leaders who understand the complexity of the world in which they are operating; who demonstrate agility and resilience in responding to rapidly changing scenarios; and who see the connections between seemingly independent events, understanding how decisions in one area have longer-term impact on business accountability and social responsibility. Organizational success is dependent on having a pipeline of talented people who are able to lead effectively in this milieu. The challenge facing professionals working in leadership and management development, organization effectiveness, and human resources development is to recognize the need for new approaches that foster the development of these capabilities across the organization.

As "Chief Curriculum Architect for Personal and Managerial Effectiveness" for a British multinational this was the challenge I faced. Working from a base in Hong Kong, I was charged with developing a new core management and leadership curriculum for the top 3,000 managers and leaders who led 60,000 employees and managed operations in 60 countries. The organization focused their business on the emerging markets, and most managers and leaders who would be attending were living and working in Asia, Africa, and the Middle East. People were leading and managing teams both from their own country of origin and beyond. While an American might be working in Thailand, I was just as likely to be meeting a Zambian who was working in Botswana; an Indian in Dubai; a Kenyan in Hong Kong; a Japanese in New York; an Australian in Singapore; or a Malaysian in London.

My charter was to create a curriculum that would prepare these culturally diverse global leaders for the exigencies of the twenty-first century: "Not just a different leadership program, but a leadership program that would make a difference" (K.S. Tsang, [2001] Head, Organization Learning, personal communication). To respond in a meaningful way to the organization's needs, I drew on the latest research in adult learning—transformative learning, leadership—transformational leadership, and relationship—the feminist "ethic of care" to develop an approach to leadership development that focused on perspective transformation.

Transformative learning offers a well-researched approach that supports the development of adults. While most of the research until recently has focused on an educational setting, the theory offers organizations a conceptual framework for developing requisite leadership capabilities for the twenty-first century. Transformative learning theory incorporates a constructivist focus on individual development, rational thought, and reflection, while bringing to the fore the importance of cultural context, group learning, and discourse. It suggests a learning process for developing socially responsible, clear-thinking decision makers who use critical reflection to challenge assumptions (their own and others'), increase their understanding of complex situations, question conformity, embrace change, and align their actions toward the betterment of society. By creating an environment where learners may experience "disorienting dilemmas," challenging dialogic conversations and opportunities for conscious expression of empathy, participants in a transformative learning process gain awareness of their personal beliefs, values, and feelings. By engaging with others in this learning, they gain an appreciation of a range of beliefs, values, and feelings and recognize that perceptions form the basis for the actions we take.

Transformational leadership was introduced in a Pulitzer Prize–winning treatise by Burns (1978), who described this form of leadership as "a structure of action that engages persons, to varying degrees, throughout the levels and among the interstices of society." Burns placed the study of leadership openly in the realms of both human development and social responsibility, noting that it emphasized emotions and values and acknowledged the importance of the role of the leader in making events meaningful for followers.

Bass's (1985) work on transformational leadership became the primary scholarly source for research in this arena. Drawing on Burns's conceptual representation, Bass conducted an open-ended survey interviewing 70 senior executives to identify the characteristics of transformational leaders and establish a conceptual framework for subsequent research. As Bass noted in discussing his findings:

Many of these individuals—all were men—indicated that the transformational leader they could identify in their own careers was like a benevolent father. . . . The leader provided a model of integrity and fairness with people and set clear and high standards for performance. He encouraged followers with advice, help, support, recognition and openness. He gave followers a sense of confidence in his intellect, yet was a good listener. He gave autonomy to followers and encouraged their self development. . . . He was seen as firm and would reprimand subordinates when necessary. . . . Such a leader could be counted on to stand up for his followers. (p. 30)

Yukl's (1999) review of transformational leadership research suggested that the theory as espoused and written about reflected a predominantly male perspective reflecting those in key positions in the 1980s and 1990s. He suggested that transformational leadership neglected to incorporate important themes including "infusing work with meaning, providing voice and discretion to followers, facilitating mutual trust and cooperation, and building group identification and collective efficacy" (p. 290).

As voice, mutuality, and relationship are tied closely to feminist theory, I sought to augment leadership research by incorporating the feminist "ethic of care." Gilligan (1982) defines the ethic of care placing the self in the activity of attachment to the other, where morality arises from the experience of connection and is seen as a problem of inclusion. Through the ethic of care, dilemmas become solvable by bringing together a network of those involved and engaging in dialogue and communication, discovering in this process of inclusion and connection new ways of understanding, innovative options, and eventual solutions.

Hence, the confluence of these three streams of theory, research, and practice—transformative learning, transformational leadership, and the feminist ethic of care—became the basis I used for developing culturally diverse leaders for the exigencies of the twenty-first century.

## What Is Required of Leaders in the Twenty-First Century?

### Act Ethically

The questionable values portrayed by leaders at Enron, Parmalat, Andersen, and the more recent "subprime mortgage" debacle suggest the need for leaders to integrate and encompass two perspectives initially presented by Weber (1964)—the ethic of ultimate ends as well as the ethic of responsibility. The ethic of responsibility has been the driving ethic in business and is actualized by taking calculating and rationalist approaches to business that focus on meeting short-term outcomes and serving the interests of a few at the potential expense of the many (Burns, 1978).

In a world experiencing the devastation of natural disasters; economic upheaval; civil unrest; the long-term impact of AIDS, wars, and worldwide terrorism, organizations can no longer afford to continue taking only this short-term perspective. To create sustainable practice, leaders in global corporations need to consider their daily actions in light of the needs of all stakeholders, including the community and society at large, balancing short-term gains with a longer-term perspective—the "ethic of ultimate ends"—and leading to behavior that serves the greater good and higher purposes. It is the balance of acting from both the *ethic of responsibility* and the *ethic of ultimate ends* that leaders need to portray in the twenty-first century (Weber, 1964; Burns, 1978).

## Be Personally Courageous

In today's global enterprise, managers and leaders are required to have the courage to offer their perspective and voice challenges when strategy is being planned and actions are first being implemented. It is no longer enough for managers and leaders simply to ask, *How do we do this?* and *Are we doing it right?* Managers and leaders in organizations that will survive and thrive need to consistently inquire, *Why are we doing this?* and *Are we doing the right things?* (Argyris, 2000; Fulmer & Keys, 1998). When the answers do not seem to make sense, then courage is required to surface "the untold and untellable stories."

## Transform Organizations into Places for Innovation

Freire (1970) identified cultures of oppression as situations where people are objectively exploited or hindered from the "pursuit of self affirmation as a responsible person" (p. 55). When money alone is used as the primary form of recognition and reward, people lose an aspect of their humanity and their creative ability. In this, environment creativity and innovation are diminished. To foster cultures of engagement and innovation, leaders need to know and honor those who work on their teams, appreciating their differences, recognizing their strengths, and positioning them for success.

## Give Voice to Others

It is the leaders' role to create an environment where each member of the team accepts responsibility for the team's success. To do this, the leader needs to be able to engage the team members in dialogue, discovering through a process of inclusion and connection innovative options and effective solutions. When people give voice to their thoughts, when they are able to offer alternative views without fear of reprisal, then it becomes possible for dilemmas to be deconstructed and solved considering responsibility to a range of stakeholders.

### Lead a More Diverse Workforce

As multinational corporations flatten and morph into "globally integrated" organizations that relocate jobs and people worldwide with the goal of "moving work to the places with the talent to handle the job and the time to do it at the right cost," reporting lines reflect the transformed horizontal and transnational nature of business (Palmisano, 2006, p. 127). And further, as developed populations reach retirement age without sufficient numbers of youth to replace them, immigration in North America, Western Europe, Singapore, and Japan reflects the increasing diversity of people moving to developing countries to assume professional roles. The result of these two factors in combination creates an increasingly diverse workplace requiring leaders who recognize that team members and stakeholders are likely to be different from the self in gender, race, culture, geography, and first language. In this milieu, the leader is challenged to learn to work with and value the differences each person on the team brings.

In the 24/7 approach to work and the knowledge worker roles that have emerged in this and the prior decade, organizations are calling on leaders in the twenty-first century to (a) act ethically; (b) be personally courageous; (c) transform organizations to cultures of innovation; (d) give voice to others; and (e) lead a more diverse workforce. Leaders will need to recognize their ever-increasing importance in creating environments and cultures where actions are ethical, where views are voiced with the courage of one's conviction and people feel valued for who they are and their talents. It is in this setting that innovation will flourish and sustainability will be fostered.

## What Is Required for Leadership Development in This Milieu?

### Instrumental Knowledge by Itself Is Not Enough

Learning based on the experience of acquiring skills and knowledge without contradicting prior learning or raising questions as to the assumptions of what is being taught (instrumental learning) on its own is not effective in developing leaders. And yet, in this organization and many others, leadership development curricula rely heavily on this approach supported by the limited inclusion of communicative training—to build awareness of others and establish shared group norms. Building leadership competency by offering tool kits detailing structured processes and effective responses is a necessary but insufficient means of leadership and management development.

By defining the challenges leaders face, it became clear that a shift in the focus of training toward emancipatory approaches that focus learning on the higher purpose would foster broadened worldviews, increase complexity in understanding, and develop leaders who are effective in creating an environment for high performance.

### Building Self-awareness, Mindfulness, and Respect for Others Is Key

The leadership curriculum was being redesigned to align with new organizational branding and values. Leaders across the organization were called on to be "courageous, responsive, international, trustworthy and creative." And the board agreed that strong leadership at every level would be based on building self-awareness, mindfulness, and respect for others. This was supported by Brown and Posner (2001), who concluded that,

> Leadership development programs and approaches need to reach leaders at a personal and emotional level, triggering critical self-reflection, and providing support for meaning making including creating learning and leadership mindsets, and for experimentation. Transformational learning theory can be used to assess, strengthen, and create leadership development programs that develop transformational leaders. (p. 279)

### Transformative Learning Serves as a Foundation

The decision to include transformative learning as the basis for the new leadership curriculum required a translation of its largely conceptual principles into practical dynamics that would be able to drive learning design. To do this, an in-depth review of the literature of transformative learning was undertaken, and six dynamics were identified across the range of writings as key and important in perspective transformations (Geller, 2004)

In 1998, Taylor reviewed 46 studies that involved Mezirow's model of perspective transformation in their purpose or conceptual framework. He conducted a second review in 2003 with 20 additional studies. From his analysis, he identified transformative learning as a meaning-making process unique to adulthood. And in 2005, Taylor reported again at the third Transformative Learning Conference noting:

> Found essential to making meaning is understanding of one's frame of reference, the role of the disorienting dilemma, critical reflection, dialogue with others, and conditions that foster transformative learning to name a few. It is these assumptions about transformative learning . . . [that] reveal a picture of transformative learning theory that is . . . complex and multifaceted. (p. 287)

Building on Edward Taylor's analytical reviews and the work of others, Geller (2004) suggested that there are five dynamics of transformative learning that will form the basis for the design of leadership development: (1) building self-awareness and understanding the role of frame of reference in the process of meaning making; (2) recognizing critical thinking as a central tenet for decision making; (3) incorporating praxis, the process of reflecting on action, as a planned activity; (4) integrating empathic and reflective dialogue in a collaborative context, providing a foundation for trust; and (5) appreciating cultural diversity.

## Understanding the role of frame of reference in the process of meaning making

At the core of effective leadership is the self. "The self" experiences others and the world through frames of reference. These are sociocultural beliefs, values, and perspectives acquired (usually in childhood) through our family of origin, cultural assimilation, and stereotypic representations within our society. Left unexamined, our frames of reference limit our experiences, our approach to problem solving, and our decision making.

## Recognizing critical thinking as a central tenet for decision making

Brookfield (1987) proposed that people became critical thinkers through a four-phase process: (1) the triggering event and critical reflection may occur spontaneously in response to disorienting dilemmas; (2) appraisal offers a period of self-reflection where we seek to understand what has transpired or is transpiring, identifying what we know and assume about the experience and in the process becoming indirectly aware that our current set of values, beliefs, and assumptions results in disconnects; (3) through exploration we seek out new ways of being and acting, learning through dialogue to understand others' perspectives and the assumptions behind them; and (4) learning from the experience, we gain insights and change our frames of reference to reflect our understanding of the experience with new meaning. Through the process of critical thinking, the leader is freed to explore and imagine a range of alternatives and experience current circumstances with a new way of seeing that offers options and choices not previously recognized. Innovation is fostered, and with it comes a *"reflective skepticism* . . . . [Evidenced] when we refuse to accept that the justification for an action is simply 'That's just the way it is' or 'that's how things are done'" (Brookfield, 1987, p. 21). Critical reflection incorporating reflective skepticism leads to informed commitments after a period of questioning, analysis, and reflection and is where the proposed action is measured for congruence with reality as we know it.

## Incorporating praxis—the process of reflecting on action—as a planned activity

Praxis is the process for learning through the reconstruction of experience. Dewey (1916) described the fundamental process of education as activity to engage the learner in a continuous and alternating cycle of investigation and exploration, followed by action "grounded on this exploration, followed by reflection on this action, followed by further investigation and exploration, followed by further action, and so on" (Brookfield, 1986, p. 15). And Argyris and Schon (1992) noted, "All human beings—not only professional practitioners—need to become competent in taking action and simultaneously reflecting on this action to learn from it" (p. 4) while in process.

When action and reflection are integrated, actions are considered not in light of "how do we do this," but rather become about "what do we believe taking this action will do; why are we doing this; what don't we know about taking this action; what alternatives are there that we have yet to consider?" In this process, withholding action until time is taken to consider its implications and longer-term impact allows for a fuller understanding of what is proposed as well as consideration of other possible alternatives. By incorporating the third practice—praxis "stimulates interest among followers to view their work from new perspectives to be innovative by questioning assumptions, reframing problems, and approaching old situations in new ways" (Bass & Avolio, 1994, p. 2).

## Integrating empathy and reflective dialogue in a collaborative context

Dialogue introduces critical thinking as a group process. It provides the group a focus on inquiry and understanding rather than planning and action. By inviting in all voices and encouraging the exploration of diverse perspectives, dialogue provides a foundation for new approaches, ways of thinking, and resolution of conflicts. Mezirow (1990) acknowledged that the dialogic process requires empathy. Freire (1970) voiced this by describing that dialogue is the act of creating a special and significant understanding.

> Founding itself upon love, humility and faith, dialogue becomes a horizontal relationship of which mutual trust between the dialoguers is the logical consequence. . . . [It] leads the dialoguers into ever closer partnership . . . trust is established in the group by dialogue . . . [and] true dialogue cannot exist unless the dialoguers engage in critical thinking . . . thinking which discerns an indivisible solidarity between the world and the people and admits of no dichotomy between them . . . thinking that perceives reality as a process, as transformation (pp. 90–93)

While discussion is prevalent in most organizations, dialogue is not present in any plan-ful way. Dialogue establishes a process for exploration for encouraging voice and participation and for developing creative responses to situations, while empathy provides a foundation for mutuality, collaboration, and trust. Together these two dynamics form the basis for developing high-performing teams.

## Appreciating cultural diversity

"Because context seems to play such a significant role in shaping transformative learning, it would seem just as obvious that a participant's culture would have an impact as well" (Taylor, 2000, p. 310); but as Taylor noted in two analytical reviews of the literature, "much is still not known about the role of difference and transformative learning" (p. 3) as almost all studies to date have been conducted in North America. Bringing a fresh view to the literature, Davis (2006) provides recent insights into the transformation of perspective by non-American expatriate educators working transnationally for 5–25 years on all continents. She notes

> major findings supported learning and growth related to cultural difference and disorienting dilemmas. Perspective transformation was expressed by most of the participants and changes to their perceived identity becoming more than their own culture, which affirmed their becoming intercultural. (Davis, 2006, p. 8)

To understand how intercultural experiences may lead to perspective transformation and foster transformative learning within a planned curriculum, Hofstede (1997) noted that intercultural communication abilities start with "the recognition that I carry a particular mental software because of the way I was brought up, and that others brought up in a different environment carry a different mental software for equally good reasons" (p. 230). Hofstede suggested that intercultural appreciation can be taught but requires that people have openness to alternative perspectives, a high tolerance for uncertainty, emotional stability, and an ability to distance oneself from one's personal beliefs. Hofstede's specification of attributes for intercultural competence seemingly aligns with the learning outcomes in the transformative learning process and becomes the final dynamic from transformative learning to foster leadership development.

Figure 9.1 provides a visual representation of the dynamics of transformative learning that form the foundation for program design based on this adult learning perspective.

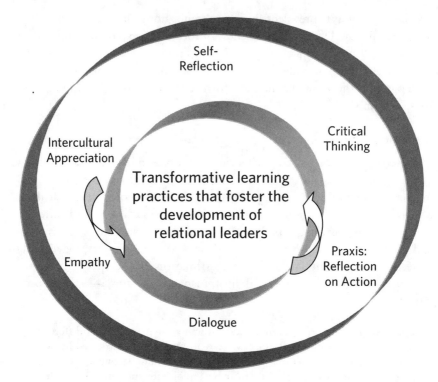

Figure 9.1: Six practices of transformative learning

The six dynamics provide a basis for content design of leadership develop-ment. These dynamics also need to be lived by those facilitating learning pro-grams.

### Developing Relational Leaders

The needs of twenty-first century leaders align to practices identified in a theo-retical model-building study by Geller (2004). Geller's model of relational lead-ership applies transformative learning to the design of leadership development curricula with a goal to consciously foster changes in assumptions, beliefs, and perspectives that may lead to measurable shifts in attitudes and behaviors. A brief description of her model follows the visual representation.

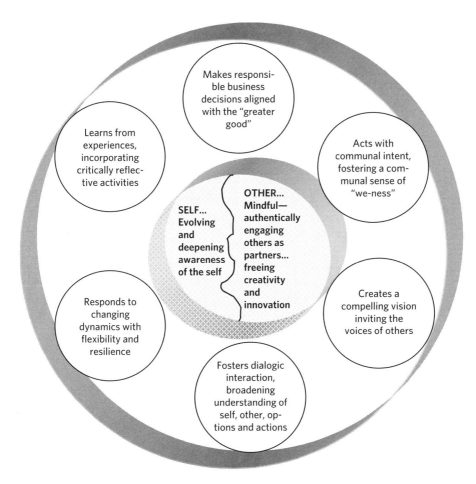

Figure 9.2: Model of relational leadership for twenty-first century leaders (Geller, 2004)

## The Self and the Other: The Keystone for Relational Leadership Development

The keystone of this model is the mutuality of the self and the other. With an evolving and deepening understanding of self, beliefs, and values, the relational leader identifies current frames of reference and deconstructs them to gain an increased awareness of how familial, cultural, and stereotypic beliefs influence the meaning made from experiences. As the leader begins to experience the myriad options and choices that exist and when the world is experienced from another's point of view or with different assumptions, he gains an appreciation of alternative perspectives.

The relational leader continually deepens self-understanding—values, beliefs, and premises—and in taking time to hear and understand the other is opened to new ways of seeing and experiencing others and the world. By amplifying self-understanding in relation to others, the relational leader becomes adept at authentically engaging with them. In these interactions, the relational leader's courage is displayed not only in the willingness to express personal views but also in valuing the voices and opinions of others. The leader presents his or her perspective as only one of the several possible ways of understanding an issue and not as the only answer. The leader focuses on bringing others into the conversation, seeking to build an understanding of the complexity of issues and to incorporate a diversity of views, generating a broader range of possible outcomes.

Through this process of empathic understanding and mutual responsiveness, both become known through the broadening of personal and contextual understanding. As Bass and Avolio (1994) find in their research, this consideration for the other emerges as a consistently important aspect, contributing to both satisfaction and business productivity. The relational leader learns that caring about the other, being mindful, and involving them fully in the work process frees creativity, innovation, and positively impacts "hard" business results.

## Identifying the Defining Practices of Relational Leaders

With the evolving self-understanding and the involving mindfulness, the relational leader builds a strong web of connection amongst team members and with stakeholders. The relational leader fosters a shared commitment to mutually defined goals centered in an ethical context. To accomplish this, the relational leader has expertise in six practices.

### The relational leader acts with communal intent fostering a collective identity

The relational leader draws on knowledge of collectivist cultures and builds a collective sense of the group. Communication in collectivist cultures is contextual and circular and focuses on creating shared understanding well suited for collaboration. Unexplored, this style of communication may be experienced as indecisive, indirect, and slow by those who speak from an individualistic context. It is primarily expressed by men from Eurocentric countries and tends to be a linear representation well suited to short-term task completion but is limited in developing inclusive relationships. Unexplored, it tends to give those from communal societies the impression that those from individualistic cultures seem both simple-minded and arrogant.

Relational leaders understand and consciously communicate from both the individualistic and collectivist styles. They learn to use circular language and stories to broaden their options and build their effectiveness as leaders. They understand that this approach is uniquely suited for collaboration and for developing an appreciation of the complexity of desired outcomes and presenting problems. Goal attainment is defined with the group and each member of the team is able to fully articulate desired outcomes. Task accomplishment is determined through collective understanding, and individual roles become flexible morphing as needed to assure successful accomplishment of goals. Group success transcends autonomous actions, responding to the need for flat, flexible, and networked structures in most global organizations.

### A co-created and compelling vision aligns work activities with a higher purpose and to the greater good

By giving voice to others and encouraging open consideration of a range of perspectives, each member of the team becomes actively involved in strategy development. This collaborative process aligns with a recent emphasis in business to drive strategy formation out of the boardroom into the depths of the business. As co-creators of the compelling vision, each person on the team assumes responsibility for its accomplishment. It serves as a standard against which group and individual performance is reviewed. Actions toward the attainment of desired outcomes are aligned to it and it becomes a shared source of pride.

### Dialogue is a process of discovery that promotes mutually responsive perspective sharing

Dialogue offers an alternative approach to leader-led discussions that by their implicit, hierarchical nature limit open interaction. The relational leader employs dialogue to gain clarity on the complexities of situations and to increase the potential options and outcomes available. In holding dialogic conversations, a collaborative work team is able to establish shared meaning and develop innovative solutions incorporating a broad range of perspectives that respond to the increasing complexity of the twenty-first century.

### The relational leader responds with flexibility and a resilient spirit to the myriad changes

Acknowledging that globalization creates a 24/7 workday and requires negotiated adjustments in both work and personal life, the relational leader considers the needs of the self, the family, and the organization, in the process, clarifying and agreeing on boundaries with key stakeholders. Acts of nature and acts of terrorism, devaluing currency, war and civil unrest, and economic crises all have serious implications for the organization and specific impact on daily business activities. For these and other reasons, the relational leader understands that well-developed plans will frequently be challenged, halted, or required to change. The leader engages others in understanding the impact of external changes, fostering flexibility and building resilience across the team.

### Learning to think in new ways is a requisite

In the face of turbulence, chaos, and change, learning to think in new ways becomes the basis for all relational leadership practices. The relational leader accepts personal responsibility for keeping his or her knowledge current and building an increasing appreciation of the complexity of his or her world. The relational leader establishes time for self-reflection, considering this an important aspect of each day.

In reflecting "in action," the relational leader seeks through partnership with the team to identify "what is working" to share positive lessons and best practices. By facilitating conversations on what's getting in the way of success and encouraging the team to make "midcourse" corrections, the relational leader fosters a dynamic approach to task accomplishment. Reflection "on action" is a process used by the relational leader that leads to sharing best practices, highlighting heroic moments, identifying changes for related work, and celebrating success.

### Acting ethically

Making decisions with a view toward short-term business results while at the same time considering the longer-term impact and the greater good of society, the relational leader has both a financial responsibility to the shareholders and a social responsibility to local communities and society. Neither can exist alone as both hold critical importance and guide decision making and actions.

### *Developing Relational Leaders Through Application of Transformative Learning Dynamics*

Through the inclusion of transformative learning dynamics in leadership development curricula, an organization establishes a common foundation for increasing levels of reflective action, intercultural appreciation, employee engagement, and ethical action, all of which may positively influence business performance. By consciously integrating transformative learning dynamics into learning interventions, leadership capabilities are enhanced, and leaders learn to question assumptions; become more accepting of diverse perspectives; broaden understanding of situations; consider the complex interrelationships that impact business decisions, and gain more self-understanding.

## The Role of the Facilitator in Transformative Learning

Embracing a transformative learning approach to leadership development may necessitate a shift in the role of learning consultants. In addition to being content experts and skills-focused trainers, learning consultants are required to have requisite expertise as adult educators with knowledge of transformative learning theory and process facilitation. Self-awareness and empathy are key attributes for these individuals. And much like organization development consultants, they need to be capable of introducing and fostering processes that encourage personal reflection, critical thinking, dialogue, and intercultural communication.

Learners in the transformative learning process primarily learn from each other. The adult learning consultant becomes a "facilitator of reasoning in a learning situation and a cultural activist fostering the social, economic, and political conditions required for fuller, freer participation in critical reflection and discourse" (Mezirow, 2000, p. 63).

Applying transformative learning to curriculum design and delivery for multinational corporations and other organizations places a focus on crafting learning that builds manager and leader capabilities to identify and leverage the unique skills of current and potential staff; to create work environments to fully engage individuals and teams and improve business results; and to respond with agility to changing business processes and approaches. As Brooks (2004) notes, suggesting directions for future research on transformative learning and human resource development, that

> The theory readily applies to research on management and leadership development, where a change in level of conscious awareness is appropriate, such as managing across national boundaries, learning to be part of a diverse workforce, adjusting to mergers and acquisitions, dealing with complexity, motivating others, making sense of work in an era of downsizing, involuntary reassignments and changes in the psychological work contract. (p. 220)

### *Examples of Transformative Design and Facilitation*

While it is not possible to detail the full curricula for learning interventions for frontline managers, middle managers, senior managers, and executives, this chapter concludes by providing some examples of how these practices have provided the basis for planned transformative learning interventions with leaders at different levels in an organization. The following experiences are meant as exemplars and are not inclusive of all possibilities. Nor are any of these experiences enough in themselves; each of these experiences must fit and flow with what comes before and what follows in the learning intervention to create a safe holding environment to experience "disorienting dilemmas," in a communal context that allows for praxis, dialogue, the expression of empathy, and the recognition of diversity.

## Creating learning partnerships that frame the experience of mindful interactions

Creating learning partnerships with individuals from different cultures is a way of showing the value for developing meaningful interactions. Through the design of an "appreciative interview" conducted by peer managers, the learning partnership provides each person with a view of herself/himself through the eyes of a colleague—"an interested but dispassionate person who sees both positive and negative in a broader context" (David Carder, designer, 2002). The partnership is a highly structured, supportive affiliation for coaching in which encouragement and challenge are given and received in confidence. In this application, the partner is a colleague in the same organization with a different reporting line, thus, there is shared knowledge of the contextual realities of the work setting with planned difference to encourage exploration of a range of perspectives.

A key aspect of this collaboration involves personalizing the experience of a 360° process and conducting it as a partnered interview process that focuses queries on the strengths of the other. Each person in the partnership is asked to identify three to five key people (boss, colleagues, associates, and customers) to be telephone interviewed by the partner who follows a given interview format.

The initial process with those in partnership is as important as the interviews themselves; it is about establishing a mutually responsive and empathic relationship. Partners, who are unknown to each other prior to the experience, are asked to hold conversations first to share insights on themselves; they are encouraged to set ground rules for how they will work together and agree on a plan of action to which each commits. Setting the context is a critical part of the pre-interview process, and the partners are encouraged to share background information on their leadership performance.

The partner personally contacts the people identified and conducts the interview. The interviewer then has the responsibility for reflecting on the information provided and synthesizing it in preparation for sharing it in a one-to-one extended conversation held within a larger face-to-face learning intervention. Over a three-hour period, the two partners meet and follow a structured approach sharing the synthesized data, offering insights, and gaining increased awareness of how each as a person and as a leader is experienced by self and others.

The conversations require mindfulness of the other, empathy and mutual responsiveness, respect and even appreciation for difference, and an ethical approach to confidentiality and naturally incorporate elements of dialogue, praxis, and reflection. As the approach used is based on "appreciative inquiry" and the "strengths" of each manager, the outcome for each member of the partnership is an extended development conversation focused on what they do well, increased awareness of his or her personal impact on stakeholders, and recognition of the strengths valued. In parallel and introduced indirectly, each person is provided with powerful, positive experiences as well as the structure, tool, and process for coaching team members in the work setting. By the conclusion of the conversations, a caring and mutually supportive collegial and coaching relationship is generally established that often extends well beyond the boundaries of the formal learning setting.

## Using art as a means to learn about the self, other, and dialogic practices

Having established a level of trust in learning partnerships and introduced aspects of dialogue, performative art becomes the basis for learning more about the self and for gaining an appreciation of difference. Through the activity of mask making, the partners build deeper self-understanding mutual responsiveness to each other, emphasize the importance of reflection, and create a sense of community.

Using plaster cast materials and working with the learning partner, each person creates a form of the other's face. This is a highly personal process and requires maintaining mindfulness of the other's thoughts (Can I allow myself to be touched? Am I claustrophobic? Will I be able to breathe?) and the self's thoughts as well (Is this mask good enough? Am I doing it right? I've never touched another man's face before). The activity requires empathic responsiveness to the other. Because it is a two-way process where each partner makes a mask on (and for) the other, mutuality and care are essential.

After the masks are made, a range of craft materials are provided. Participants are encouraged not to be plan-ful and not to do a self-portrait, rather, to use the mask as a canvas for free expression. When the decorating is done, small groups of people come together to dialogue and share their story of the mask.

A group member describes several elements of his or her own mask and suggests what those elements represent—"I put yellow paint on first because I wanted the mask to be sunny, but it didn't look right, so then I layered on other colors and as I think about it, the sunshine is there, but hidden to others who frequently experience other emotions." Others in the group are invited to say what they see in a mask—"Your mask really has a depth to it; the glitter is like your personality shining through, it's similar to the way I experience you." The process creates a context for people to explore their own personalities with others through art and appreciation. It requires the safety of trust, empathy, and care to work in this business setting and becomes a metaphor for leaders to understand what caring interaction includes.

The final aspect of this experience is a conversation between the partners. The partner holds the other's mask and queries from behind it—"What am I to you?" "What do you need from me?" and "What do you want to say to me?"—allowing time for reflection; asking each question multiple times allows for a deepening awareness of the self. It is experienced in the moment, with people gaining insight from this personal conversation with the self.

While throughout the experience, people have simply "trusted the process," at its conclusion leaders note the value of developing an evolving sense of self experienced within the context of this process. As a Hong Kong colleague noted, "This is the first time I have really connected to myself so directly, I've been so busy working and doing for the company and my family that I never took time to understand my own needs. . . . I'm going to hang this mask up at home and ask myself these questions regularly, I want to stay in touch with myself!"

## Action learning brings experience of the model from head to heart

Once a strong sense of community is established, an action learning project allows for focused application of the leadership practices. An action learning project in the context of a broader learning intervention provides a challenging arena for applying the engagement practices of relational leadership to the "real work" of planning, implementation, and evaluation. Participants "try out" new ways of building a team, they work collaboratively to establish a compelling vision, they conduct planning sessions incorporating dialogue seeking to fully engage both minds and hearts, they incorporate time into the process for reflection in action, and the experience is debriefed through structured application of appreciative inquiry, storytelling, metaphors, and visual time lines as new ways of reflecting on action.

A well-designed action learning project resembles the complexity, ambiguity, and level of challenge of the leader's real work. Real challenges emerge throughout the preparation and implementation of the action learning project that directly evoke behavior in a real context. Time-based delivery with an external client establishes a context that requires both flexibility and resilience.

Participants have the opportunity to freely participate in critical reflection and discourse and gain the experience of balancing action needs with relational needs when taking action.

In an action learning project, leaders develop deeper self-knowledge because they can "play themselves" in the experience. While a number of powerful learning experiences can be achieved through participants taking on a role, an action learning project allows them to become much more conscious about how they truly operate. And community-based action learning projects intensify experience through exposure to emotionally rich circumstances that provide the opportunity to feel real compassion and act ethically.

The following case example gives further insight into this experience. That this program was held in Botswana and attended by diverse participants from five African countries is not directly relevant to the story but does indicate the universality of the experience of perspective transformation. The group of 20 senior managers in the learning intervention in Botswana were given the task to plan a "learning and fun experience for 30 youth who had lost both parents to AIDS and were now living with extended families and receiving government support." The project was prearranged to be a one-off half-day event and the planning time was limited to one day (occurring over an evening, an afternoon, and a subsequent evening).

With the encouragement of his colleagues in the group, the Chief Financial Officer (CFO) from one country stood up and assumed the role of project manager. Earlier in the workshop, he and a colleague had suggested that this multinational corporation had lost its focus on business results and was spending way too much time on the soft stuff—centennial celebrations, satisfaction surveys, values campaigns, and global social responsibility projects.

Early in the social responsibility project process, passions in the room were high as three people fervently expressed concern that a short program for "these helpless youth" (an initial assumption about the client population) would cause more harm than good, and the three called for the group to do nothing unless it was tied to a longer-term purpose and involvement. Others in the group disagreed vehemently, suggesting that attention to teens living in extended families from caring leaders in the community would by itself serve an important purpose. The CFO, in his self-described "move to action" style, was driving the group to a quick decision on what (if anything) they would do, and he said, "Let's take a break and when you return we will vote on the action we will take." People were clearly divided and emotions had been running high for over an hour and many, uncomfortable with conflict, desired a quick resolution, so nobody disagreed with his suggested approach.

During the break, the CFO sought counsel from the facilitators. The facilitators asked several questions: "What do you think the level of engagement will be if you vote and move to action now? How might the elements of dialogue and developing compelling vision support the group's actions? [and] What other options might you have at this point?" The CFO reflected on the questions and at the end of the break went back to the group to suggest that as there were generally two different views being expressed on what should be done, perhaps more time to consider both options would be beneficial. The group dialogued on this and collectively agreed to break into two task teams for the remainder of the evening meeting, each developing a singular plan.

When the facilitators saw a small group of participants in the restaurant at 9:30 p.m. that evening, their concern was running high. Each group had a plan, but there was no agreement across the groups. The next morning was a planned learning session, and the group was introduced to a model for paradox management (another element of this particular program), and the facilitators used the paradox management matrix to identify the upsides and downsides of each plan. Data were now available to the full team and both groups had expanded understanding of the range of possible options.

The CFO took over again at midday as the group returned to its planning time period. He began the second planning session calling for formal reports from both groups. At the same time, four members of this leadership group went off to interview five youth from the group of 30 to gain a first-hand understanding of the clients and to find out what they valued. Late in the afternoon on this final planning day, this team of four came back with data from the youth and the data matched with aspects of both plans. By combining elements of both plans, the half-day activity was set in the context of a larger, continuing commitment that this organization had to a local orphanage. The youth were recognized as determined young people overcoming adversity and seeking to have fun and to learn through an interaction with successful bankers.

Debriefing was done through a series of four different approaches to praxis. The CFO remarked during the debriefing that early in the process he had to face his need for action and his concern with the conflicting perspectives voiced. After speaking with others and reflecting on the questions they asked, he noted that his suggestion to reach consensus by voting probably was not in the group's best interest. By trying out the engagement practice of dialogue and allowing the options to be fully considered, he found the commitment and engagement of the group at decision time to be incredibly high. From this experience, he expressed a newfound respect for allowing time for dialogue, recognizing the value in disagreement and his role in managing conflict and outcomes. He described how his perspective had shifted and what this meant for him and his finance work team in the work setting. As a more relational leader, he was now open to view work from new perspectives, to be innovative and creative by questioning assumptions, reframing problems, and approaching old situations in new ways.

## Conclusion

Integrating the dynamics of transformative learning into the design of leadership development curricula provides a basis for personal transformation through broadening perspective, identifying values and beliefs, and illuminating cultural differences. Through this process, organizations may see changes in attitudes and behavior in individuals, greater appreciation of difference and recognition of diversity, and increased levels of team engagement and productivity.

And those impacted take time to reflect on where they are best positioned to do work that has the greatest meaning. As the relationships established at this learning program are significant, people tend to stay in touch with one another. Several months after a workshop in Singapore, this note was sent to the participants and facilitators.

> I have moved roles since we met and am now working back in Sales as opposed to Operations. . . . some of the processes we did made me think about where I was heading and how fulfilled I was in my role. After I returned to work, I began to seek out ways to position myself more in alignment with my strengths.

Deidre, email

The challenge an organization faces in electing to incorporate a transformative learning approach is that employees will take responsibility for themselves and their career. And sometimes this may lead a valuable employee to end their relationship with the organization when they determine that their life's purpose is elsewhere.

> It's a year since we met at that glorious hotel in London. Trust everyone is doing fine and still engaging. . . . I will be leaving the organization on Friday to follow my dreams. I'm going back to Uni [university] for a year to train as a secondary school music teacher. Quite a change but one I'm looking forward to. I was thinking of this a year ago and insights from our workshop definitely helped me progress the idea. Thank you!!

Niecie, email

Transformative learning provides a process to develop leaders to become more self-aware, able to foster stronger relationships with others, and consider both the short-term and long-term impact of decisions. It is an approach to adult learning that "makes a difference" to the individual, the team, and the organization.

# References

Argyris, C. (1993). *Knowledge in action: A guide to overcoming barriers to organizational change.* San Francisco: Jossey-Bass.

Argyris, C. (2000). Can we discuss this? Why flawed advice persists. *Training, 37*(1), 48–49.

Argyris, C., & Schon, D. A. (1992). *Theory in practice: Increasing professional effectiveness.* Jossey-Bass higher and adult education series. San Francisco: Jossey-Bass.

Bass, B. M. (1985). *Leadership and performance beyond expectations.* New York: Free Press.

Bass, B. M., & Avolio, B. J. (Eds.) (1994). *Improving organizational effectiveness through transformational leadership.* Thousand Oaks, CA: Sage.

Brookfield, S. D. (1986). *Understanding and facilitating adult learning: A comprehensive analysis of principles and effective practices.* San Francisco: Jossey-Bass.

Brookfield, S. D. (1987). *Developing critical thinkers: Challenging adults to explore alternative ways of thinking and acting.* San Francisco: Jossey-Bass.

Brooks, A. K. (2004). Transformational learning theory and implications for human resource development. *Advances in Developing Human Resources, 6*(2), 211–225.

Brown, L. M., & Posner, B. Z. (2001). Exploring the relationship between learning and leadership. *Leadership and Organization Development Journal, 22*(5), 274–280.

Burns, J. M. (1978). *Leadership.* New York: Harper & Row.

Carder, D. (2002). Comment. FORUM Corporation, Boston, MA.

Davis, A. (2006). *Cross-cultural experiences of intercultural expatriate teachers: From cultural difference within disorienting dilemmas to shared meaning.* Doctoral dissertation. Santa Barbara, CA: Fielding Graduate University.

Dewey, J. (1916). *Democracy and education.* New York: Macmillan.

Freire, P. (1970). *Pedagogy of the oppressed.* New York: Herter and Herter.

Fulmer, R., & Keys, J. (1998). A conversation with Chris Argyris: The father of organizational learning. *Organizational Dynamics, 27*(2), 21–32.

Geller, K. D. (2004). A Model of Relational Leadership Development for Multinational Corporations in the 21st Century. 192pp. *UMI Proquest Digital Dissertations* (Number: AAT 3158283).

Gilligan, C. (1982). *In a different voice: Psychological theory and women's development.* Cambridge, MA: Harvard University Press.

Hofstede, G. (1997). *Cultures and organizations, software of the mind: Intercultural cooperation and its importance for survival.* New York: McGraw-Hill.

Mezirow, J. (Ed.) (1990). *Fostering critical reflection in adulthood: A guide to emancipatory learning.* San Francisco: Jossey-Bass.

Mezirow, J. (Ed.) (2000). *Learning as transformation: Critical perspectives on a theory in progress*. San Francisco: Jossey-Bass.

Palmisano, S. J. (2006). The globally integrated enterprise. *Foreign Affairs*, May/June (85) 127–129.

Taylor, E. W. (1994). Intercultural competency: A transformative learning process. *Adult Education Quarterly, 44*(3), 154–174.

Taylor, E. W. (2000). Analyzing research on transformative learning theory. In J. Mezirow (Ed.), *Learning as transformation: Critical perspectives on a theory in progress*. San Francisco: Jossey-Bass.

Taylor, E. W. (2003). *Looking back five years: A critical review of transformative learning theory*. Paper presented at the Columbia Teachers College Conference on Transformative Learning. New York: Columbia University Press.

Taylor, E. W. (2005). Making meaning of the varied and contested perspectives of transformative learning theory. In D. Vlosak, G. Kilebaso, & J. Radford (Eds.), *The Proceedings of the Sixth International Conference on Transformative Learning*. Michigan State University and Grand Rapids Community College.

Tsang, K. S. (2001). Personal communication, October 13. Standard Chartered Bank, Hong Kong.

Weber, M. (1964). *The theory of social and economic organization*. In T. Parsons (Ed.), New York: Oxford University Press.

Yukl, G. (1999). An evaluation of conceptual weaknesses in transformational and charismatic leadership theories. *Leadership Quarterly, 10*(2), 285–305.

# Section 2 Summary

## Looking through the Lens of Culture, Difference, and Diversity

*Kathy D. Geller*

Recognizing the innate power of "disorienting dilemmas" inherent in the challenge to communicate across difference, the chapters in this section offer a view to how culturally diverse experiences provide an important context for transformative learning. Focusing on individual, community, and organizational contexts, these chapters introduce the reader to: (a) a culturally responsive model for transformative learning experiences at the individual or community level with people of color; (b) how successful long-term work life experiences in nonnative cultures become the basis for transformation of individual boundaries and conscious reframing of both one's self-view and worldview; (c) recognizing the opportunity that a diverse workforce offers for challenging everyday assumptions and reflexive responses to our social world; and (d) applying the dynamics of transformative learning for developing relational leaders across Asia, Africa, and the Middle East.

The authors draw from a variety of theoretical perspectives that provide and relate to the applicability of transformative learning in culturally diverse contexts incorporating Festinger's concept of *cognitive dissonance*—recognizing the incongruity between aspects of what one knows and what one encounters and suggesting that this concept is echoed in descriptions from Mezirow's *disorienting dilemma,* Brookfield's *trigger event,* Taylor's *disconfirmation,* and Cranton's *confusion and withdrawal;* Hall's anthropological articulation of *intercultural communication*; Pearce's conception of the Coordinated Management of Meaning framing communication as a social act that permeates actions between the interactive cross-cultural experiences of everyday life and intercultural communication; Kim's notion of *integrative theory* placing personal communication at the center of the structure of cross-cultural adaptation; and Bray et al.'s view of *cultural inquiry* offering a systematic structure for individual and community learning from lived experience; Gilligan's notion of the *feminist ethic of care* reflecting on the importance of being in relation with others; and Burns's representation of *transformational leadership.*

A range of perspectives are offered across the four chapters. Green Fareed synthesizes transformative learning and collaborative inquiry, suggesting from her work with a community inquiry with "strong Black women" that "culture does matter." She offers the reader a model for "culturally relevant transformative learning." Davis suggests an integrated, holistic understanding of transformative learning related to communication, culture, consciousness, and difference in her model of ENRICHED Dialogue. In their REAL Model, Wasserman and Gallegos depict how destabilizing entrenched habits and exploring new, more creative paths of engaging leverage diversity and inclusion. Finally in her model of "relational leadership development," Geller proposes six dynamics of transformative learning as a framework for developing relational leaders across the world.

Although diverse in concepts and focus, the four chapters share four common characteristics in fostering cultural diversity by creating (1) *culturally sensitive* learning *environments* (2) that offer space for *critical reflection through inquiry and dialogue* leading to (3) a recognition of culturally diverse *frames of reference* and *broadened worldviews* that indicate that (4) *culture matters.*

*Culturally sensitive learning environments* provide a basis for understanding how different people in the same environment may be living very different lives. Wasserman and Gallegos noted that "in a diverse environment, it is easy to assume that we are all having the same experience and that the organizational culture is the same for each of us. The data we collect in conducting organizational assessments clearly indicate that people, although working in the same building (literally or virtually), live very different narratives."

Broadened worldviews supported by culturally sensitive environments establish the best conditions for transformation of perspective. As Green Fareed notes, these settings offer a "gradual depth of reflection [that] is especially important for strong Black women because it allows them time to transition from busy lives focused on the needs of others, to time focused on self-reflection."

*Critical reflection through inquiry and dialogue* suggests a learning process to challenge assumptions (one's own and others'), increase understanding of complex situations, question conformity, and embrace change. Wasserman and Gallegos suggest that dialogue is the basis for creating traction and insuring meaningful contact in relationships by reflecting on current relationships, assumptions, and situations; expanding awareness across differences; building agility in behavior and ways of engaging; and learning from shared stories that transform individuals and organizations. Geller contrasts discussion and dialogue in organizations noting that "dialogue establishes a process for exploration for encouraging voice and participation and for developing creative responses to situations. . . . Together these two dynamics form the basis for developing high-performing teams." To bring transformative learning into action, it is necessary in these environments to communicatively join together to deconstruct, reflect, reframe, and reconstruct concepts in order to understand and perceive multiple perspectives from which to co-construct shared meanings and new directions.

*Frames of reference* offer ways of making meaning and are acquired in our family of origin, through cultural assimilation and stereotypic representations within our society. Davis offers "We seek to communicate our identities as part of who we are, and who we are is continually evolving due to our everyday interactions and experiences. These myriad communicative experiences transform our identity and how we label them, for example, 'now I am a world citizen, I'm Canadian-Chinese or Chinese-Canadian whatever, you become more British, and I have so many perspectives, more complemented, more mixed, more overlapped.'" The making anew of the perceptions of oneself, consciousness, relationships, and difference lead to the common within us all. Green Fareed draws from Kegan's constructive-developmental view of frames of reference as a way of knowing that moves from a place where we are captive of our perspective to a place where we can be in relationship to it. Her process in a community of inquiry provided learning from a developmental view where the women examined how they were "'had by'—'subject to' the ethic . . . of being 'a strong Black woman'" or captive to seeing only the positives aspects of this role and moving to a place where they could be "in relationship" with the concept through the course of the cultural inquiry dialogues. Frames of reference, according to Geller, suggest that the core of effective leadership is in knowing yourself and honoring others, noting that when the leader's frames of reference are left unexamined this limits the leader's experiences, acceptance of cultural difference, as well as his or her approach to problem solving and decision making.

*Culture matters* indicates that "successful long-term living/work experiences and engagement within nonnative cultures facilitate participants knowing themselves more, 'who I am,' which leads to transformation with the deconstruction, reflection, and reframing of their self-view [identity]. . . . Their points of view changed and also how they perceived the world and acted in it." And Green Fareed notes that the overall outcomes of the strong Black woman inquiry group "clearly show that *culture does matter* when designing community-based learning experiences with people of color. . . . So what were the factors that contributed to the women openly sharing aspects of their lives as strong Black women and experiencing warmth, a sense of belonging, and a transformative learning experience? It was the cultural factors because culture *truly* does matter!"

Community inquiries with women of color, reflections on lived experiences with expatriate educators, leveraging diversity to enhance employee engagement, and developing leaders through praxis and dialogue show the applicability of the principles of transformative learning in a range of settings.

# Section 3

Animating Awareness Through the
Expressive and Performative Arts

# Chapter 10

## Storytelling and Transformational Learning

*Annabelle Nelson*

According to Mezirow, transformational learning changes problematic frames of reference to make them more inclusive. Using inclusive frames is more likely to be "more true or justified." This definition of transformational learning is similar to Trungpa's definition of wisdom. Trungpa says that wisdom is the ability to perceive reality as it is. Transformational learning then is aimed at helping humans become wise by removing the clutter in the mind that interferes with clear perception and actions (Mezirow, 2003, p. 59; Trungpa, 1991).

Mezirow's theory is in the realm of communicative learning where knowledge is about mutual agreement and is gained through critical self-reflection. Drawing on Habermas, Kegan, and Bruner, Mezirow's work examines conscious, cognitive thought stemming from rationality. Critical self-reflection is a logical process, even though moral dimensions that have an affective dimension are important to Mezirow. Other learning theorists, however, add other dimensions to the process of adult learning. Knowles, sometimes known as the father of adult education, places his theory of andragogy in a holistic model of learning stemming from Dewey, Lewin, and Combs's work. In a holistic model of learning, emotional, physical, and spiritual factors are as important as mental or cognitive factors. The components of Mezirow's and Knowles's models may differ, but the end product is the same—learning that allows a human to perceive in a wise manner for the benefit of the self and others (Mezirow, 2003; Knowles, Holton, & Swanson, 1973).

Eventually through transformative learning, a person has access at times to the cognitive state that Kegan calls interindividual. In this stage, a person perceives others as value-oriented, systems-generating people, and the person has a universal orientation of fellowship with other humans. In the interindividual stage, a human naturally can capture Mezirow's transformational learnings of tolerance, sensitivity, reciprocity, and clarity of one's own preferences. According to the holistic learning theorists such as Knowles and Rogers, this type of learning must include experiential, emotional, and spiritual components as well as shifts in the actual cognitive schema of the human mind in perceiving reality. The limited frames of reference that impede wisdom fall away in the developmental process. Transformative learning has a number of mini state shifts within the human mind where the limited frames of reference that Mezirow talks about are imploded, so the barrier to directly perceiving the reality around a person is eventually gone (Kegan, 1982; Knowles, Holton, & Swanson, 1973; Rogers, 1961).

This chapter details how storytelling can be a tool in transformational learning and developmental changes. The first sections of the chapter are to set the stage by showing the origin of storytelling in indigenous societies and in detailing the purposes of storytelling. The next sections present the role of storytelling in building emotional resiliency to promote psychological maturity, so that an individual's defensive frames are not impairing learning. Following this are sections showing how storytelling promotes spiritual development through metaphoric knowledge and expanded intelligence, allowing intuition in the unconscious to be active in conscious awareness. Identification with archetypes as a means for further spiritual development is then reviewed. Finally research that supports the use of storytelling for transformational learning in youth is presented.

## The Indigenous Roots of Storytelling[10]

In indigenous societies, all creation originates from some form of myth that directly correlates to the natural environment surrounding them. This central myth places nature at the center of existence, therefore, all subsequent stories are nature based. Most creation stories reference a point of origin or center, where all life emerged (Cajete, 1994).

The view that they were one with nature allowed indigenous people to become keen observers and quickly recognize cyclical patterns in nature. The seasons, availability of game, gathering of plants, sprouting seeds, the lunar and solar cycles, and the menstrual cycle were constant reminders of the Earth's circular patterns. These patterns led indigenous people to visualize circles and hoops in describing or artistically expressing these patterns. This overlapping

---

[10] Information in this section is used with permission from John Farmer's Master of Arts thesis, *StoryTeaching*, 2006, Prescott College, Prescott, AZ.

and connected image or concept of circles and hoops became a template for relationships, myths, and stories (Allen, 1986).

Indigenous stories most often examine the complex mythological relationships between animal deities, humans, and the environment. It is understood that all events affect the future and, therefore, have deeper meaning and give stories access to multiple realities. It is also understood that every action has ramifications, both positive and negative. Inside the indigenous view of interconnectedness is the concept of concentric effect and reciprocity. Cajete explains that there was an instinctual understanding that to take life from these groups of animals, one must give back as well (Cajete, 1994).

Stories work in a circular fashion as in the metaphor of the hoop. Every story has an introduction or education, followed by an event or conflict, then followed by some sort of resolution that is also a return to the beginning or to the place and time for the next story to start. In this circular fashion, stories mimic the earth, the moon, the seasons, the cosmos, as well as human life, the psyche, and human stories.

The shaman's role in tribal cultures came in many different forms. The commonality that shamans shared in many societies seems to be that of near-death experiences, insightful visions, or intense dreams. Shamans shared their wisdom gained by "journeying" to different spirit worlds during altered states of consciousness through stories originating in the indigenous models of education relying on storytelling to transmit cultural practices, religion of the creation, day-to-day skills, and values bonding the tribe and perpetuating its existence. All storytelling stemmed from the creation story, making all education spiritual and ultimately transformational (Black Elk & Lyon, 1991).

The hope and intent for many indigenous cultures was simply to live "the way" or "the path" in as happy and successful a way as possible. Contrary to today's concept of all education being career training, indigenous societies were aware of innate gifts in the individual and nurtured those gifts toward a place and time that would allow the individual to contribute more effectively to the group. Education was considered a community process. Using storytelling as initially developed in indigenous societies can bring community awareness and a spiritual view of connectedness to nature back to education in a holistic manner.

## Purpose of Stories

Storytelling is an oral account that sets it apart from literate traditions of learning and knowledge. Storytelling can involve a folktale, a performance by a professional storyteller, a cultural story by an elder, a story around the dinner table of what happened to a child when he or she was three, a sharing at an Alcoholics

Anonymous meeting, an original story of what happened on a trip, or an event from childhood or from an ancestor's life. All humans are natural storytellers as evidenced by the presence of storytelling in all cultures around the planet. Stories have been used by all societies since ancient times to teach cultural bonding and spiritual interconnectedness. Storytelling is also the traditional method in societies of transmitting values and establishing cultural identity and self-concept. The light that all people are born with is brightened further with the wisdom that has been passed down from person to person in stories. This wisdom includes heroes and heroines, great feats, the spirit of perseverance, the character traits of discipline and courage, the ability to laugh at failures, accepting help when it is offered, and never giving up hope. Stories portray human fears and adversities in vivid terms. They do not deny, avoid, or flinch from the tests in life. In fact, the tests are often the core of the most potent stories. By providing maps of facing adversity, stories can heal the pain from abandonment, violence, racism, alienation, blocked opportunities, and negative expectations. Stories give humans a vehicle to express the pain and then transform it with the archetypes and symbols of strength embodied by the main characters.

Some of the purposes of stories are the following:

1. Respect for all of life, including respect for self, family, community, tribe, and planet.

2. The interconnectedness of all life.

3. The coherence in one's life from the past and the hope in one's life for the future.

4. The awareness that adversity will come in life.

5. The goals of building a life in harmony and balance with nature.

6. The ability to laugh at pitfalls.

7. How to stay safe.

8. Identification with a group or tribe.

9. Character traits such as courage, perseverance, ability, and bravery.

10. Role modeling by characters of withstanding negative forces and overcoming adversity.

11. Acceptance of one's role or destiny in life.

From these purposes, it is clear that storytelling can assist people in finding psychological stability in their lives within the context of the scope of human experience. Stories tell humans where they came from and where they are going.

## Storytelling and Emotional Resiliency

Understanding the stages in a story shows how stories work to give listeners emotional resiliency. With emotional resiliency, a human has a strong sense of self, such that the pitfalls and adversity of life do not overwhelm the person. This leads to psychological growth since the person's psyche energy is not bound up in defending the ego. With a strengthened ego, limiting frames in the mind used for ego defense are released so as to allow clear perception for transformational learning.

Most stories use the hero-heroine stages documented by Joseph Campbell who studied stories from cultures from all over the world (Campbell, 1972). These are the stages:

1. **Normal:** Life is in a steady state. Then a "call to adventure" happens that changes everything.

2. **Separation:** The character must leave home or family to prove his character or to help others.

3. **Tests:** The character goes through very serious tests that prove his or her character. These initiations include battles, dismemberment, journeys into the unknown, and being abducted. The character often has "helpers" during these tests.

4. **Return:** The hero or heroine returns after the initiation to his or her society, community, and family. By surviving the tests, the hero or heroine gives hope that others can survive. The hero or heroine brings back knowledge or a symbol or accomplishes a great feat that will help the community and family.

## Graphic of Hero's Journey

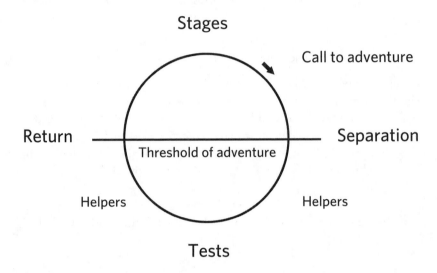

Figure 10.1: Hero's Journey

Before the **call to adventure** above, life starts out in a normal manner for the main character. Then something happens that skews everything, a different reality apart from what the main character knows as normal is beginning. The story of the Buddha is an apt example to illustrate these stages. Before becoming the Buddha, he was a pampered prince. However, there was a call to adventure in his story when he accidentally visits a place where untouchables live, showing him for the first time the suffering in the world. The Buddha *separates* from his life as he knows it and goes off on a journey to find the meaning of life. The separation stage in stories shows that life changes, sometimes in abrupt and painful ways. It also shows that people change and grow as a result of their interactions in life.

In the next stage, the main character endures many *tests*. In the example of the Buddha's story, he nearly starved from fasting too much, people beset him in the wilderness and his own faith was severely tested. The tests in stories are very difficult; in some of the old cultural stories, for example, there are brother battles, duels with dragons, or being swallowed by a whale. The severe tests in stories make it clear to the listener that adversity abounds in life. Hearing the tests in stories allows listeners greater acceptance of life's traumas and gives them a map of how to face them and hope that one will emerge, survive, and thrive through tests. In stories, people can experience the trauma of life in a safe manner, since a story is a third-person account of events instead of the listener's actual life events. Stories of abusive parents, rape, abandonment, divorce, betrayal, disloyal friends, messages of inadequacy and ignorance, poverty and societal oppression lose their sting when it is happening to a mythical character. However, listeners can use the story to extricate the demons besetting their individual lives vicariously and see how characters map the healing and integration of traumatic experiences. A third-person account removes the feelings of shame and inadequacy since people are talking about a character outside of themselves.

The best part of the stage model is the *helpers* component, since stories show that helpers naturally come to people during these tests. For example, the Buddha had the help of sages who told him to take the middle way, the path of moderation, and he had spiritual insight that gave him the direction to meditate to realize the truths of the eightfold path. In European folktales, the enduring love of a dead parent is often the main helper, as in the case of Cinderella's father, for example, who inspires her to live her values even though she is abused. Helpers can also be characteristics of the main character—for example, Cinderella's work ethic or the Buddha's perseverance. Often the tests bring out hidden characteristics.

The final stage in stories is the *return* stage, in which the main character has transformed in some way and returns to the earlier normal state. But it is a new normal, usually with an internal transformation (transformational learning), which is a gift back to the community. The transformation of the main character with new insights, new characteristics, or enhanced strength enriches the entire community. For example, the Buddha returned to society but he was changed; transformed from spiritual insight, which he could teach others, he has brought back a gift to his community in his "new" being. Cinderella took her role as a queen, supporting her king and her country, with the new realization that she did not deserve abuse and that she was no longer a victim. This transformation happens even for listeners who are not living adversities of mythic proportions that the Buddha or Cinderella lived.

All humans experience tests in life such as the death of a parent, financial crises, a divorce, or difficulties at work. The hero-heroine stages inform this adverse experience by encouraging listeners to look for helpers. These helpers can be personal character traits, a teacher or friend, strokes of luck, or spiritual guidance from a deity or a loved one who has passed. The stages also foretell that there will be a return. People will come out of the test and be different than can be imagined and take a different role in family or society.

Because of the strength of the stages of stories, listening to stories and beginning to learn to tell stories can actually impart emotional resiliency. Since stories are in the nonrational, unconscious realm and since metaphors and symbols work at an unconscious level, the meaning or morale of a story need not be explained.

Some of the resiliency factors that stories impart are the following:

1.  **A sense of inner strength:** Stories bond people with their geographic, cultural, and family realities by giving values and "ways of being" that humans in the listener's situation have used for centuries. Through this stories pass on cultural affiliation.

2.  **Future orientation and sense that the internal and external worlds are predictable:** Stories give a sense of continuity with the past and give patterns to use in the future.

3.  **Ability to laugh at one's self:** Story characters such as coyote and Brer Rabbit often make fools of themselves but also win out in the end, showing mistakes are a normal part of life.

4.  **Problem-solving skills:** Attitudes, character traits, and even actions that help people face and thrive in the face of adversity are showcased in stories.

5.  **Character traits:** Stories show that courage, love, kindness, vulnerability, weakness, strength, perseverance, fear, and anger are all part of the human condition and can serve to propel personal transformation and change. The characters in stories can also serve as role models to the listeners to inspire hope and motivation.

There is a story called Cinderlad, where a princess is placed on a glass hill to see which knight can accomplish the goal of riding up the glass hill and retrieving the golden apples on her lap to prove himself worthy of being her husband and the future king of the land. The only knight that can accomplish this is the youngest son of a poor family who is called Cinderlad since he sits in the ashes of the family hearth. But he is the only son brave enough to face the terrible pestilence that has ruined his family crops for many years. Through his acts of bravery, he receives three horses and three coats of armor, awarded by the monster (pestilence), which he uses to retrieve the three golden apples. The image of the glass hill may be simply a shiny, glittering symbol to a young child. But over time, that image, a princess on a glass hill with three gold apples in her lap, grows into a symbol of purity and the hope to strive for one's best as an adult. These seeds of symbols and metaphors grow into resiliency tools over time.

Stories help people find symbols for a strong self-identity and a cultural affiliation. Heroes' and heroines' endeavors create models of problem-solving skills and become role models for youth. Stories told by family members strengthen ties to kin and community and capitalize on the family as a resiliency factor. Stories build a sense of self, establish cultural affiliation, and construct a sense of personal power.

After the characters experience the dire fates in stories, listeners see the forces that are necessary to withstand negative forces and succeed. It is interesting to note that stories teach that the most help from others comes from the heart of our favorite characters as well as from the heart of the storyteller. Almost always in favorite stories, the most significant help is based in spiritual beliefs and spiritual entities. Love from a parent or from someone acting in the mentor role, even though that person is no longer present, is the next most significant factor in helping people succeed. Learning to love others also helps our heroes and heroines succeed. This affective dimension of stories aids transformational learning.

## Storytelling and Metaphoric Knowledge

Storytelling originated in oral traditions as noted earlier. This is a very important point. The knowledge stories convey is different than the knowledge from literate traditions, where knowledge is written in a book. In oral traditions, knowledge comes from the storyteller and is equated to wisdom where to know and to love are the same. Stories can actually hold wisdom, defined as the integration of knowledge with the heart. Storytelling communicates from the heart of the storyteller to the heart of the listener. Parker clarifies with the following quote, "When the blood, or life essence, springs from the emotional center of the heart, uniting with the mental principle, intuition arises" (Benally, 1988; Trungpa, 1991; Parker, 1993, p. 41).

Metaphors and symbols represent knowledge in a nonliteral manner that allows them to carry multiple meanings. Stories then contain emotional and spiritual content unlike literal, linear knowledge content. Thorton compares indigenous creation stories to scientific explanations of origins. He states that these are two parallel knowledge systems, from different paradigms, that do not contradict each other, but each holds its own unique knowledge (Thorton, 1987).

Tafoya explains that stories plant symbols in the listeners' unconscious mind. Over time these symbols grow to a new meaning to the listener, giving intuitive insight to the rational mind, and focus for emotional growth. Tellers need not end a story with the-moral-of-this-story-is conclusion, since the metaphors and symbols are planted in the unconscious mind (Tafoya, 1982).

Metaphors and symbols are in the realm of the nonrational unconscious mind and as such can enhance nonrational learning. Richard Restak reports that only 10% of the brain's 6 billion neurons and 100 trillion neural connections are used by the conscious mind. This means that the unconscious takes up a vast amount of the total brain mass. If the unconscious can be accessed for learning, students' potentials will be much greater and teachers' jobs will be much easier since more mind potential is available for learning. Since metaphors are processed in the nonrational unconscious parts of the brain, using metaphors in stories allows a teacher, guide, or facilitator to actually communicate "underneath" the limited frames of reference in the conscious mind, thus speeding transformational learning (Nelson, 1998b, 2003; Restak, 1984; Hart, 1983; Pribam, 1981).

## Storytelling and Expanded Intelligence

Expanded intelligence actually is the intuitive process that occurs when a human experiences a state of consciousness unbounded by time and space. This is also called a liminal state where there is a feeling of interconnectedness to other forms of creation. The experience of an energetic wholeness fills the mind-body. Sometimes expanded intelligence happens in dream states or peak experiences. In this intelligence, ambiguity is tolerated and judgment is suspended about what is and is not reality. Spiritual feelings of unity occur and insights and "ahas" may pop into the mind. During storytelling, the storyteller, by merging with the archetypal patterns contained in stories, creates a liminal space speaking from the heart as well as the head, which allows listeners to merge with this space and transcend their normal waking consciousness. Therefore, through storytelling, a person can experience an expanded intelligence allowing the possibility of spiritual insight. This in turn can fuel transformational learning by injecting new awareness in the individual's cognitive development. Using cognitive terminology, a cognitive dissonance can occur since the spiritual insight counters the individual's usual cognitive schema of the world and self-concept, propelling accommodation to a new level of consciousness (Nelson, 1993; Campbell, 1972; Houston, 2000; Kegan, 1982).

In the Hindu Vedantic model of the mind, there is a portion of the mind called the buddhi, which translates from Sanskrit as "wisdom" or "the wisdom faculty." The buddhi is outside of conscious awareness but can be contacted or opened through altered states of consciousness. Since storytelling awakens expanded intelligence, it can in turn contact the buddhi to move a person toward wisdom. However, through the storytelling experience, an individual could have glimpses of new states of cognitive development that are transformative. In essence, the individual could experience a preview of the states to come, setting the stage for accommodation of the current stage into a more expansive one, such as Kegan's interindividual stage (Rama, Ballentine, & Ajaya, 1976; Kegan, 1982).

Storytelling can be a tool to slowly move human consciousness into a state of unity and interconnectedness. Woodman and Dickinson say humans are at the brink of a paradigm shift, wherein moving into a state where the spiritual self is the locus of development and interconnectedness will mark consciousness. Storytelling could be a tool to move this paradigm shift along (Woodman & Dickson, 1996).

## Storytelling and Archetypal Identification

Storytelling can help a person identify with an archetype, since listeners are intuitively drawn to certain characters in stories. Through storytelling, a person can find an archetype with which he or she feels an intuitive connection. An archetype is an energy pattern in the collective consciousness. An archetype is a basic blueprint of the personality in the energetic domain, that liminal dimension without time and space orientation. An archetype is a generic way of being and has a recognizable collection of character traits. As such, it is a character type that is discernible across humans, such as a teacher, elder, child, a fool, a monster, an artist, and so forth. It can also be an entity from myths or religions. Some Jungians say humans live "in front of an archetype," which is to say we have an archetype that is propelling and motivating us. In other words, humans are trying to become a given energy pattern to help propel development. By listening to stories, a person may "find" an archetype or a main character that he or she identifies with. A person can develop a strong fascination with an archetype that is almost an itch that needs to be scratched, that is, it doesn't go away. Finding an archetype in this manner can help a person use the archetype to speed psychological and spiritual development (Edinger, 1992).

By identifying with an archetype, the conscious mind can focus on the energy pattern of the archetype to open the unconscious mind. This clears an opening between the conscious and the unconscious mind to receive insight.

The following is an example of using an archetype for personal growth. I once made up a story with Sophia as the main character. People liked the story, so I started researching who Sophia was. Maria-Louise von Franz, a Jungian therapist, called Sophia the self-knowing primordial cause or the energy from "the archetypal world after whose likeness this sensible world was made." She also says that Sophia is the fundamental archetype or the blueprint of the material, sensible world. Sophia is derived from the Greek word *sophizesthai* [one who is wise]. Her name is also derived from the Greek word *sophos* [to be of the same kind], possibly indicating that all of life is of the same kind as Sophia. Working with this archetype, Sophia, helped me experience certain states of wisdom that could in turn possibly help transform the topography of the mind to a more holistic state of awareness toward a different cognitive level, such as Kegan's interindividual level (Von Franz, 1985, p. 155f, 1996; Cady, Ronanad, & Taussig, 1986).

A person can choose to work consciously with an archetype for both psychological and spiritual development. Ways of working with archetypes could be finding stories, imaging the archetype in the mind, finding emotions that the archetype evokes in the body to sense and release, drawing the archetype, or moving the archetype. Possibly the simplest way to work with an archetype is finding a picture and a story about the archetype. Archetypal identification can aid transformational learning by clearing a channel between the conscious and unconscious mind so that limited frames in the conscious mind, which impede intuitive insight, are removed.

## Storytelling, Health Education, and Transformational Learning

Researchers have used storytelling to promote transformational learning in youth to choose mental strength amidst peer pressure for destructive behaviors. By telling stories of their experiences, youth can gain strength from the cultural myths that create structure and patterns for their lives. Storytelling taps unconscious emotional material and memories that contain salient content about an event. As Nelson puts it, "through metaphoric knowledge stories are maps about life. These maps show what qualities create what events" (1998, p. 1). Research by Lieblich, Tuval-Mashiach, and Zilber suggests that stories can lead to expression of three distinct stages: "before and after a major life change, with a much shorter mediating stage that could be called the experience of transition" (p. 107). This perspective of narrative research echoes the stages of storytelling detailed above, which show the transformation of the main character after tests and helpers prompt the character's return (Houston, 2000; Krueger, 2004; Campbell, 1972; Nelson, 1998a; Lieblich, Tuval-Mashiach, & Zilber, 1998).

Nelson and Arthur found that the Storytelling for Empowerment model based on storytelling and interactive activities was effective in decreasing Latino 12–15-year-olds alcohol and marijuana use from once a month to never. African psychologists have documented storytelling to increase safe sex skills. They worked with 13–14-year-olds in Nairobi, Kenya, also used a storytelling and role play approach about sexual behavior, and documented increases in sexual self-efficacy scale (i.e., refusing advances, using safe sex practices). Several narrative-oriented HIV prevention programs report that story or narrative allows teens to clarify their personal values as a means for making decisions about self-destructive behaviors. This research shows that storytelling is a practical tool for helping youth learn values, gain spiritual strength, and develop skills to protect their health and grow into adults (Nelson & Arthur, 2003; Nelson, 1998b; Balmer, Gikundi, & Rachier, 2002; Balmer et al., 1997; Morrill et al., 2000; Nelson, 2005).

## Summary

Storytelling as an ancient human technology has great utility to the transformational learning field. Stories give a movement and direction to people's lives by nesting experiences in the grand scope of human history, evoking power and protection for both emotional and spiritual growth. By understanding the purposes and structures of stories, teachers and facilitators can use stories to help listeners gain emotional resiliency and teach people to find helpers in their lives to transcend adversity. The storytelling experience creates expanded intelligence and liminal spaces to help listeners and tellers experience states of consciousness that are unitive and that can propel transformation of cognitive schemas toward an interconnection with reality. Finally by identifying with archetypes in stories and consciously evoking those archetypes in their lives, listeners can access more connection with their wisdom faculties. Although not giving applied practices for using storytelling, this article may prompt teachers and facilitators to use storytelling more in a variety of learning settings (Mellon, 1992).

# References

Allen, G. P. (1986). *The sacred hoop: Recovering the feminine in American Indian traditions.* Boston: Beacon Press.

Balmer, D. H., Gikundi, E., & Rachier, C. O. (2002). The evaluation of an adolescent programme based upon a narrative story, role plays and group discussion in Kenya. *Journal of Psychology in Africa; South of the Sahara, the Caribbean & Afro-Latin America, 12*(2), 101–118.

Balmer, D. H., Gikundi, E., Billingsley, M., Kihuho, F., Kimani, M., Wang'ondu, J., & Njoroge, H. (1997). Adolescent knowledge, values, and coping strategies: Implications for health in Sub-Saharan Africa. *Journal of Adolescent Health, 21*(1), 33–38.

Benally, H. (1988). Diné philosophy of learning. *Journal of Navajo Education 6,* 7–13.

Black Elk, W., & Lyon, W. S. (1991). *Black Elk: The sacred ways of a Lakota.* San Francisco: HarperSanFrancisco.

Cady, S., Ronanad, M., & Taussig, H. (1986). *Sophia: The future of feminist spirituality.* San Francisco: Harper and Row.

Cajete, G. A. (1994). *Look to the mountain: An ecology of indigenous education.* Skyland, NC: Kivaki Press

Campbell, J. (1972). *The hero with a thousand faces.* Princeton, New Jersey: Princeton University Press.

Edinger, E. (1992). *Ego and archetype.* Boston: Shambhala.

Hart, L. A. (1983). *Human brain and human learning.* New York: Longman.

Houston, J. (2000). Myths of the future. *The Humanistic Psychologist, 28*(1–3), 43–58.

Kegan, R. (1982). *The evolving self: Problem and process in human development.* Cambridge, MA: Harvard University Press.

Knowles, M. S., Holton, E. F., & Swanson, R. A. (1973).*The adult learner: The definitive classic in adult education and human resource development.* Houston, Texas: Gulf Publishing Company.

Krueger, M. (2004). Using self and story to understand youthwork. *Child and Youth Services, 26*(1), 25–48.

Lieblich, A., Tuval-Mashiach, R., & Zilber, T. (1998). *Narrative research: Reading, analysis and interpretation.* Thousand Oaks, CA: Sage.

Mellon, N. (1992). *Storytelling and the art of imagination.* Rockport, MA: Element.

Mezirow, J. (2003). Tranformative learning as discourse. *Journal of Transformative Education, 1*(1), 58–63.

Morrill, C., Yalda, C., Adelman, M., Musheno, M., & Bejarano, C. (2000). Telling tales in school: Youth culture and conflict narratives. *Law & Society Review, 34*(3), 521–565.

Nelson, A. (1993). *Living the wheel: Working with emotions, terror and bliss with imagery.* York Beach, ME: Samuel Weiser.

Nelson, A. (1998a). *Storytelling for prevention.* Evergreen, CO: The WHEEL Council.

Nelson, A. (1998b). *The learning wheel: Holistic and multicultural lesson planning.* Tucson, Arizona: Zephyr Press and the WHEEL Council.

Nelson, A. (2003). Circle relationships of intelligence. *International Journal of Learning,* 10, 693–712.

Nelson, A. (2005). Multicultural model of HIV prevention for youth. *International Journal of Learning,* 11, 1555–1564.

Nelson, A., & Arthur, B. (2003). Decreasing at-risk youth's alcohol and marijuana use. *Journal of Primary Prevention,* 24(2), 169–180.

Parker, K. L. (1993). *Wise women of the dreamtime: Aboriginal tales of the ancestral power.* Rochester, VT: Park St. Press.

Pribram, K. H. (1981). *Language of the brain: Experimental paradoxes and principles of neuropsychology.* New York: Brandon House.

Rama, S., Ballentine, R., & Ajaya, S. (1976). *Yoga and psychotherapy: The evolution of consciousness.* Honesdale, PA: Himalayan International Institute.

Restak, R. M. (1984). *The brain.* New York: Bantam Books.

Rogers, C. (1961). *On becoming a person: A therapist's view of psychotherapy.* New York: Merrill.

Tafoya, T. (1982). Coyote's eyes: Native cognition styles. *Journal of American Indian Education, 21*(2), 21–33.

Thorton, R. (1987). *American Indian holocaust and survival: A population history since 1492.* Norman, OK: University of Oklahoma Press.

Trungpa, C. (1991). *The heart of the Buddha.* Boston and London: Shambhala.

Von Franz, M.-L. (1985). *Aurora consurgens.* Princeton, New Jersey: Princeton University Press.

Von Franz, M.-L. (1996). *The interpretation of fairy tales.* Boston: Shambhala.

Woodman, M., & Dickson, E. (1996). *Dancing in the flames: The dark goddess in the transformation of consciousness.* Boston: Shambhala.

# Chapter 11

## Bodymindfulness for Skillful Use of Self

*Adair Linn Nagata*

## Intercultural Communication as Transformative Learning

Living in Japan since 1970, I discovered a talent of which I had been unaware. I seem to have had an innate ability to disturb the famous Japanese sense of *wa*, the harmony existing in a group situation before I appear on the scene. My presence, especially my arrival in the group, would often result in a change in the atmosphere and what was happening, a shift in the conversation, and—in a worse case—a dispersal of the people assembled there. After a while, I began to realize that these things did not just happen; something I was doing was causing them.

When I had the opportunity to do doctoral study in human development, I found myself researching a question related to these communicative and relational difficulties that I was seeking to understand. Gradually, I realized that the problem was a combination of my way of doing and, more fundamentally, my way of being, but I wondered how I could change such basic things about myself. It seemed that if my international marriage to a Japanese man were to survive, if I were to be able to raise my children honoring both their Japanese as well as their U.S. heritage, and if I were to be able to work well with mainly Japanese people, I needed to learn new ways of communicating.

As I tried to understand what I was experiencing and what might be necessary to shift it to a more satisfying and effective way of communicating with Japanese people, the research question that eventually emerged took the following form: What is the embodied experience of being in empathic resonance with another person in an intercultural interaction? My mindful inquiry (MI) into this mysterious phenomenon resulted in a change in my way of being that was also expressed in new ways of doing things. Since beginning to teach at the university level in 2002, I have aspired to promote this holistic kind of transformative learning experience for my students, who are mainly Japanese but also include men and women with diverse cultural backgrounds and nationalities (Bentz & Shapiro, 1998).

In calling for a reconceptualization of the transformative learning process, Taylor (1997) emphasizes the significance of whole person learning by quoting the following: "awareness and use of all the functions we have available for knowing, including our cognitive, affective, somatic, intuitive, and spiritual dimensions." Like Taylor, Boyd and Myers, Cranton, and Dirkx have found that affective and other extrarational aspects of human experience had been neglected in transformative learning theory as articulated by Mezirow. They have integrated depth psychology, particularly that of Jung, into their approaches to transformative learning (Taylor, 1997, p. 49; 2000; Boyd & Myers, 1988; Cranton, 2000; Dirkx, 2000; Mezirow, 1991).

These critics have been described as proponents of holistic transformation theories by Lennox, who noted that holistic transformation theorists have not reached a consensus on a definition of transformation, but "they tend to conceive of it as involving more of a whole person shift or a shift in consciousness that extends beyond mere ideation" (p. 32). She quoted an articulation by O'Sullivan, Morrell, and O'Connor as a tentative definition of what they term integral transformative learning:

> Transformative learning involves experiencing a deep, structural shift in the basic premises of thought, feeling, and actions. . . . Such a shift involves our understanding of ourselves and our self-locations; our relationships with other humans and with the natural world; our understanding of relations of power in interlocking structures of class, race, and gender; our body-awarenesses; our visions of alternative approaches to living; and our sense of possibilities for social justice and peace and personal joy. (Lennox, 2005; O'Sullivan, Morrell, & O'Connor, 2002, p. 11)

This definition resonates with my pedagogical intention to promote the development of interculturalists who are aware of using their whole selves as instruments of communication. Who is an interculturalist? My simple definition is a person who is committed to trying to communicate across significant differences of various types. Interculturalists typically have a personal stake in communicating in a more satisfying way with some of the people who are important in their lives who do not speak the same language natively or do not share the same culture or have other significant differences. They are often motivated to continue developing their relational skills as they encounter and process differences and difficulties that they neither yet understand nor know how to manage skillfully. They are usually willing to make an ongoing effort to communicate to avoid or resolve misunderstandings. They are typically open to new experiences (Nagata, 2004, 2005, 2006a, 2006b).

Being an interculturalist has become my practice, a commitment to a way of pursuing a personally important conceptual ideal that leads toward a higher level of functioning. I think of my daily communication as walking meditation, that is, being aware of what I am doing during all my interactions every day. This is my ideal; although admittedly not always possible, it is very practical because it reminds me to try to figure out my own assumptions and shift my approach when something is not going well.

When we communicate, all aspects of our selves—body, emotion/feeling, mind, and spirit—are involved, whether we are conscious of them and use them skillfully or not. If we are unconscious of our feelings, our emotions may leak out in our paralanguage, facial expressions, or movements and send messages that contradict the verbal content of what we are saying. If we are unaware of our bodies, our body language may reveal our thoughts and emotions in ways that are not congruent with the text of our speech. Because nonverbal communication is typically beyond our awareness, when we are sending mixed messages—conflicting nonverbal and verbal signals—people have a tendency to believe the nonverbal ones. If we are not sensitive to intuitive inspirations, we miss a source of mysterious energy that can promote our creativity and connections to larger frames of meaning that may sustain us beyond the usual limits of our physical and emotional endurance.

O'Sullivan, Morrell, and O'Connor's definition of transformative learning is particularly relevant to my emphasis on bodymindfulness, the process of attending to all aspects of the bodymind in order to grasp the holistic personal meaning of an internal event and to use the resultant understanding to communicate skillfully. This understanding of transformative learning includes both rational and extrarational aspects. In my own case and those of my students—most of whom are Japanese working adults who are pursuing a graduate program in intercultural communication studies—the learning process I promote is intended to facilitate integration of the whole person (O'Sullivan, Morrell, & O'Connor, 2002; Nagata, 2004, 2006a).

O'Sullivan recommends that each author using the term *transformative learning* specify her definition, and I will articulate my approach in this chapter by connecting my developmental intention with concrete pedagogical practices. Following Lennox's usage of *integrative,* I am calling this approach *integrative* transformative education rather than *integral* because the latter term often refers to a specific tradition (O'Sullivan, Morrell, & O'Connor, 2002; Lennox, 2005; Ryan, 2005; Esbjörn-Hargens, 2006).

## Mindful Inquiry for Integrative Transformative Learning

### Research Methodology and Conceptual Framework

Mindful inquiry is an essentially, but not exclusively, qualitative research approach formulated by Bentz and Shapiro. It incorporates four knowledge traditions described as follows:

- Phenomenology: description and analysis of consciousness and experience

- Hermeneutics: analysis and interpretation of texts in context

- Critical social theory: analysis of domination and oppression with a view to changing it

- Buddhism: spiritual practice that allows one to free oneself from suffering and illusion in several ways, such as becoming more aware (p. 6)

MI is based on 13 philosophical assumptions. My research applications of them are detailed in Nagata, 2003, 2004, 2005, 2006a, 2006b.

The process of pursuing an MI begins with identifying a personally important question that intrigues or troubles us and proceeds by using the four knowledge traditions as applicable during the inquiry. The methodology of MI is characterized by circular movement that spirals into new experiences and understanding and returns repeatedly to different aspects of them on other levels or in other contexts. There is no fixed order for using them. They can be employed flexibly according to the learner's need in any setting. An MI question can provide a focus throughout a course that helps students to identify and to engage with whatever they are learning that is most relevant. The MI question may remain the same, may evolve into a slightly different question as new understandings emerge, or may change significantly, even completely.

## Scholar-Practitioner's Integrative Transformative Learning

The MI I pursued as my doctoral research provides an example of the distinction between rational and extrarational knowledge related to the phenomenon I was researching, which I termed *embodied empathic resonance*. In my dissertation, I described the cultural anthropologist Hall's explanation of the concept of synchrony as follows:

> In *The Dance of Life*, Hall describes the work of William Condon. Condon coined the term *entrainment* to describe the internal process that makes synching possible, wherein one central nervous system drives another or they do so reciprocally. Self-synchrony is the manifest observable phenomenon of a rhythmic internal process linked with the brain waves. It is associated with al-

most everything a person does and can be seen most clearly in a unity between speech and body motion. In painstaking research on the synchronization of movement and the human voice, Condon demonstrated that when people converse there is both self and interpersonal synchrony that operates at the level of the brain waves. When summarizing the importance of Condon's research, Hall writes: "If you can't entrain with yourself, it is impossible to entrain with others, and if you can't entrain you can't relate." (Hall, 1983, p. 167; cited in Nagata, 2002, pp. 91–92)

As helpful as finding this articulation of a phenomenon that had been out of my awareness was, reading about the concept of entrainment did not mean that I was then capable, either intrapersonally or interpersonally, of this process of the bodymind that is typically unconscious. My dissertation can be read as the story of what and how I learned about entrainment and resonant communication.

My early attempts to use the understanding I was developing were not always successful. Reflecting in writing on what I was learning—working with imagery, focusing, and Asian methods of self-cultivation such as tai chi and yoga, all the while trying repeatedly to implement my insights in practice—eventually moved me to a somatic-emotionally based level of knowing that I was able to trust as a guide to action (Gendlin, 1981).

Gendlin articulates this deep level of experience and how working with the holistic *felt sense* is an integrative approach to releasing new energy for change.

> Focusing is not an invitation to drop thinking and just feel. That would leave our feelings unchanged. Focusing begins with that odd and little known "felt sense" and then we think verbally, logically, or with image forms but in such a way that the felt sense shifts. When there is a body shift, we sense that our usual kind of thinking has come together with body-mind, and has succeeded in letting body-mind move a step. (p. 160)
>
> . . .
>
> The holistic felt sense is more inclusive than reason. . . . It is your sense of the whole thing, including what you know, have thought, have learned. . . . Thought and feeling, ought and want, are not now split in it. (p. 165)

As I worked in the constant flux and flow of corporate life at the intercultural interface at that time, I found that my felt sense is an excellent inner guide. Additionally, Gendlin's phenomenological work provided a theoretical context for my understanding of the efforts required in the internal organizational consulting work I was doing (Nagata, 2000; Gendlin, 1991).

This workplace description from my article "Resonant Connections" that detailed some of my integrative efforts in my work life provides an example.

The emotional connection I felt with my colleague sometimes had negative content that blocked our work productivity and sometimes positive that led to speedy and creative resolution of a complex issue. I can see now that throughout we were resonating with each other's varying emotional vibrations, which increased their intensity. We were never indifferent to each other. (p. 29)

In that article, I continued to reflect on the process in which I was engaging:

Like Gendlin's open space that exceeds the existing concepts, I tried to pause and hold open the possibility that something would emerge into that space and time that would take me beyond my current understanding. Problems seem to arise when I am operating just from concepts, the ideas in my head. I have begun to honor the opening into the unknown that being existentially present in the unfolding experience in connecting with another person might create. (Nagata, 2000, p. 29)

I found myself relying on my felt sense, especially when first encountering situations. Attending to the felt sense in the present moment guided my self-management by alerting me that I was nearing the end of my comfort zone, the limits of what I thought I knew and could do. Recognizing resonant somatic-emotional sensations of dissonance and consonance helped me to make the effort to hold myself open to the situation presently unfolding and to create containers for the interaction in process, both within myself and between me and the other person. I have come to value bodily signals as warnings that I am moving toward the unknown, a place of high energy and tension. Focusing on the felt sense of a situation brings implicit material into consciousness and permits more skillful communication.

These messages from my bodymind promote its further integration by moving me beyond what I have come to call the *bodymindset*, my existing pattern of being in my bodymind. *Bodymind* is a term for the totality of self, encompassing all physical, mental, emotional, and spiritual functions. Wilber uses this term for the *centauric self*, the total psychophysical organism resulting from the integration of the differentiated body and the ego-mind of the earlier stages. I will use bodymind in the sense of our given, undifferentiated natural heritage and *Bodymind* to refer to the integrated functioning achieved by self-cultivation (Dychwald, 1986; Pert, 2000; Wilber, 1996).

Trust in the deep knowing of one's bodymind builds confidence because it is readily available and can be quickly utilized simply by being present to it. The bodymind mediates inner experiences and outer circumstances, thus guiding alignment with the flow of the situation. I found trusting the felt sense of my bodymind to be a reliable compass. The greater openness, fluidity, and trust I began to experience in my bodymind enhanced my work as an internal organizational consultant and took me beyond what I had thought I was capable of. My whole being was absorbed in my MI so that I reached a new level of embodied understanding.

When I recently read Hall's description of his way of being with the Navajo, I not only recognized the underlying concept of synchrony but also recalled situations in which I had embodied it similarly in my behavior.

> I soon acquired the habit of opening the door quietly in the Navajo way, squeezing in sideways so as not to let in too much light or disturb the air, and waiting for the proper amount of time for people to get used to my presence. . . . It was in this context, whenever I was working with another culture, that I first acquired the habit of letting others set the tempo as well as the order of events. It is the only way to avoid some of the more flagrant errors in intercultural relations. (Hall, 1994, p. 146)

The conceptual and experiential understanding I gained through my studies combined with my lived experience in Japan integrated into a new way of being an embodied knowing that enables me both to be and to do with greater sensitivity to cultural differences and human relations in general. My understanding deepened to the holistic level of the *Bodymind*, which I could not have reached just by reading and reflecting on the concepts explained (Wilber, 1996).

Developing understanding that encompasses the whole self has often been considered a spiritual practice as this passage by Hindu scholar and meditation teacher Easwaran explains:

> Because, "as a man thinketh in his heart, so is he," not as he thinketh in his head. There is a vast distance from the head to the heart. In the Greek and Russian Orthodox traditions, they say that whatever spiritual knowledge you have in your head must be brought down into your heart. This takes many, many years. (Easwaran, 1997)

Spiritual references reflecting wisdom from many traditions are included in my teaching as they reveal commonalities across differences and reinforce commitment of interculturalists to ethical principles of respect and dignity for all human beings.

The above description of my integrative transformative learning includes mind, body, emotion/feeling, and spirit. This learning involved my whole self and was transformative to a different level of consciousness and way of being in the world.

## Pedagogical Approach

MI has been my choice of intercultural education approach for working with graduate students because it is particularly suitable for attempts to capture the dynamic, developmental, and complex nature of communicating with people of diverse cultures. MI is the answer to my pedagogical research question of how to help students to cultivate their self-reflexivity and voice as researchers. MI is a learner-centered approach to pursuing research that is personally meaningful and intellectually rigorous. Once learned, it can be used in any setting through-out life.

## Reflective and Self-Reflexive Practice

### Reflection and Reflexivity (Gadamer's Hermeneutic Circle)

Educators Nakkula and Ravitch's *Matters of Interpretation* guides students to un-cover their assumptions and biases and to put their reflections to work in doing their research and pursuing their professional practice. Their explanation of philosopher Gadamer's hermeneutical circle as diagrammed below is useful in understanding the cycle of action and reflective interpretation for application in human relations.

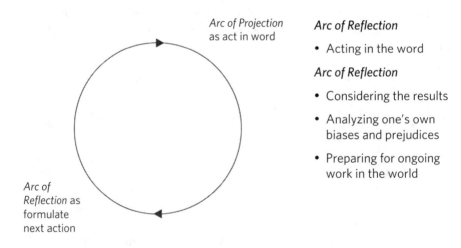

*Arc of Projection* as act in word

**Arc of Reflection**

• Acting in the word

**Arc of Reflection**

• Considering the results
• Analyzing one's own biases and prejudices
• Preparing for ongoing work in the world

*Arc of Reflection* as formulate next action

Figure 11.1: Gadamer's hermeneutic circle applied to human relations, based on *Matters of Interpretation* by M. Nakkula and S. Ravitch, 1998

Reflecting on action is an iterative approach to processing our lived experi-ence for increasing self-awareness and skillful future self-management and communication. It is a recognizable cycle for interculturalists and a concept that scholar-practitioners can easily grasp and apply in the reflective writing that is required throughout my courses.

The power of this hermeneutic process comes from cycling through acting to reflecting. Once patterns of thought, feeling, and behavior have been identified through reflective writing, they can be spotted when in play during relationships. Because intercultural communication involves encounters with different rules of communicative interaction, understanding what is taking place is often especially challenging. The link between theory and practice is self-reflexivity, a type of self-awareness that I conceive of as an accelerated form of hermeneutic reflection that has been ingrained by ongoing effort (Nagata, 2005).

Although the intrapersonal effort or inner work is similar, self-reflection is after the fact; self-reflexivity is in the moment, and feeling is likely to have more immediacy so it may be easier to grasp its role. To be reflective is to sit and think about what took place after it is completed: our role in it, others' reactions, and our responses to them. This can be done through thinking, writing, or speaking. One goal of engaging in reflection is to learn from our experiences to improve the quality of our interactions in future encounters (Fisher-Yoshida & Nagata, 2002).

Since intercultural communication is typically practiced in the moment, face-to-face self-reflexivity can be more valuable than self-reflection. Cultivating the ability to be self-aware of feeling and its impact on thinking (or the reverse) and then adjusting what we are doing and saying right then may confer immediate benefits. If we approach all our interactions as walking meditation, we have ongoing opportunities for the integrative transformative learning of cultivating ourselves as a *Bodymind* by expanding our consciousness and refining our communication skills.

## Promoting Bodymindfulness

I identified three components that have been incorporated into promoting self-reflexivity in my teaching: bodymindfulness, metacommunication, and communicative flexibility. I will discuss bodymindfulness here as an example of the extrarational component of my educational approach (Nagata, 2004, 2005; Mindell, 1990; Wood, 2007; Bolton & Bolton, 1996).

*Bodymindfulness* is a word I coined. The term *bodymind* emphasizes the systemic, integral nature of lived experience, and mindfulness is a Buddhist concept and practice of cultivating awareness. Awareness has two components: attention and intention. Awareness includes a flow of biological information that can help us relate more skillfully. Bodymindfulness can be used to attend to this type of information, somatic-emotional sensations that are often out of awareness, especially during an interpersonal interaction when our attention may be focused on another person or on a group of people. Typically words grab our attention, and bodily experience drops into the background, out of consciousness. We usually need to make a conscious intention to be bodymindful. Although much of our bodily experience is beyond our awareness most of the time, we can become conscious of it if we focus our attention on it (Nagata, 2002; Chopra, 1994; Young, 1997; Pert, 2000; Leder, 1990).

Bodymindfulness applies to recognizing information that comes from all aspects of the self and how the various kinds may interact, but I have emphasized somatic-emotional sensations because they underlie our intrapersonal experience and are typically subconscious and neglected. Engaging in bodymindfulness is a process of attending to somatic-emotional sensations that may also include the felt sense, the holistic personal meaning of an internal event. It is a way of tuning into prelinguistic experience prior to a sense of separation of body and mind. It can help us become more conscious of all aspects of our being and reveal deep layers of our experience of them and their interactions. Bodymindfulness can alert us to information that might otherwise go unnoticed so that we can use it resourcefully in the moment. Later in this chapter, I will explain how I teach it.

Intrapersonally, bodymindfulness is a way of cultivating the ability to *metacommunicate*. Interpersonal communication scholar Wood defines metacommunication as "communication about communication" (p. 31), but my focus in regard to self-reflexivity is more intrapersonal, that is, on being conscious of how we are communicating as we communicate or shortly thereafter. Mindell, a Jungian psychologist who works on global conflict resolution, describes the aspect of metacommunication that appeals particularly to me as an interculturalist seeking a larger view of self and context. He writes, "the more you work on yourself, the less you will identify with only one part, and the more you will metacommunicate" (p. 85). Working to strengthen this ability has often helped me to step outside my cultural confusion, frustration, and attendant misunderstandings that were grounded in identifications and assumptions that were unconscious until I stumbled over them (Wood, 2007; Mindell, 1990).

Nakkula and Ravitch offer a thoroughgoing method of clarifying bias and overcoming blind spots that affect our human relations. As Ravitch details, efforts at significant personal development often begin with recognizing discomfort. Cultivating bodymindfulness has been my emphasis in helping students recognize the prelinguistic basis of the information that they can gain by focusing on the sensations, feelings, and thoughts that arise when they encounter experiences that challenge their values, assumptions, and ways of communicating, both verbally and nonverbally. Bodymindfulness can help us access and understand the prerational structures of our meaning perspectives and how we express them (Nakkula & Ravitch, 1998).

My classes begin with encouragement to students to pay attention to their internal states and their overall state of being. *State of being* refers to the phenomenon other people sense as our energetic presence, which I think is based on what neuroscientist Damasio terms *background emotions*. Background emotions are internal states that are engendered by ongoing physiological processes and/or interactions with the environment, which are experienced with feelings of fatigue, energy, excitement, wellness, sickness, tension, relaxation, surging, dragging, stability, instability, balance, imbalance, harmony, and discord. Damasio uses the metaphor of a musical score to describe various levels of conscious behavior. His diagram starts from the bottom with wakefulness and rises through background emotions, low-level attention, focused attention, specific emotions, specific actions, to verbal report at the top. Background emotions are part of the bass line of somatic tonality, and specific emotions add varied higher notes. *Somatic tonality* is a term I coined for the emotional tone of our state of being (Damasio, 1999; Nagata, 2002).

*Energetic presence* is our living presence and the message it communicates, whether or not we are conscious of it. This is variously described as the atmosphere we create, the *vibes* others get from us, or the field or aura surrounding the personal space around the body. Educator and aikido instructor Leonard refers to this as our "own personal electromagnetic signature" (p. 14) (Nagata, 2002; Palmer, 1999; Feinstein, 1998; Leonard, 1986, 1997; Nagatomo, 1992; Yuasa, 1993).

When discussing the rhythmic, synchronic process of entrainment that occurs within and between people, Hall writes, "Rhythmic patterns may turn out to be one of the most important basic personality traits that differentiate one individual from another" (p. 164). I repeatedly remind my students to pay attention to their own energetic presence—and those of their classmates and teacher—as it provides a subtle and important foundation for verbal communication (Hall, 1983).

## Quaternity Model

I adapted the Quaternity model of human development from Carl Jung to describe the components of presence that are the expression of the state of being of the human bodymind. The model uses a circle to represent wholeness, the totality of our potential consciousness. The words near the circumference are labels for four aspects of human being. When these four are differentiated and ordered in proper relation to each other as shown here, our state of being can become integrated and we may achieve a synthetic unity on a higher level. The model is only a tool for understanding, and my intention is to promote an ideal for integrated, not fragmented, functioning of self (McLaren, 2000; Nelson, 1993; Schwartz-Salant, 1995).

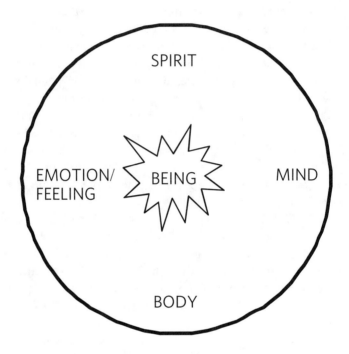

Figure 11.2: The Quaternity model of the bodymind.
Adapted from *Living the Wheel* by A. Nelson, 1993, p. 38.

The definitions used as starting points in presenting this model are as follows:

- **Consciousness**: a person's entire inner experience: thoughts, sensations of the body, emotions, visions of the spirit

- **Being:** sometimes called *self*; the integral state of all aspects of the self; may be cultivated to a higher than usual level of human functioning

- **Mind:** the part of a person that reasons, thinks, imagines, feels, wills, perceives, judges, and so forth; the part of us that pays attention

- **Body**: a person's physical structure and material substance; the body gives bounds to the personality and provides a vehicle for life

- **Emotion**[11]: a complex collection of chemical and neural responses forming a distinctive pattern, an automatic response to a stimulus, that changes the state of the body proper and the state of brain structures that map the body and support thinking. The purpose is to place the organism in circumstances conducive to survival and well-being.

- **Feeling**: the perception of a certain state of the body along with the perception of a certain mode of thinking and of thoughts with certain themes. "Feelings let us mind the body."

- **Spirit**: incorporeal, transcendent aspects of human being; connection with a larger creative source of meaning, the universe, or the divine (Nelson, 1993; Damasio, 1994; 2003).

## Use of Self as an Instrument of Communication

Face-to-face communication is an integral expression of all aspects of our bodymind. We need to be mindful that we use our whole self when we communicate. To be an effective intercultural communicator, it is necessary to develop consciousness of all aspects of our bodymind so that we can use all of our inner resources skillfully, even when we are not speaking. Cultivating bodymindfulness through conscious breathing promotes being present in the moment and experiencing connections between these four aspects of being. Doing inner work at this deep level can be both integrative and transformative.

## Bodymindfulness Practice

Attention to and care for our bodymind affects our internal state. Breathing consciously is the simplest, most fundamental way to tune into our current state, to care for, and to calm ourselves. Cultivating bodymindfulness with conscious breathing also helps us recognize the interaction and mutual influence that body, emotion/feeling, mind, and spirit have on each other. The following figure introduces these ideas prior to my teaching the Bodymindfulness Practice, an exercise for self-attunement.

---

[11] Damasio's distinction between *emotion* and *feeling* is particularly useful for interculturalists. Emotions are actions or movements that precede feelings. Many are public and perceptible by others as they occur in the face, the voice, and specific behaviors. These displays provide particularly valuable cues for interculturalists, especially when they are learning new nonverbal codes. Feelings are always hidden, like all mental images necessarily are, the private property of the organism in whose brain they occur. (Damasio, 1999, 2003)

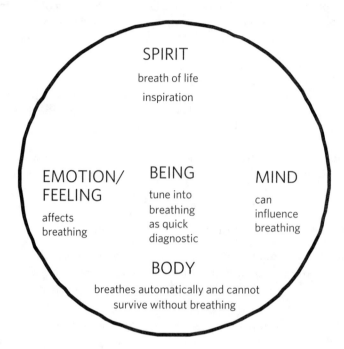

Figure 11.3: Breathing as the connector of the aspects of being of the bodymind.

The Bodymindfulness Practice, a seemingly simple exercise, clears a space for turning attention inward and making contact with our own energy. It promotes development of awareness of our bodymindset and offers a means of shifting it so that our presence is more poised and effective in conveying a desired message congruently.

Bodymindfulness Practice instructs us to

- Be present in the moment: *Be here now.*

- Tune into your breathing and see what it tells you about your current state of being.

- Breathe more deeply and evenly.

- Set your intention for your participation here.

- Use bodymindfulness to **Be here now!**

The Bodymindfulness Practice is a means of diagnosing our own internal states, attuning to our sensations, feelings, thoughts, and inspirations and then shifting them if deemed desirable. It is a distillation of Asian practices that can be done anytime, anywhere, at no cost, and in the complete privacy of our own bodymind. The Bodymindfulness Practice can be used whenever we enter a new space or begin to interact with someone. It can provide an orientation to the context of that moment. Ideally, it becomes a means of ongoing self-monitoring and attunement, which are both essential for self-reflexivity in the varied situations interculturalists may encounter, and it promotes skillful communication.

## The Practice of Intercultural Communication as Walking Meditation

Most of my graduate students are working adults in their 20s to 50s who are seeking a catalyst for change in their lives. They are knowledge workers whose professional work depends on their skillful use of self. The work that they are currently doing or that they aspire to typically ranges across education: interpreting and translating; consulting, coaching, and facilitating; business; law; and NGOs.

My students are multilingual and often focused on the importance of language learning, but my emphasis on nonverbal communication usually begins to fascinate them. In trying to understand how to communicate in Japanese with Japanese people, I particularly attended to the nonverbal aspects of my interactions since the people around me often seemed to be communicating without words. Because I was socialized in the mainstream U.S. culture, I expected the most important part of the message to be carried in words. I realized I had to discover and develop other resources in myself in order to communicate well. Teaching bodymindfulness has provided a way to bring tacit knowledge into awareness and to use it intentionally to promote better communication, especially when people have not mastered a common language.

Anderson's (2000) work on intercultural differences in nonverbal communication identifies *State* as one of four sources of influence on interpersonal behavior. The other three are *Culture, Situation*, and *Traits*. He theorizes that Culture and Traits are enduring, and Situation and State are transient. Culture and Situation have an external focus and Traits and State an internal one (Anderson, 2000).

State, a transient phenomenon with an internal focus, is what I have tried to bring to my students' attention. Attending to and attuning to one's inner states have been my emphasis in promoting more skillful communication. Of these four influences, our state is likely to be easier for us to influence quickly than the others.

The Bodymindfulness Practice is intended to help my students develop a holistic self-awareness that will serve them in the moment during intercultural interactions. I urge them to think of intercultural communication as walking meditation if they want to become interculturalists who can manage unexpected communication situations on their feet when they are actually occurring.

## Student Experiences of Bodymindfulness

The following analysis is intended to reveal the effects of incorporating bodymindfulness into my classroom teaching of graduate communication courses in English. It is based on the reflections of 21 recent students in response to the following question: While using bodymindfulness and paying attention to your breathing during or outside class, have you observed anything new about your inner state and how it affects your communication?

Data were collected from written reflections required after each class, presentations, and final reflective papers. Content analysis was used to identify the themes described below that reveal the overall structure and flow of the students' experiences. While bodymindfulness is only a small part of what I teach, one third of the students noted in their final course evaluations that it was what they would remember most (Creswell, 2003).

Students' observations focused on (1) attending to their inner states and (2) using the resulting awareness to attune themselves and do the inner work necessary to (3) align their actions with their intentions to communicate in more appropriate, effective, and satisfying ways. The quotations below reveal these inner moves that may also shift how they interact with other people.

## Attending to Inner States

Experiencing uncomfortable bodily sensations and unpleasant emotions and feelings were noted and sometimes related to other aspects of being a bodymind. Brief class exercises led the students toward making these connections, particularly concerning how they were communicating.

Students reported using bodymindfulness outside class when tired, confused, or upset, when hurrying, when waiting in line or riding a rush hour train, when arguing with someone or listening to troubled friends, when anxious while making a presentation, when struggling to concentrate, and so on. They also used it to relax, to calm themselves down, and to promote sleep. Yoshioka used it to do her research on bodymindful listening in intercultural dialogues (Yoshioka, 2006).

The following observation shows how common physical symptoms were understood in relation to a metacommunication on self and communication.

A few weeks ago I caught a cold, and although the cold has more or less gone away, I am still cursed with a cough which I find has held me back in communicating with other people. If I talk for long, my throat becomes dry and I start to cough, and so I am talking less frequently. The significance of this is that my physical state is having an effect on my self-esteem, which in turn is affecting the way I communicate with other people. (Shek)

These insights can support skillful self-management when feeling unwell and discouraged as an alternative to contagiously spreading personal distress in relationships.

As the following two quotations illustrate, students varied in whether they were more aware of their bodily condition and how it influenced other aspects of themselves, especially their minds, or how mental states affected their bodies and feelings.

I have noticed that my mental condition is directly and immediately influenced very much by my body state. Whenever I breathe deeply and regularly, I become calm and at the same time keen towards many subtle things around and inside myself. I feel more positive and brimming with hope about the outer world as well as the inner world, both other people as well as myself. I feel myself more lively in this space and harmonious with people and the environment. (MT)

Through understanding bodymindfulness, I have realized that I am such a bodymind, which means that the state of my mind is immediately represented/inscribed onto my body, which sometimes I do not like that much. (Morita)

Recognizing which aspect of ourselves is likely to take precedence in our awareness can alert us to other areas that have been neglected and need to be cultivated so that they become more readily available inner resources.

## Attuning with Awareness

Using bodymindfulness to attend to breathing is the first step to becoming aware of inner states and their relation to outer contexts. Then bodymindful breathing can be used to attune and shift those states as desired. The following discoveries by Asano took place over several weeks and represent a typical emphasis on becoming calm and making choices regarding communication. The second paragraph is an overall reflection in her final paper.

I think, owing to bodymindfulness, I calm down in communicating with people, even when I am worried about something or was rushing just before that. I come to pay attention to my own breathing, not only during using bodymindfulness but also during communication. . . . Above all, I have come to recognize my current condition by using bodymindfulness, so that I can fit myself to each particular situation as much as I can. I believe that such a practice is really useful not only to myself but also to others that I am communicating with. I feel that it has a kind of unlimited possibility for communication.

By encountering and practicing bodymindfulness, I have learned to face myself steadily, and I, accordingly, have come to know how I am expected to behave under a certain circumstance. The knowledge of my own state of being helps me to communicate with others much better than before. Not only my own whole atmosphere but also the ways in which I consider others as well as the ways in which I talk have altered.

When considering the class topic of conflict, we practiced tuning into the *inner aura*—Gendlin's (1981) term for the felt sense of another person, object, situation, or idea—of different people that we imagined relating to. We noted changes in our inner states related to communicating with people who are *uppers*, whom we experience as positive about us, in contrast to *downers*, people who seem negative about us (Gendlin, 1981; Wood, 2007, p. 48). One student wrote:

When I thought about a person who was an upper for me, I felt something warm in my body. When I started to think about a different person who was a downer for me, my body felt coldness inside. Usually, I try not to think about the downer person, but while doing bodymindfulness, I could think about the person calmly, at least more calmly than usual. And, I could think why the person was a downer for me, or how I could have better communication with the person. . . . I think that I always lose calmness when I communicate with the downer person, and that might have a bad effect on my utterances and behavior.

This exercise also resulted in insights about how she evaluated another person and how that evaluation might change. There is a suggestion here of accessing new inner resources for improving communication. Knowing how to deal with negative anticipation about communicating with someone is a critical skill for professional people.

Yoshioka described how bodymindfulness influenced her inner states and helped her become neutral in outlook.

I am feeling back on form after trying bodymindfulness. Inhaling, I feel as if I am charging my energy to be in a better state, and exhaling, I sense that my aspects of feelings, emotions, and body are calming down and becoming a state of zero. The exhaling process reminded me of my imagination of a process of clearing muddy water of a lake. I wait for the muddy water to become transparent and its wave motion to be quiet on the surface. After a while, my vision goes close to check the bottom of the lake to see if the water is transparent and also goes back to watch the surface of the lake to see if the beautiful trees and the sky are reflected there as they are. I repeat this movement of looking back and forth and try to come into a neutral state. (Yoshioka, 2006, p. 46)

Her use of bodymindfulness has evolved into a way to metacommunicate and to shift her inner state.

## Aligned Action

Some of the students emphasized how bodymindfulness gave them a new sense of being as shown above, and others focused more on new ways of doing. In both cases, the result was usually improved communication skills. Students often noted how their state influenced the way they communicated, particularly in the relationships that were most important to them.

> The relationship between mood and my communication style is very strong. When I am in some extreme emotion, like excited or angry, the urge to talk will become uncontrollable. Sometimes I quarreled with my girlfriend not really because of the stuff that we debated, but because of the tone, too loud a voice, or some inappropriate, harsh term I used.

> Controlling my breathing could help to eliminate the influence of mood and lower the possibility of misunderstanding or even a quarrel. Paying attention to my breathing by counting always makes me calm, and then I could really start to reflect before talking. (JL)

As the result of learning bodymindfulness, Taniguchi, who works as a facilitator, realized the importance of preparing himself differently for his work.

> I tried bodymindfulness at the office before meetings. It is interesting that I plan to design the meeting place, the attendants' circumstance and the control of it as a facilitator without paying attention to my self. Whereas the place is for all the attendants including the facilitator her/himself, it happens easily that I ignore myself—a particularly influential member.

> After acknowledging it, I try to consider the position or the meaning of myself at the meeting and to control my attitude toward the meeting members by managing my condition using bodymindfulness.

This sense of realization of something fundamental that had not been obvious prior to using bodymindfulness was expressed by many students.

Hamelitz, a full-time student who has a young family and a growing business, wrote, "Mindful breathing really has become part of my life. It really helps me in starting the day right and in dealing with potentially stressful situations." He uses it to set his intention for the day by making a conscious choice on how to approach whatever the day will bring as well as by using it as things unfold. He feels it is becoming a way of life for him.

Shimano did his master's thesis about the successful NGO project on blind migration and human trafficking in Cambodia where he did an internship. Bodymindfulness was particularly important because his ability to speak Khmer was limited, and he had to use interpreters when interviewing Cambodian people. In a presentation reflecting on his studies, he described his transformative learning experience that prepared him to do the complex development communication work he aspires to at the Japan International Cooperation Agency (JICA), where he is now employed (Shimano, 2006a, 2006b).

> What I learned most through my experience in the courses I took is bodymindfulness. Studying about intercultural communication is much easier than putting it into practice. My NGO experience in Cambodia was tough at first. Even though I could understand that there were differences, it was difficult for me to comprehend and to adopt them. The bodymindfulness practice and theories that I learned were really helpful in giving me an inner sense of myself and in noticing resonance in relationships that helped us to understand each other more. Using them, every day I continue to learn something even though I experience the same things. . . . As I utilized bodymindfulness by keeping a journal and diary and realizing my inner sense, qualitative research and person-centered interviewing made it possible to recognize the basics of HCC's projects' successful points. . . . For me, each day is a journey to be a better interculturalist—to communicate well using bodymindfulness within myself intrapersonally, interpersonally with others, and interculturally wherever I find myself.

These reflections about three years of work reveal the connection between a shifting state of being and the resulting change in what it is possible to do in the world.

## Conclusion

Bodymindfulness is a discovery made while engaged in a mindful inquiry, and it is a valuable approach for researchers who want to pursue their own MIs. Bodymindfulness is a practice particularly suitable for integrative transformative learning because it focuses us at a deep, prereflective level where we can begin to understand the sources of our perceptions, interpretations, and behavior. Bodymindfulness offers us ways to recognize and to shift our inner states whenever and wherever needed as we lay down our paths while journeying through life.

People interested in learning more about intercultural communication are referred to SIETAR (Society for Intercultural Education, Training, and Research) <http://www.sietar.org/>, which has organizations in various parts of the world, and to the Summer Institute for Intercultural Communication (SIIC) <http://www.intercultural.org/>, where a wide variety of workshops are offered in the summer. As a recommendation of a specific course, Personal Leadership: Making a World of Difference (sm), is offered at SIIC and elsewhere, http://www.plseminars.com/. It is an approach to leading oneself toward one's highest and best and includes significant emphasis on cultivating all the aspects of self that make up the bodymind.[12]

---

[12] These papers are posted at http://www.humiliationstudies.org/whoweare/board03.php#nagata

## References

Anderson, P. A. (2000). Cues of culture: The basis of intercultural differences in nonverbal communication. In L. A. Samovar & R. E. Porter (Eds.), *Intercultural communication: A reader,* 9th edition, pp. 258–270. Belmont, CA: Wadsworth.

Bentz, V. M., & Shapiro, J. J. (1998). *Mindful inquiry in social research.* Thousand Oaks, CA: Sage.

Bolton, R., & Bolton, D. G. (1996). *People styles at work: Making bad relationships good and good relationships better.* New York: AMACON.

Boyd, R. D., & Myers, J. G. (1988). Transformative education. *International Journal of Lifelong Education, 7,* 261–284.

Chopra, D. (1994). *The seven spiritual laws of success.* San Rafael, CA: Amber-Allen.

Cranton, P. (2000). Individual differences and transformative learning. In J. Mezirow & Associates (Ed.), *Learning as transformation: Critical perspectives on a theory in progress,* pp. 181–204. San Francisco: Jossey-Bass.

Creswell, J. W. (2003). *Research design: Qualitative, quantitative, and mixed methods approaches,* 2nd edition. Thousand Oaks, CA: Sage.

Damasio, A. R. (1994). *Descartes' error: Emotion, reason, and the human brain.* New York: Avon Books.

Damasio, A. R. (1999). *The feeling of what happens: Body and emotion in the making of consciousness.* New York: Harcourt Brace.

Damasio, A. R. (2003). *Looking for Spinoza: Joy, sorrow, and the feeling brain.* Orlando, FL: Harcourt.

Dirkx, J. M. (2000). Transformative learning and the journey of individuation. *ERIC Clearinghouse on Adult, Career, and Vocational Education* (Information Series No. 223). Columbus, OH: Ohio State University Press.

Dychwald, K. (1986). *Bodymind.* New York: Jeremy P. Tarcher.

Easwaran, E. (1997). *Words to live by.* Accessed on May 26, 2006, from http://www.nilgiri.org/Html/Thoughts/today.html

Esbjörn-Hargens, S. (2006, Winter). Integral education by design: How integral theory informs teaching, learning, and curriculum in a graduate program. *ReVision, 28*(3), 21–29.

Feinstein, D. (1998, Summer). At play in the fields of the mind: Personal myths as fields of information. *Journal of Humanistic Psychology, 38*(3), 71–109.

Fisher-Yoshida, B., & Nagata, A. L. (2002). Developing reflective/reflexive transcultural practitioners. Unpublished manual for workshop at Society of Intercultural Education, Training, and Research (SIETAR) Japan.

Gendlin, E. T. (1981). *Focusing,* 2nd edition. New York: Bantam Books.

Gendlin, E. T. (1991). Thinking beyond patterns: Body, language, and situations. In B. den Ouden & M. Moen (Eds.), *The presence of feeling in thought,* pp. 21–151. New York: Peter Lang.

Hall, E. T. (1983). *The dance of life: The other dimension of time.* Garden City, NY: Doubleday.

Hall, E. T. (1994). *West of the thirties: Discoveries among the Navajo and Hopi.* New York: Doubleday.

Leder, D. (1990). *The absent body.* Chicago: University of Chicago Press.

Lennox, S. L. (2005). Contemplating the self: Holistic approaches to transformative learning in higher education. Dissertation Abstracts International, *66*(7), 2492A. (UMI No. 3184473)

Leonard, G. (1997, Autumn). Living energy. *IONS: Noetic Sciences Review, 43,* 8–15.

Leonard, G. (1986). *The silent pulse: A search for the perfect rhythm that exists in each one of us.* New York: Bantam Books.

McLaren, K. (2000). *Emotional genius: How your emotions can save your life* [Cassette recordings]. Boulder, CO: Sounds True.

Mezirow, J. (1991). *Transformative dimensions of adult learning.* San Francisco: Jossey-Bass.

Mindell, A. (1990). *Working on yourself alone: Inner dreambody work.* London: Arkana.

Nagata, A. L. (2000, Spring). Resonant connections. *ReVision, 22*(4), 24–30.

Nagata, A. L. (2002). Somatic mindfulness and energetic presence in intercultural communication: A phenomenological/hermeneutic exploration of bodymindset and emotional resonance. *Dissertation Abstracts International, 62*(12), 5999B. (UMI No.3037968)

Nagata, A. L. (2003). Mindful inquiry: A learner-centered approach to qualitative research. *Journal of Intercultural Communication, 6,* 23–36.

Nagata, A. L. (2004). Cultivating confidence in public communication: Teaching bodymindfulness and sensitivity to energetic presence. *Journal of Intercultural Communication, 7,* 177–197.

Nagata, A. L. (2005). Promoting self-reflexivity in intercultural education. *Journal of Intercultural Communication, 8,* 139–167.

Nagata, A. L. (2006a). Cultivating researcher self-reflexivity and voice using mindful inquiry in intercultural education. *Journal of Intercultural Communication, 9,* 135–154.

Nagata, A. L. (2006b). Transformative learning in intercultural education. *Rikkyo Intercultural Communication Review, 4,* 39–60.

Nagatomo, S. (1992). *Attunement through the body.* Albany: State University of New York Press.

Nakkula, M. J., & Ravitch, S. M. (1998). *Matters of interpretation: Reciprocal transformation in therapeutic and developmental relationships with youth.* San Francisco: Jossey-Bass.

Nelson, A. (1993). *Living the wheel: Working with emotion, terror, and bliss through imagery.* York Beach, ME: Samuel Weiser.

O'Sullivan, E. V. (2002). The project and vision of transformative education: Integral transformative learning. In E. V. O'Sullivan, A. Morrell, & M. A. O'Connor (Eds.), *Expanding the boundaries of transformative learning,* pp. 1–12. New York: Palgrave.

O'Sullivan, E. V., Morrell, A., & O'Connor, M. A. (Eds.). (2002). *Expanding the boundaries of transformative learning.* New York: Palgrave.

Palmer, W. (1999). *The intuitive body: Aikido as a clairsentient practice,* revised edition. Berkeley, CA: North Atlantic Books.

Pert, C. B. (2000). *Your body is your subconscious mind* (cassette recordings). Boulder, CO: Sounds True.

Ravitch, S. (1998). Becoming uncomfortable: Transforming my praxis. In M. Nakkula & S. Ravitch (Eds.), *Matters of interpretation: Reciprocal transformation in therapeutic and developmental relationships with youth,* pp. 105–121. San Francisco: Jossey-Bass.

Ryan, J. (2005, Fall). The complete yoga: The lineage of integral education. *ReVision, 28*(2), 24–28.

Schwartz-Salant, N. (1995). *Jung on alchemy.* Princeton, NJ: Princeton University Press.

Shimano, T. (2006a). *Cambodian villagers' mindset change and empowerment: The case of Healthcare Center for Children (HCC) human trafficking and blind migration.* Unpublished master's thesis, Rikkyo University, Graduate School of Intercultural Communication, Tokyo, Japan.

Shimano, T. (2006b, May 28). From case study to thesis about NGO internship. Paper presented at the meeting of the Rikkyo Intercultural Communication Society, Tokyo, Japan.

Taylor, E. W. (1997). Building upon the theoretical debate: A critical review of the empirical studies of Mezirow's transformative learning theory. *Adult Education Quarterly, 48*(1), 34–59.

Taylor, E. W. (2000). Analyzing research on transformative learning theory. In J. Mezirow & Associates, *Learning as transformation: Critical perspectives on a theory in progress,* pp. 285–328. San Francisco: Jossey-Bass.

Wilber, K. (1996). *The atman project: A transpersonal view of human development,* new edition. Wheaton, IL: Quest Books.

Wood, J. T. (2007). *Interpersonal communication: Everyday encounters,* 5th edition. Belmont, CA: Wadsworth/Thomson Learning.

Yoshioka, M. (2006). A phenomenological exploration of bodymindful listening through intercultural dialogue with Chinese individuals. Unpublished master's thesis, Rikkyo University, Graduate School of Intercultural Communication, Tokyo, Japan.

Young, S. (1997). *The science of enlightenment: Teachings and meditations for awakening through self-investigation* [Cassette recordings]. Boulder, CO: Sounds True.

Yuasa, Y. (1993). *The body, self-cultivation, and ki-energy* (S. Nagatomo & M. S. Hull, Trans.). Albany: State University of New York Press. (Original work published 1986–1991)

# Chapter 12

---

## Dreamscape: A Multimedia Collaboration Method

*Tiffany von Emmel*

## Introduction

This chapter describes the Dreamscape method and a case story of its use with an organization of international systems scientists. With the goal of offering new approaches to transformative learning and organization development, I describe the Dreamscape process and three theoretical frameworks that inform the design and facilitation: relational design principle, the interactivist model, and four kinds of transformative knowledge.

Dreamscape offers an approach to group collaboration and organizational cultural transformation. Specifically, the dreamscape is designed to facilitate four kinds of transformation: connectivity, new meaning, embodiment of values, and adult development. While the group level is the primary focus, individual transformation also is facilitated in practice. Although there are not yet extensive data to support the claim of individual transformation, many individuals have self-reported breakthrough thinking, growth, connections, healing from alienation, increased self-efficacy, and agency.

As a social project, the Dreamscape also has broader social cultural intentions. The long-term purpose of spreading the use of this open source group method is to seed life-sustaining forms of knowledge in communities, institutions, and organizations dedicated to developing a peaceful, just, and healthy planet. Over time, this cultural work can spark new practices of change makers, consultants, adult educators, artists, activists, and facilitators.

## The Performative Turn of Knowledge

The Dreamscape is situated at the forefront of an exciting knowledge evolution. Briefly, I map out here the "performative turn" within the social sciences and why it matters. In the last decades, there has been a burgeoning paradigm shift underway in the social and behavioral sciences. In the ongoing linguistic turn of knowledge in the social sciences, knowledge has been thought of as socially constructed via conversation and speech acts, metaphors and narratives; knowledge is logocentric; knowledge is representation. Over the last 20 years, another turn has been underway in the social sciences, which I call the "performative turn." Communities of scholars and practitioners are pioneering this turn in education, communication studies, psychology, organization development, and sociology (von Emmel, 2005).

The Dreamscape is a response to a problem with organizational knowledge. In the performative turn, scholars and practitioners have realized that there are critical problems with knowledge-creation that impact the self, culture, and the natural environment. Controlling patterns in knowledge production interfere with the relational dynamics of life. With institutional knowledge, modern subjectivity has patterns of passivity, alienation, fragmentation, consuming modes of desire, impoverished imagination, shallow perception, limited time perspective, and the disappearing of relational ways of knowing (Touraine, 2000; Griffin, 1995; McLaren, 1988; Orr, 1994; Abram, 1996; Sewall, 1999; Adam, 1996; Petranker, 1998; Tulku, 1979; von Emmel, 2005).

The key to the problem is in how knowledge is coupled to the subject's modes of desire, time, agency, and perception. As a way out, knowledge can be reconstituted from non-Eurocentric, multicultural, ecological, and feminist perspectives: from representation to participation, from abstraction to action, from value-neutral to value-specific. Participative inquiry, also known as Action Research, has been at the forefront of practice in this turn. In the performative turn, knowledge is relationally shaped, as is the case in the linguistic turn, that is, social construction. The difference is that in the performative turn, knowledge is what is *done* in relationship, not just what is said or written. Knowledge is historical, aesthetic, ecological, emotional, and embodied. Knowledge is not "discourse." Knowledge is the "concourse" of participation. Knowledge is a performed activity. This "concourse" of relational responsiveness is improvisational and fluid (Hershock, 1996).

| Linguistic turn | → | Performative turn |
|---|---|---|
| representation | → | participation |
| mind | → | embodied |
| subject/object | → | action |
| value subjective | → | value-specific |
| interpretation | → | activism |
| language | → | relationship |

Table 12.1: The Performative Turn

Most importantly, knowledge is value-specific. The kind of knowledge that society generates does matter. It has ethical consequences for the well-being of the world. There is a coupling between institutional knowledge, subjectivity, and social ecological well-being. To address the knowledge problems, the interdisciplinary field of performance studies has in the last 10 years developed the area of art as a critical social research method. The arts for thousands of years have been powerful in generating life-affirming knowledge. Theater, dance, and visual art are able to touch people in a way that traditional quantitative or qualitative research does not. Action Research in the social sciences has also been at the forefront to address the knowledge problem (Adam, 1996; Park et al., 1993; Reason & Bradbury, 2001; Shotter, 2003, 2004).

While the social and behavioral sciences have taken a "performative turn," the arts have gone through a parallel change in the last decades, with the influence of feminist and multicultural art. In many instances, social science and participatory arts blend and merge. Genres of art have sprung up and moved away from object-oriented representation to the activity of participation. Art for change, rather than art for art's sake, is coming to the forefront. These genres are variously called community art, interactive art, site-specific art, improvisational art, and environmental art. Suzi Gablik explains that the "connective aesthetics" of these art forms are transformative for public participants. For example, the last "world fair" for the arts, the Documenta 11, displayed many such projects. Art and research are reclaimed as "by the people, for the people." It is at this fruitful intersection of art and science where the Dreamscape project stands (Gable, 1995, 2002; Documenta, 2002).

## Theory Development of the Models

The Dreamscape process is facilitated with a set of models that can serve to both describe and prescribe actions. The models below are grounded in the understanding that knowledge is about relationship. The methods reflect that learning is embodied and embedded in a social ecological spiritual context.

Learning is an active practice of deep engagement. The models are grounded in theory that is relational and embodied in perspective—perspectives from ecological, feminist, Buddhist, African, queer, and body-based knowledge theory (von Emmel, 2005).

To develop this theory and methodology, I used arts-based research methods in my doctoral research. For three years in Berlin, Germany, I used group physical theater improvisation as a site and as a research method. This unique type of improvisation has been extensively reported as transformative in practice. Using performance ethnography, I researched the experience of transformation in the art, the organizing choreographic principles, and facilitation by way of an action research project. This enabled me to track different conditions of knowledge than hegemony offered. Group improvisational dance asserts participation, instead of representation, in the forming of knowledge. An experimental art form, this cultural practice also asserts the aesthetics of its historical context of radical democracy, African, Asian, feminist, Buddhist, ecological, and somatic ways of understanding. This unique condition of knowledge allowed me to consider the activity of this context as I defined what is "knowledge" and "transformation" (Brinkmann & von Emmel, 2002, 2003; von Emmel, 2001; Martin, 1998; von Emmel & Seashore, 2003; Zaporah, 1995; Foster, 2002; Denzin, 2003).

The results of the research have been the relational design principle, the interactivist model, and the four knowledge theory. Below, I outline first the five phases of the Dreamscape as a process and then the tools.

## Mapping the Process

Now, it is time to shift to the nuts and bolts of the Dreamscape. Over time, a Dreamscape process has five parts. In the table opposite, I give a thumbnail overview of the characteristics of these five parts.

In the beginning, a design team collaboratively decides on the objectives and creates the first element, an interactive "Environment." To use a theatrical analogy, the stage is built. The next element is "Interaction tools and Costumes." Participants are given at entry a shared frame and tools with which to interact. The third element is "Interactivism." Throughout the project, the facilitators act as interactivists and promote interactivism as the community engages in visual art-making and performance practices. Similar to a theater production process, this art-making evolves into a meaningful "Community Finale," element four. What participants generated earlier now becomes the choreography, scripts, and props of the Community Finale. And finally, comes an integrative and generative phase, "Digital Engagement." A short video or photograph from the dreamscape materials is made as an evocative digital conversation tool and distributed via social networks, blogs, video podcasting, and in real-time events. Used strategically, this digital cultural artifact serves to influence the social environment as an important condition of transformation.

| Phases | Function | Ways of Knowing | Kinds of Knowledge |
|---|---|---|---|
| 1. Create environment<br><br>Three physical spaces for inquiry at three system levels: | Inquiry of planet:<br>*What do you care for?* | *Audio:*<br>Voices of participants interviewed by facilitators | Develop relational knowledge: empathy |
| | Inquiry of community<br>*Who are we?* | *Visual:*<br>Social sculpture of objects made by community | Create representational narratives and images |
| | Inquiry of self<br>*How does a healthy system feel?* | *Kinesthetic:* play, rest, movement sessions, meditation | Cultivate tacit embodied understanding |
| 2. Use Interaction tools and costumes | Entry into transition, provide interaction tool and shared frame | Verbal, text, and aesthetic | Create a shared social context for transformation |
| 3. Interactivism | Mobilize use of self | Participants are guided by facilitators to practice experimental performative activity | Develop responsive knowledge: develop the capacity to respond |
| 4. Community finale | Group ritual | Participatory activity Or performance | Mark transition, build community, embody values, mobilize commitment |
| 5. Digital engagement | Influence the future via social networks | Digital cultural artifact | Generate narratives, aesthetics, and inquiry |

Table 12.2: The 5 phases in the Dreamscape

## Relational Design Principle

The relational design principle is used by the design team to create the design of the Dreamscape. In designing the learning environment, it asks the practitioner to consider three dimensions: (1) Knowing, (2) Participation, and (3) Perception:

1.  Engage multiple ways of *knowing*. Each person is unique in learning styles, culture, ethnicity, age, gender, discipline, physical ability, sexual orientation, religion. Surfacing diversity can create conditions for transformation. By creating an open space of not-knowing, diversity becomes a fertile field for learning. *Ask: How do we acknowledge, respect, and engage different ways of knowing?*

2.  Engage diverse ways of *participation*. Deep participation does not mean that all participation looks the same. Some participants may participate in more passive observation. Many will participate with guided help. Some may want to proactively initiate new kinds of participation. *Ask: How do we design for different kinds of participation?*

3.  Engage an ecology of *perception*. Engaging kinesthetic, aural, and visual senses in a multimodal interplay can be transformative for individuals, groups, and the environment. Each person's perceptual system is different. There is more robust learning as more diversity is engaged. Multimodal practice allows individuals to gain more awareness (Markova, 1996; Halprin, 2003).

Mobilizing the body's perception is also a way to engage the environment, as well as a group and the individual self. The body is shared by humanity. The body is also the human site of the earth. The body is part of the larger whole of life. The body's perception is coupled with the environment—in each breath we take, in each step, and in each vision. Therefore, offering ways to engage the body more deeply is the key to the people side of sustainability. Ask: *How do we design for the kinesthetic in particular, as well as for the auditory and visual? How do the kinesthetic, auditory, and visual modes interact in relation to the self, group, and environment?* (Shapiro, 2002; von Emmel & Seashore, 2003; Abram, 1990, 1996).

## Interactivist Model: Facilitation of Collaboration

The principle above requires evolving structures and support that can fluidly shift to support an ever-changing situation. The interactivist model offers this support. It reflects the organizing principles of group improvisation. While this model is very useful for group facilitation or educational design, it is also useful for practitioner interactions in networks and loosely coupled distributed fluid organizations. The interactivist model offers a tool for how a practitioner can facilitate change in each moment in a system by their use of self. By choosing to enact the self in an improvisational way, we continually adapt our design to the changing mode of involvement in the present moment and in the unfolding future.

Within the field of Organization Development, the interactivist model is a "use of self" theory. "Use of self" refers to how the practitioner consciously acts in a relationship in order to facilitate growth and development. Use of self involves increasing awareness and making choices that have generative influences (Mattare, Seashore, Shawver, & Thompson, 2004; C. Seashore, Curran, & Welp, 1995; E. Seashore, 2006; von Emmel & Seashore, 2003).

The interactivist model has five dimensions: *Connect, Attend, Respond, Interpret, and Design.* The dimensions are sequential and interdependent. To *Connect* is the foundation of improvisation. To connect involves opening the heart. It involves physical relaxing into the flow of relations. To *Attend* to this ground is the active engagement of perception. Connecting and attending lead the act of responding. To *respond* is the creative craft of shaping form. To *interpret* is the trace activity that follows responding. To interpret is to make distinctions between forms such as narratives and images. To interpret is reflective and representational. To *design* is the self-reflexive act of adjusting the shared understandings of how a group or individual acts—*who, where, how, and what* of performance. It is a meta-activity that involves assessing the flow of the performance and making choices that foster a more satisfying performance. This involves all of the senses, including thinking.

| Practice | Focus of Collaboration | Group Facilitation |
|---|---|---|
| **Connect** | Heart, feeling, sensation | *Softened muscles, slow heart rates, open sensation* |
| **Attend** | Perception | *Track developments, notice what's unfolding* |
| **Respond** | Aesthetic crafting of time and place with "architecture, feel, music" | *Make choices to act within the context of the situation: recycle, develop, shift, intensify, transform, deconstruct, join, contrast, play with* |
| **Interpret** | Meaning, cognitive frames, patterns | *Ask: what are stories? Images? Patterns?* |
| **Design** | A reflexive meta-activity | *Iteratively adjust the design: who, where, when, how i.e., tighten design, open design, recycle design* |

Table 12.3: Interactivist model

These dimensions reflect the dimensions of activity in group improvisation that allow it to evolve and to sustain itself. The dimensions have some resonance with the collaborative creativity model of Lawrence Halprin, an environmental architect, as well as with David Kolb's learning cycle. Pragmatically, the use of the model is similar as well. In learning design, this model can be applied in a linear cycle, as with Kolb's learning cycle. My colleagues and I have applied the interactivist model in different settings—with artists, in consulting and leadership coaching, in strategy sessions, in the classroom with graduate students, in the organizational design of our own organization as well as the Dreamscape. To make the model more accessible for the reader, I will refer to the dimensions in the case below (Halprin, 1969; Kolb & Fry, 1975).

## Four Kinds of Transformative Knowledge

The Dreamscape is designed to generate four kinds of transformative knowledge. In the case story, each of these was represented in the self-reports by participants:

1. **Relational Knowledge**: *Cultivate intimacy, relationship, and integration.* This kind of knowledge is fundamental for addressing the problems with institutional knowledge. It is also the basis of forming other kinds of knowledge. It is the idea that knowledge is relationship. In the case study, community building, new connections, and healing of alienation were the most frequent reports by participants (Palmer, 1993).

2. **Practical Knowledge**: *Create robust aesthetic know-how.* By practice and repetition, people learn to embody tacit knowledge. Tacit knowledge is the embodiment of values. By practicing participatory arts, participants practiced moving as a fluid complex ensemble (Polyani, 1983; Varela, 1999).

3. **Representational Knowledge**: *Make meaning together; Identify patterns and stories.* Taking both social construction and liberation pedagogy seriously, we involve participants in both appreciative inquiry and critical reflection. In the case story, participants had new theoretical insights about systems theory, and art gave them a rich language (Shotter, 1994; Freire, 1970).

4. **Responsive Knowledge**: *Stimulate innovation and adult development.* Based on Vygotskyan activity theory and East Asian thought, Responsive Knowledge treats knowledge as action. As they practiced performance skills, participants were learning to live with agency as the gap between the habits and possibilities unfolded (Engestrom, 1999; Shotter, 2000; Varela, 1999; Vygotsky, 1978).

Articulating further the knowledge forms is not practical within the scope of this chapter. To read a thorough discussion, please see other sources (Park, 2001, 2004; von Emmel, 2005).

## A Dreamscape Case Story: An Organization of Systems Scientists

This specific dreamscape was designed with and for an international association of systems scientists. Each year, the organizational members meet in a different country. We involved hundreds of organizational members in a Dreamscape for one week during their fiftieth annual meeting.

I was a member of the planning committee for this fiftieth meeting. The committee expressed that it wanted creative processes to help the organization to break out of old patterns, to heal the fracturing within the community and to enliven the organization. The president expressed her desire for a community finale that participatively involved the members. In response, I offered that we could design and facilitate a Dreamscape (von Emmel, Brinkmann, & Dreamfish, 2006)[13].

## Interactivism on the Dreamscape Team

The design of the design team itself was essential to the success of the intervention. First, creating diversity and a wide range of competence on the team was one factor. Secondly, choosing key influencers in the client system was also crucial. With this intent, I formed a design team that was about 50% professional artist-facilitators and 50% client members of the organization and their graduate students. To follow the relational design principle to create diversity on our team was key. We spoke many languages and had different sexual orientations and ethnicities. Expertise on our team included transformative learning, visual arts, dance, theater, digital technology, photography, somatics, organization development, improvisation, and systems thinking. The artists whom I chose for this project have graduate degrees in transformative learning, organization development, or psychology.

Our entire process reflected the interactivist model. Below, I give examples of each dimension during the first phase of the project.

1. Connect: Relationship is the ground of interactivism. The first phase of our design process focused on building community, within our own team first and then again when onsite with the organization. At our first team meeting, we met on the site where the Dreamscape would be created and made a ritual, speaking our intentions for the project. We then had a dinner party and created artful group-forming activities. In the language of the model, this phase emphasized the dimension of "Connect."

---

[13] In this case story, the dreamscape was produced by Dreamfish and realized by these individual team members: Dietmar Brinkmann (co-design), Tiffany von Emmel (concept and co-design), Patty Nason (photography), Sam Bower, Billy Cauley, Brian Collentine, Todd Johnston, Alexander Laszlo, Kathia Laszlo, Sue Lebeck, Paul Loper, Denzil Meyer, Ava Square-Miller, Steve Tellium, Pien van den Herik, Lucille Whitaker, and Barbara Widhalm.

Figure 12.1: The Team

2.  Attend: We mobilized diversity and attended to what felt enlivening. We asked individuals on our team to lead the team in activities that reflected their own expertise and ways of knowing. This allowed members to differentiate as unique individuals on the team and to have influence on the design process. This widened the team's awareness of choices available in the design process. I encouraged members to attend to the host of possibilities that were present. We paid attention to what felt enlivening. This choice reflects relational activity theory. This strategy is similar to Appreciative Inquiry in the generativity of approach. As we moved along in this divergent phase, ideas converged and patterns emerged. For the improvisers on our team, tracking this process and being comfortable with the unknown were easier to deal with. However, for those who preferred tighter structure and were new to improvisation or group process, the openness of this dimension was more challenging (Shotter, 2002; Cooperrider, 1995).

3.  Respond: As we gained awareness of what felt enlivening to participants and our dream team, we responded to it with choices and action that affirmed these directions. We set the design and implemented.

4.  Interpret: We then made meaning about our choices. We made stories about why a choice worked or didn't work. We critically reflected on decisions. This dimension reflects Mezirow's transformative learning theory, in which critical reflection is the process by which transformative learning happens (Mackenzie, 1998; Mezirow, 1990, 1991).

5.  Design: The design process was emergent and as flexible as we could make it. Because we used a lot of physical materials and construction was involved, a "tight design" of preplanning was critical to building the environment, tools, and costumes. More "open" design was possible with the interactivism onsite with the participants.

Below, I explain the design of the space, purpose, and activities.

## Environments

We designed the installation to engage 3 system levels in creative inquiry—planet, community and self. In the open grassy site near the main conference building, three canopies stood as contexts for three unique explorations. The Planet was placed in the center.

### THE PLANET Canopy (green marbles, green flags)

*System level:* the planet.
*Way of knowing:* sound and words.

Figure 12.2: The Planet Canopy

*Purpose:* The Planet focused individuals' attention on their relationship to the planet and how to serve the planet. It had two purposes: (1) to create knowledge of sustainability, democracy, and complexity and (2) to mobilize our collective responsibility.

*The Space:* A 16 ft. green globe became a horizontal landscape to explore. A 10'x10' canopy was inside the landscape. Inside the canopy, four special sound speakers with MP3 players were hung from the ceiling. Because these speakers projected a narrow band of sound, an intimate sound experience was created for the listener.

*The Activity:* Facilitators assigned to this station wandered throughout the conference and asked participants to be interviewed and audio-recorded. Creating a learning relationship with the participant, the interviewer focused on the theme "What is your dream for the planet?" Participants voiced wishes and feelings for the planet. With the intent to create an emotionally moving relational sound experience, the audio-recordings were then edited and played from the speakers. A soundscape of voices for the planet grew. Sitting within the space, participants listened to the feedback of their own voice and the voices of the community.

## THE BEEHIVE Canopy

*System level:* the community.
*Way of knowing:* visual arts.

Figure 12.3: The Beehive Canopy

*Purpose:* To serve the community of participants and the organization, the Beehive intended to (1) facilitate both unity and diversity in the community and (2) carry forward the creativity of this fiftieth meeting into the future of the organization.

*The Space:* A 22'x20' canopy stood on the grass. Card tables, covered with butcher paper, and chairs stood underneath. A wall of chicken wire was fastened to one side.

*Activity:* Each participant was given a Tyvek hexagon, in which to dream a future for the planet and what role can we as a community play. In the Beehive, participants made collages, colored them, and wrote on them. Participants pinned the hexagons in relation to other hexagons to make a honeycomb.

Figure 12.4: Making meaning

Individuals also reflected on other hexagons by writing on strips of yellow paper and wearing them as badges. The honeycomb grew during the week: *What is this organization's honeycomb to give the world?* Finally, during our community ritual on Friday, the hexagons were then used as props on sticks to signify carrying forward the dreams.

## THE POOL Canopy

*System level:* the self.
*Way of knowing:* fluid kinesthetic movement.

Figure 12.5: The Pool Canopy

*Purpose:* (1) to mobilize individual creativity, energy, and balance and (2) to facilitate reflection.

*Activity:* Reflection and play. Early morning, meditative movement was facilitated. In the evening, we swayed to music and had fun. This area had a playful fountain of water with chairs around the pool.

## Interaction Tools and Costumes

To immediately set initial conditions for involving participants in the dreamscape, we needed an interactive process that would engage them from the start. At registration, in each participant's bag was a set of instructions on how to dreamscape and a necklace to hang around the neck. The necklace held three marbles (green, yellow, and blue). These were held in a round tin at the end of a red conference necklace. The necklace was an invitation to three kinds of exploration in the dreamscape. When individuals came to a canopy, they could drop their marble into a tube of water (blue, green, or yellow) at each site. The marbles could be recycled as instruments in the performance and be taken home as evocative artifacts.

## Interactivism

To facilitate the organization's capacity to connect and to respond, we engaged participants in interaction in several ways. We created a role for this function, a performance troupe. Every morning, during the large plenary sessions with the 300 scientists in one room, the troupe invited the audience in a call-and-response activity as a design for bringing each speaker to the podium. Secondly, for three nights, we held evening movement and percussion sessions, in which 20–50 participants participated. At dawn each day, we led meditation and reflective movement sessions in the Pool canopy.

Liminality can frame a zone for new behavior, what Vygotsky calls a zone of proximal development. Therefore, we designed the dreamscape to be situated at the margins of the space and for our interactivism to be present in the transitions. We came out in the beginnings and in the endings, in the early morning and twilight hours, in the spaces at the margins and in the paths to and from the meeting sessions. The dream team performed an interactive performance at the end of the community banquet, in which the community of scientists boogied, jammed, sweated, and prayed for the planet.

## Community Ritual

The art-making in the physical installation shaped the emergent design of the community finale on Friday in which the community created a celebratory closing with song, percussion, movement, narrative, and sculpturing of place.

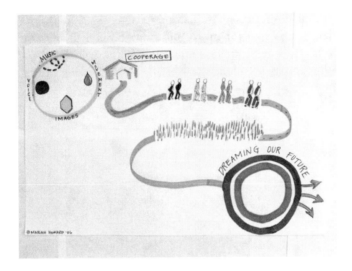

Figure 12.6: The Community Finale

## Digital Engagement

During the Dreamscape, our team members were taking photos and recording video and audio interviews. These then were fashioned into digital content to be used to stimulate further conversation. To do so, we posted a slideshow of this Dreamscape on Dreamfish.com and on the Flickr photo-sharing site at http://flickr.com/photos/dreamfish. Dreaming our Future is the next phase of this particular Dreamscape. It is a five-minute video that will highlight the dreams of the participants of the fiftieth anniversary conference of the systems sciences. To be used to seed new dreams and conversations in communities worldwide, these digital forms, freely distributed via social networks, support the sprouting of new forms of collaboration and knowledge creation.

## Conclusion

This chapter has offered an introduction to the Dreamscape as a method and as a set of principles and tools. These tools have been developed to support the work of adult educators, consultants, leaders, and facilitators in the work of helping groups and organizational networks to thrive. As part of the performative turn of knowledge, these tools are not to be reified but remixed freely to suit the particular needs of a given situation. Ironically, the fixity of a map or model has a smack of hegemony. However, I believe that to protect and give rise to that which does not speak, knowledge activism requires representational knowledge about nonrepresentational knowledge. As a final note, I must say that the Dreamscape is a lot more fun in practice than it is on paper. The Dreamscape is one way to create knowledge that is enlivening and healthy for an organization and its stakeholders—serving the well-being of the earth and its people.

# References

Abram, D. (1990). Perceptual implications of Gaia. In A. H. Badiner (Ed.), *Dharma Gaia: A harvest of essays in Buddhism and ecology.* Berkeley: Parallax Press.

Abram, D. (1996). *The spell of the sensuous.* New York: Vintage Press.

Adam, B. (1996). Re-vision: The centrality of time for an ecological social science perspective. In S. Lash, B. Szerszynski, & B. Wynne (Eds.), *Risk, environment and modernity: Towards a new ecology.* Thousand Oaks, CA: Sage.

Brinkmann, D., & von Emmel, T. (2002). Improvisation lab notes 1. Unpublished manuscript, Berlin, Germany.

Brinkmann, D., & von Emmel, T. (2003). Improvisation lab notes 2. Unpublished manuscript, Berlin, Germany.

Cooperrider, D. (1995). Introduction to appreciative inquiry. In W. French & C. Bell (Eds.), *Organization Development,* 5th edition. New York: Prentice Hall.

Denzin, N. K. (2003). *Performance ethnography: Critical pedagogy and the politics of culture.* Thousand Oaks, CA: Sage.

Documenta, M. F. V. a. (2002). *Documenta 11-Platform5: Austellung/Exhibition Kurzfuehrer/Short Guide.*

Engestrom, Y. (1999). Activity theory and individual and social transformation. In Y. Engestrom, R. Miettinen, & R.-L. Punamaki (Eds.), *Perspectives on activity theory.* Cambridge: Cambridge University Press.

Foster, S. L. (2002). *Dances that describe themselves: The improvised choreography of Richard Bull.* Middletown, CT: Wesleyan University Press.

Freire, P. (1970). *Pedagogy of the oppressed* (M. B. Ramos, Trans. 2003 edition). New York: Continuum.

Gablik, S. (1995). Connective aesthetics: Art after individualism. In S. Lacy (Ed.), *Mapping the terrain: New genre public art.* Seattle: Bay Press.

Gablik, S. (2002). *The re-enchantment of art.* New York: Thames and Hudson.

Griffin, S. (1995). *The Eros of everyday life: Essays on ecology, gender, and society.* New York: Anchor Books.

Halprin, D. (2003). *The expressive body in life, art, and therapy: Working with movement, metaphor and meaning.* Philadelphia: Jessica Kingsley.

Halprin, L. (1969). *The RSVP cycles: Creative processes in the human environment.* New York: George Braziller.

Hershock, P. D. (1996). *Liberating intimacy: Enlightenment and social virtuosity in Ch'an Buddhism.* Albany: State University of New York Press.

Kolb. D. A., & Fry, R. (1975). Toward an applied theory of experiential learning, in C. Cooper (Ed.). *Theories of Group Process.* London: John Wiley.

Mackenzie, G. (1998). *Orbiting the giant hairball,* 1st edition. New York: Viking.

Markova, D. (1996). *Open mind: Exploring the six patterns of natural intelligence.* Berkeley: Conari Press.

Martin, R. (1998). Dancing the dialectic of agency and history. In *Critical moves: Dance studies in theory and politics,* pp. 29–53. London: Duke University Press.

Mattare, M., Seashore, C., Shawver, M. N., & Thompson, G. (2004). Doing good by knowing who you are: The instrumental self as an agent of change. *OD Practitioner* (Fall).

McLaren, P. (1988). Schooling the postmodern body: Critical pedagogy and the politics of enfleshment. In H. Giroux (Ed.), *Postmodernism, feminism, and cultural politics,* pp. 144–173. Albany: State University of New York Press.

Mezirow, J. (1990). How critical reflection triggers learning. In J. Mezirow & Associates (Eds.), *Fostering critical education in adulthood: A guide to transformative and emancipatory learning,* pp. 1–20. San Francisco: Jossey-Bass.

Mezirow, J. (1991). *Transformative dimensions of adult learning.* San Francisco: Jossey-Bass.

Orr, D. W. (1994). *Earth in mind: On education, environment and the human prospect.* Covelo, CA: Island Press.

Palmer, P. (1993). *To know as we are known.* San Francisco: Harper.

Park, P. (2001). Knowledge and participatory research. In H. Bradbury & P. Reason (Eds.), *Handbook of Action Research: Participative inquiry and practice.* Thousand Oaks, CA: Sage.

Park, P. (2004). Foreword. In *Freire, P. Letters to Christina,* Korean edition.

Park, P., Brydon-Miller, M., Hall, B., & Jackson, T. (Eds.) (1993). *Voices of change: Participatory research in the United States and Canada.*

Petranker, J. (Ed.) (1998). *The light of Knowledge: Essays on the interplay of knowledge, time and space.* Berkeley: Dharma Publishing.

Polyani, M. (1983). *The tacit dimension.* Gloucester, Mass.: Peter Smith.

Reason, P., & Bradbury, H. (Eds.) (2001). *Handbook of action research: Participative inquiry and practice.* Thousand Oaks, CA: Sage.

Seashore, C., Curran, K., & Welp, M. (1995). *Use of Self as an instrument of change.* Paper presented at the Organization Development Network conference, Seattle.

Seashore, E. (2006). Awareness Choice Matrix, pp. AU/NTL Use of Self course. Bethel, Maine.

Sewall, L. (1999). *Sight and sensibility: The eco-psychology of perception.* New York: Jeremy Tarcher.

Shapiro, S. B. (2002). The body: The site of common humanity. In S. B. Shapiro & S. Shapiro (Eds.), *Body Movements: Pedagogy, Politics and Social Change,* pp. 337–352. Cresskill, NJ: Hampton Press.

Shotter, J. (1994). *Conversational realities: From within persons to within relationships.* Paper presented at the Discursive Construction of Knowledge Conference.

Shotter, J. (2000). Seeing historically: Goethe and Vygotsky's 'enabling theory-method'. *Culture and Psychology, 6*(2), 233–252.

Shotter, J. (2002). *Cartesian change, chiasmic change: The power of living expression.* Paper presented at the Second International Conference on the Dialogical Self: Meaning as Movement, Gent.

Shotter, J. (2003). The intellectual legitimacy of participatory action research: Its grounding in 'the interactive moment.' *Human Systems, 14* (http://pubpages.unh.edu/~jds/ActionRes.htm), 1–22.

Shotter, J. (2004). *The embodied practitioner: Toward dialogic-descriptive accounts of social accounts of social practices.* Paper presented at the seminar series: The Role of the Social Sciences Today.

Touraine, A. (2000). *Can we live together?* Stanford: Stanford University Press.

Tulku, T. (1979). *Time, space, and knowledge.* Berkeley: Dharma Publishing.

Varela, F. (1999). *Ethical know-how: Action, wisdom, and cognition.* Stanford: Stanford University Press.

von Emmel, T. (2005). *Somatic performance: Relational practices and knowledge activism of bodies improvising.* Unpublished dissertation, Fielding Graduate Institute, Santa Barbara, CA.

von Emmel, T., & Seashore, C. (2003). *Improvisation lab: Sustainability as a use of self practice.* Paper presented at the Sustainable Organizations: Organization Development Network conference, Portland, Oregon.

Vygotsky, L. S. (1978). *Mind in society.* Cambridge, MA: Harvard University Press.

Zaporah, R. (1995). *Action Theater: The Improvisation of presence*: Berkeley, CA: North Atlantic Books.

# Chapter 13

---

## Black Mama Sauce: Embodied Transformative Education

*Hameed (Herukhuti) S. Williams*

Speaking from a Western framework of reality, it was 21 years ago that I started my journey to recognize, understand, and internalize the transformative educational praxis and paradigm that I have named Black Mama Sauce. From an Afrocentric and non-Western informed ontology, this relationship between Black Mama Sauce and I started before my birth when my spirit made the decision to enter into the earthly plane as a physical being. I am highlighting this dual reality of Afrocentric (non-Western) and Western (U.S.-based) to underscore the dual consciousness from which I write, theorize, and work as a scholar-practitioner. It is from this perspective that this chapter on embodied transformative education has been authored. In what follows, I use a combination of narrative and commentary to illustrate Black Mama Sauce as a transformative educational praxis and paradigm. Before the illustration, I begin with this conceptual and theoretical introduction of Black Mama Sauce.

### The Roots of My Practice

At the level of the conceptual, Black Mama Sauce was born of struggle for freedom, liberation, justice, and equality. I am neither its creator nor its owner. Black Mama Sauce is a product of the work of many cultural workers, activists, community organizers, and revolutionaries who have literally and ideologically devoted their lives to social justice. In the summer of 1964, the Student Non-violent Coordinating Committee (SNCC), with the support of others, created Freedom Schools to "develop the idea of alternative education . . . young people in Mississippi [having] a forum in which they could really think through and discuss problems which were really important for them." The Freedom Schools were a part of a larger project to transform the interior and exterior worlds of the citizens of Mississippi. Conceiving education as a process of empowerment, SNCC developed a curriculum that was informed by a sociopolitical analysis of society and the structures of oppression that were propped up in U.S. society (Moses, 1990, p. 194; Rachal, 2000).

Several years later, the Black Panther Party for Self-Defense (BPP) was formed to, in part, "raise the consciousness of the people and motivate them to move more firmly for their total liberation." Though it contrasted with the nonviolent ethos with which SNCC was founded, adding militancy to their educational process, BPP held that its main function was "to awaken the people and teach them the strategic method of [resistance]" (Newton, 2002a, p. 209).

The "leading" Western-centric (United States, Canada, western Europe) theorists of transformative education have not referenced this tradition of transformative education and, therefore, they cannot be used in articulating a theoretical basis for this, a radical and revolutionary form of transformative education concerned with the struggle for freedom, liberation, justice, and equality. At the level of the theoretical, Black Mama Sauce can be understood through the lenses of Black feminist thought and decolonizing queer theory (Cranton, 1994; Mezirow, 1978a, b, 1989; O'Sullivan, 2004a, b).

Within this theoretical matrix, struggle and resistance are necessarily embodied/spiritual/erotic. Embodiment in the context of Black Mama Sauce is twofold. In part, it is the primacy of conscious action, the engagement of liberatory activity in the world in an effort to transform the material and social realities of the oppressed and the privileged and to learn what liberation means in the process. Black Mama Sauce as transformative education addresses the same concern articulated by Newton (2002c), "to lift the level of consciousness of the people through theory and practice to the point where they will see exactly what is controlling them and what is oppressing them, and therefore see exactly what has to be done—or at least what the first step is." As such, theory becomes both a process and a product of the process (Newton, 2002c, p. 191). Christian (1990) explained:

> For people of color have always theorized—but in forms quite different from the Western form of abstract logic. And I am inclined to say that our theorizing (and I intentionally use the verb rather than the noun) is often in narrative forms, in stories we create, in riddles and proverbs, in the play with language, since dynamic rather than fixed ideas seem more to our liking. How else have we managed to survive with such spiritedness the assault on our bodies, social institutions, countries, our very humanity? (p. 336)

Not all theory or theorizing is liberatory, nor all transformative education theory, but rather, as hooks suggested, "theory is not inherently healing, liberatory, or revolutionary. It fulfills this function only when we ask that it do so and direct our theorizing towards this end" (p. 61). Theory and theorizing does have a necessary role in liberatory struggle and is, as hooks (1994) maintained, "a necessary practice within a holistic framework of liberatory activism" (hooks, 1994, p. 69).

Embodiment within Black Mama Sauce also refers to the integrated understanding of the mind-body-soul in the process of liberatory transformation. Black feminist thought (e.g., the work of Audre Lorde) and decolonizing queer theory (e.g., the work of Ibrahim Abdurrahman Farajaje aka Elias Farajaje-Jones) are particularly useful in this regard. Lorde (1992) offered "the erotic as power" as a powerful theory of mind-body-soul working in unison to achieve liberation and to engage in liberatory struggle. Lorde uses the erotic to fashion a theory of transformative action powered by "those physical, emotional, and psychic expressions of what is deepest and strongest and richest within each of us, being shared: the passion of love, in its deepest meanings" (p. 80). For Lorde, "Our erotic knowledge empowers us, becomes a lens through which we scrutinize all aspects of our existence, forcing meaning within our lives" (p. 81). Farajaje-Jones took up where Lorde left off and extended the discourse into the language of decolonization that "begins with the physical/spiritual/psychological process of making our bodies and our desires our own" (Lorde, 1992, p. 83; Farajaje-Jones, 2000).

At the level of methodology, my particular practice of Black Mama Sauce is rooted in Afrocentricity and education for critical consciousness. Afrocentricity centers African cultural resources in the selection of methodological tools. Myers identified two methodological tools deployed in African epistemology: symbolic imagery and rhythm. Using these tools, Africans, from antiquity to the present, have explored self-knowledge as a basis for all knowledge. In other words, at the heart of traditional African educational systems and epistemological activities is the development of the learner's critical self-consciousness, and it is through that consciousness of self, it has been believed, that one becomes conscious of the world outside of the self (Bynum, 1999; Hilliard, 1998; Myers, 1993).

In the contemporary context, the work of Paulo Freire, Brazilian educator and educational theorist, reflects the effort to educate for critical consciousness. With the mutual goal of teaching adults how to read and how to exercise liberatory practice in their world, Freire developed an educational methodology that utilized the lived experiences of learners to both name and analyze the social world. This form of education Freire called conscientização or education for critical consciousness. Augusto Boal, Brazilian theatrical director and theorist, has extended Freire's work by using theatre games, exercises, and other theatrical techniques to not only assist people in name and analyze their social world but to also develop strategies to make changes that they feel reflect social justice. Boal's work has been culled under the name Theatre of the Oppressed (TO). I have been particularly drawn to TO because of the space it provides for embodiment and the erotic (Freire, 1997; Boal, 1979, 1992, 1998a, b).

There are, at the time of this publication, four forms of TO widely recognized in the TO community: Invisible Theatre, Image Theatre, Forum Theatre, and Legislative Theatre. Invisible Theatre involves the presentation of a scripted play based upon social issues in the real social environment of the community and in a manner such that members of the community are not aware that the action is a part of a theatrical play; the members of the community believe what is happening is real and, therefore, they respond authentically, thereby becoming part of the play. The script of the play is designed to raise consciousness around the specific social issues that are the themes of the play. Usually, these performances are scripted and rehearsed with "co-conspirator" members of the community both to create a meaningful and relevant play and to prepare for likely responses of members of the community (Boal, 1998a, pp. 121–124).

Image Theatre is the foundational form for the other forms of TO. Image Theatre is the use of the body to construct forms and images of reality that may be used to discuss and critique social reality. The approach to the body in Image Theatre is in itself liberatory; the body is liberated from unconscious movement, routine movement resulting from socioeconomic exploitation and from the reduction of the body into an automaton.

Forum Theatre is a method of analysis and strategic planning. Forum, as it is commonly called, begins with a script that depicts a person experiencing an oppressive situation that is common to the members of the community who are in attendance. The play is performed once to allow members of the community to see the oppression take place. The Joker entices and challenges members of the community to come up with alternative responses to the oppressive situation that the protagonist might employ. As alternatives are suggested, the Joker encourages and challenges those offering the alternatives to actually set into the role of the protagonist and attempt their alternatives as the play repeats with the other characters seeking the same conclusion as was presented in the first performance—the persistence of oppression. As the members of the audience, one at a time, attempt their alternatives, they are supported and offered opportunities to think out loud with the rest of the members of the community about the results of their alternative actions. Forum Theatre is a rehearsal for life; people try out strategies to issues that have real meaning in their lives in a "forum" that is relatively safe. The community gains greater insight into the issues as well as greater awareness of the options and choices available. Forum is a collaborative problem-solving, strategic-planning method.

Legislative Theatre is the legislative application of Image Theatre and Forum Theatre. In 1993, Boal became a *vereador* (legislator) in the municipal government of Rio de Janeiro. Through the use of Forum Theatre, Boal, his TO collective, the Centre of the Theatre of the Oppressed (CTO), and Workers Party of Rio de Janeiro worked in partnership with citizens of Rio to formulate municipal laws. This collaboration was responsible for the successful passage of 13 municipal laws.

Now that the conceptual and theoretical stage has been set, I turn the focus onto my experiences as a scholar-practitioner, transformative educator, and social justice cultural worker (Boal, 1998b).

## Narrative of My Practice

### Los Angeles, California, Students of Color

My first exercise of Black Mama Sauce occurred while I was attending the University of Southern California (USC). Being Black and working class at USC was challenging. The university had very little understanding of the cultural and intellectual needs of Black, working-class folks, especially of those with the cultural and political education that I had. Although I felt a sense of loneliness and isolation there, I did not immediately realize how many others were feeling similarly.

Spirit and ancestors organized the situation to allow me to organize a gathering of Black male students for Black History Month on the campus. The initial gathering of 30 Black male students was the genesis for a group that later became the Brotherhood of African men, a recognized student organization that organized support groups and cultural/political education classes at USC from 1990 to 1994. During that time, we became one of the most active groups on the campus addressing the interior world of our members while also advancing a social justice politics on the campus.

What were we doing? We were creating space for the examination of our lives, the critical analysis of our social world; at the same time, we were creating space for us to love each other. Yes, Black men loving each other. Through our listening to each other without giving advice, sharing our stories without needing to justify or explain, we created erotic connection with each other.

The experience is still with me as I write these words. It was wonderful and it was always scary. It was always scary because many of us had never experienced such deep connection with other men. The experience provided many of us with an embodied knowledge of being in community with other men, sharing the erotic with other men. The power of that experience, how quickly it was created, and the depth of its reach made the beginning of each of our sessions fill with expectation, warmth, and hope.

Our processes were simple. The support group design we used was called the Four-Part Meeting. It was designed by an organization called Network in the Schools. The support group consisted of personal affirmations, personal self-critique, action planning, and a moment of silence. In addition to the support groups, we held weekly full-day sessions on Saturdays that included Tai Chi Chuan and hatha yoga practice and political and cultural education.

The work we were doing on ourselves drove our social justice work on campus and in the local communities outside of the university walls. We organized the election of six Black students to the 18-member student senate, the undergraduate student government that controlled a budget of $1 million annually. We halted an attempt by the university to reconfigure student of color services on campus, an action that was attempted without student input. We organized a mentorship/educational program in one of the housing projects in Watts, a Black, working-class neighborhood of Los Angeles. We brought a brother from the community into our organization as he transitioned out of a gang.

As the organization grew, Black women on campus became interested in what we were doing and the Sisterhood of African Women was formed. Eventually our success was our undoing. The more successful we were, the more threatening we appeared to the agents of the status quo. We began to feel pressure coming from various aspects of the university community. As we became more successful in creating a thoughtful, unified, and effective cadre of people founded upon the values of Black Pride and Black Power, we—many of us in our late teens and early twenties—felt overwhelmed by the responsibilities of maintaining a counterhegemonic community inside of such a huge bureaucracy, one that held our degree completion objectives within its purview. Ultimately, we disbanded the organizations in an effort to make it safer for all of us involved to "graduate without incident."

### Newark, New Jersey, Elementary School Teachers

One of my very first experiences using TO as a consultant was working as a staff developer for the peace and diversity school reform program, Resolving Conflict Creatively Program (RCCP). I was assigned to an elementary school in Newark, New Jersey. The school was located in a low-income Black neighborhood. Based upon my estimation, over 90% of the students were of African ancestry. The majority of the teachers were of African ancestry and female.

The school had been included in the RCCP reform program by the local school district. At the same time, the school was under mandate to participate in another school reform focused more specifically on academic performance. This was a school community under significant pressure both from within and without. There were the economic pressures that the students and their families faced. These pressures the students brought to school with them and were evidenced in student behavior and academic performance. The teachers too faced economic pressures both personal and professional. The teachers received low pay and very little funds for school supplies.

There were also enormous pressures from the district to generate high academic performance with little funding to support such efforts. The teachers faced psychosocial and socioeconomic obstacles to which they were ill prepared to respond. Teachers, staff, parents, and students were all well meaning and good natured. But they were set in an unfair, disadvantaged position. There were various ways they responded to their circumstances. Some sought to put blinders on and set out to do what they needed to do to be as personally successful as they could, given the circumstances. Others chose to fall in line with the expectations placed on them and, therefore, stayed out of trouble. Still others chose to be resistant, to be "trouble makers." And there were some who chose to internalize the negative messages they were receiving in the system and, therefore, disappeared. I should say here that the ways that people responded in the situation were a bit more complex than I just stated. Some people used a number of approaches depending upon the specific situation rather than relying on any one particular approach. But the approaches I've identified above were present and prevalent.

I was assigned to a group of teachers who were a combination of those who volunteered for the program and those who were "volunteered" by the principal for various reasons. Being the kind of person I am—more committed to creating socially just environments than maintaining fidelity to a prescribed curriculum—I subversively deviated from the standard staff development formula designed by RCCP because I felt that the spirit of RCCP, peace and diversity reform in schools, would be better served by doing something beyond the standard intervention. I formed a regular support group meeting with the group of teachers. We met for approximately two hours each time the group gathered. Please note the significance. In many public schools, particularly in low-income communities, achieving a meeting of seven to eight teachers for two hours to support each other is unheard of. *It just doesn't happen*. It was in this group context that I introduced the group to TO—I didn't call it TO; in fact, I didn't tell them I was doing anything outside of the context of the standard RCCP formula—the Joker enters the room carrying Black Mama Sauce.

The TO method I used with the group was Image Theatre. In one of the sessions, I had the group divide into several smaller groups and construct images of their school community using their bodies. Each member of the small groups got to construct an image using himself/herself and the other members of his/her small group. This was an application of the Image Theatre technique, Image of the Images. I should say that the majority of the teachers in the group were female and of African ancestry. There was one man and two women of European ancestry. I believe most of the group was 40 or over although I never inquired about their ages (Boal, 1995, pp. 77–87).

The Image Theatre technique had a profound effect on the teachers as demonstrated by the group discussion that followed as well as my one-to-one conversations with them on later occasions. Blank faces transformed into smiles, nods, and meaningful gazes. The technique allowed the group to develop an understanding of the collective nature of their personal experiences. "Yes, that's the problem." "I feel the same way." "It's not until we sit down and talk that we realize we're not alone in this." They began to link their individual frustrations to a larger structural dynamic that fostered a general feeling of anxiety, alienation, and isolation.

For many in the group, their teaching practice changed. They began to teach without fear. Many in the group developed a sense of resolution that allowed them to manage the realities of their environment and feel more empowered. "I can only do what I can do and I have to be satisfied with that." The space of Black Mama Sauce introduced the members of the group to the concept of "breathing room." Breathing room is a term I use for the space that we can create for ourselves in environments of oppression—spaces that allow us time to connect with our needs and ourselves. If we don't breathe, we stop a vital contribution we make to the rhythm of universe. If we don't breathe, we pass on. Systems of oppression employ a mechanism that keeps us constantly gasping for air, never quite fully inhaling or exhaling. This mechanism assists in the maintenance of our disempowerment. The members of the group became more aware of how and when to create breathing room for themselves.

## Worcester, Massachusetts, Undergraduate Students of Color

For four years, I had the pleasure of working with a minority affairs office at a prestigious technical college in Massachusetts. The majority of the student population at the school was of European ancestry and male. Every summer, the minority affairs office at the school organized a two-week orientation program for incoming students of color. My portion (usually the first week) of the orientation program was designed as a forum for the exploration of personal and social identity. We covered themes related to race/culture, gender, class, and sexual orientation. The objective of the program was to offer a holistic, systematic treatment of the themes in a way that provided for self-reflection on the part of the participants as well as for a rich sociopolitical analysis of power and the ways it plays out in educational settings. It was our hope that, through this experience, students would be more able to effectively navigate the European-dominant, male-dominant culture of the college though the development of tools of observation, meaning making, synthesis, analysis, and self-examination.

The first year, I worked as a lone consultant. The following years, I worked with a Latina colleague. Over the years we experimented with uses from our original arsenal while also using methodologies and forms with which we were familiar from other contexts outside of TO. In my first year with the group, the majority of the tools I used, including warm-up and cool-down activities, were from the arsenal. I used Image Theatre mostly. In subsequent years, we used Forum Theatre to help students rehearse scenarios that were volunteered by the returning students from their personal experiences on the campus.

We experimented with the inclusion of Afrocentric ritual experience in the process to allow a deeper, richer experience to unfold for the group. Out of respect for the sacredness of such practices, I will not detail them here. But there are a few things that should be said. The ritual experiences created an out-of-the-regular-world experience that we all felt. These experiences bonded us to the process and to each other. The experiences were not religious—there was no mention of God. What we did in these times was to honor the sacredness of our lives and all life, of our humanity and all humanity. We created a context for us to touch, share, and partake in Black Mama Sauce.

The response from the students was profound. Year after year, students achieved a level of sophistication in their ability to observe, make meaning, synthesize, analyze, and self-examine that was very moving to witness. We challenged the students to apply a critical lens to their interactions as a vehicle for perceiving the larger structures and systems in schools and in society. Male students were challenged to examine the impact of male privilege and sexism within a social justice framework. Heterosexual students were challenged to examine the impact of heterosexual privilege and heterosexism within a social justice framework. Students were challenged to examine White supremacy and racial prejudice within a social justice framework. They responded with tenacity.

During the academic years following the orientation program, students acted to name and challenge structures, policies, and procedures of the institution that they deemed White supremacist, sexist, and/or heterosexist. Although inundated with work indicative of an applied science and technology college with very little in the way of social science studies or liberal arts studies, students found ways to organize and cultivate sources of support, strength, and resistance. My colleague and I were invited to facilitate annual leadership retreats for the group to aid them in their strategic planning.

In our fourth year, the original director of the minority affairs office resigned her position to pursue a doctorate and a more supportive environment in which to develop as a professional. In the wake of her resignation, the institution sought to redirect the program. My colleague and I were branded as troublemakers. We completed the orientation program under much pressure and stress. We were not expecting to come back to facilitate the annual leadership retreat for the students. The students were told as much by the student affairs administrators with whom the decision rested. We were blamed for the students being isolated/alienated from the larger campus community. Our position, and the position of the students, was that to the degree the students were isolated and alienated from the largely White male campus community, it was largely due to the institutional structures, culture, and processes that promoted and enforced White heterosexual male supremacy and European cultural hegemony.

Of course, our position did not have an effect on the decision making of the administrators "in charge." But the students made *their* decision making irrelevant. They planned to hold a leadership retreat independent of the institution in an off-campus venue and hired my colleague and me to facilitate the retreat. It was a potent moment in the development of the sociopolitical lives of these students. They had acted upon their synthesis of their individual experiences in the orientation program to act out of their own sense of empowerment and their collective critique of the system in which they existed.

### Princeton, New Jersey, Activist Youth

In 1999, I was elected to co-chair the board of Global Youth Connect (GYC), an international youth organization focused on human rights. GYC was a small organization with one full-time staff member. One of the projects we were committed to accomplishing was the Human Rights Learning Community (HRLC) for youth activists. In July of 2000, 13 youth activists from eight countries around the world (Bhutan, Democratic Republic of Congo, Jamaica, Kenya, Nepal, Nigeria, Northern Ireland, and Ukraine) came to the HRLC in Princeton, New Jersey.

Because we had limited staff and limited funds, I oversaw the hiring of the staff for the learning community and trained them using TO; I also worked as the onsite staff supervisor. The learning community staff was responsible for creating and implementing the curricula for the learning community. For my portion of the curricula, I worked with two other members of the staff (a Ghanaian-born woman and an Italian-American man) to create a workshop we called "What Are We Calling This? What Are We Gonna Do about It?" The methodology of the workshop was TO. The purpose of the workshop was to provide the participants with the opportunity to see the connections that existed between the various aspects of oppression that they experienced, to formulate a model of the international system of oppression, and to develop plans of action based upon their understanding of their shared experiences, the unique aspects of the oppression that they confronted, and the model of the international system of oppression that we constructed.

Having worked in virtual isolation, the youth activists were able to open conceptual doors that were previously closed. The workshop began the process of the youth activists recognizing that not only were they not alone but also their struggles for human rights were linked to a global struggle against the tyranny of the international system of oppression. The workshop allowed them to see the ways in which multinational corporations, organizations such as the International Monetary Fund and the World Bank, and various other players work in unison to create an international system of oppression. The youth activists also determined how their individual work contributed to a global effort for peace and justice. They used their conclusions to plan future work.

Although TO was used in various contexts throughout the learning community, this workshop, which occurred early in the program schedule, was significant in laying the foundation for what would occur later in the schedule. In addition to TO, we also utilized ritual in the learning community. Drawing upon Native American and African traditions, we incorporated ritual as a way to bring the community together, to celebrate life, and to bring our collective consciousness to those who had come before us. The member of the staff who initiated the rituals, the Ghanaian woman, did not refer to a specific deity and left room for any of us to bring our particular deities into the ritual space. For many of these rituals, I played djembe, a traditional African drum. The rhythms I chose were those that were taught to me in the Khemetic (ancient Egyptian) priesthood. Rituals allowed us to draw upon many more aspects of ourselves to learn in the HRLC.

The long-term impact of the HRLC on the participants is something I do not know. I eventually resigned from the board and lost contact with most of the HRLC participants. As for those I am in contact with, they continue to do their work and to employ much of what they learned at the HRLC. For me the true impact of the experience is not something that can be measured. The transformative learning model that we used was meant to provide a holistic effect. There is no measure for assessing the impact of what took place those 10 days and yet I know we were all forever changed by those 10 days.

## Harlem, New York, Adherence Research Subjects

Based upon a contract secured by a woman colleague of African ancestry, she and I worked on an ancillary portion of a research project in Harlem, New York. The project was designed to understand the barriers to adherence to treatment by individuals diagnosed HIV+. The research population consisted of people of color, most of whom came from working-class or poor working-class backgrounds, some of whom were former IV drug users. My colleague was contacted to work with the social work division of the research project. That division was having difficulty with getting research participants to come to group therapy sessions and other sessions provided through the division. The supervising social worker felt that TO could be a worthwhile addition. My colleague brought me in to help her on the project.

Because of the politics of the project, there were a few issues that we had to deal with in the beginning. We could not use the phrase Theatre of the Oppressed. The supervising social worker thought the title would be too intimidating to the principal investigators. Because our contribution was a part of the original research project design, the resources that were allocated to compensate us and acquire space for our work were extremely limited. There were times we were working in spaces not conducive to the work. I remember one time I got into an argument with a workman who barged right into our group during a session and refused to leave because he "had a work order to complete." Then there were the alarms that went off two or three times every session. This was not the optimal working environment.

Despite the challenges, we worked to create an environment in which the participants explored their thoughts and feelings about HIV, treatment, their doctors, the medical industry, their families, and a host of other issues. The participants developed a sense of their own subjectivity. When they first entered the process, the participants talked about their experiences as objects of the processes that they had encountered. Through the TO sessions they developed a sense of subjectivity. They talked about their experiences as subjects in the world. They began to deconstruct the processes of treatment and medicalization in which they were involved. With this new consciousness, the participants were able to critique these processes. They were telling us what the barriers were to adhering to treatment. Although the principal investigators were looking for intrapersonal barriers, the participants shared with us some of the systemic barriers that existed as well as how the systemic and intrapersonal barriers interacted to form complex barriers.

Eventually, our miniproject within the larger project would be defunded after a year. We coauthored a poster presentation for the fourteenth International AIDS Conference in Barcelona, Spain. The poster presentation allowed my colleague and me to describe the actual process we employed without omitting "intimidating" language. Perhaps for the first time the terms "Theatre of the Oppressed" and "Afrocentricity" were used at this international health conference as legitimate paradigms for consideration. Although our work did not garner us any more respect from within the project, it allowed us to present our work to an international community. Our work also helped the participants to develop a sense of efficacy and subjectivity that they previously did not exercise. Both outcomes for us were worthwhile and rewarding.

## Brooklyn, New York, Black Men Who Experience Same-Sex Desire

I took all that I had learned from my previous experiences with Black Mama Sauce and integrated them into the design of my doctoral dissertation "Our Bodies, Our Wisdom." My intention was to develop a transformative education methodology that was truly consistent with Black Mama Sauce—a methodology that could be used not only in optimal conditions (where there were no externally imposed limitations) but also in situations wherein I had to be more subtle, covert about my work and aims. "Our Bodies, Our Wisdom" began as a collaborative inquiry project that I facilitated with a group of Black men who experience same-sex desire in New York City. The group met six times over the course of a year on Friday nights through Saturdays (Williams, 2006).

Friday evenings, we ate dinner, discussed the lessons from the previous session, discussed the events of our lives since the last session, and prepared for the activities of the next day. Saturday morning started with hatha yoga. After yoga, we practiced TO, focusing our inquiry on a topic of interest for the group. In these TO-based inquiry sessions, we formed our analysis and theory of the dynamics at play in the topics of interest. We would break for a communal lunch in the middle of these sessions and then come back to finish the TO work. After TO, we prepared the space for African-based spiritual ritual. Our goal during ritual was to take what we had learned during the TO session prior to each ritual and structure our ritual focus and intention, hopefully calling forth that which was needed to bring change and transformation to the situation (Williams, 2006).

The "Our Bodies, Our Wisdom" process was so successful at addressing the issues of decolonization, embodiment, and critical consciousness during the dissertation study that I committed myself to continuing to use it as an embodied, decolonizing-transformative education methodology. Outside of the artifices of a dissertation project, "Our Bodies, Our Wisdom" has been even more powerful. During the dissertation project, we practiced hatha yoga clothed. In an "Our Bodies, Our Wisdom" series that I facilitated, again with a group of

Black men who experience same-sex desire, we practiced Sensual Yoga, which is an adaptation of hatha yoga that I've developed. Sensual Yoga combines individually practiced postures with coupled and group postures, all of which are practiced in the nude. Sensual Yoga is designed to utilize the erotic energy generated from nudity and physical contact in the development of critical consciousness and intimate engagement (Williams, 2006).

"Our Bodies, Our Wisdom" is my current practice methodology for working with Black Mama Sauce. Sixteen years after my first attempts at building community, critical consciousness, and skills for liberatory struggle in groups on the campus of USC, "Our Bodies, Our Wisdom" represents a culmination of all those years of work. It is the clearest form of Black Mama Sauce practice that I have engaged. The development of "Our Bodies, Our Wisdom" represents my own transformation as a scholar-practitioner as well. I have not only integrated meaningful theories and methods in the creation of the methodology but have also integrated various aspects of my work and myself. "Our Bodies, Our Wisdom" is my contribution to Black Mama Sauce, my contribution to transformative education, my contribution to the legacy of liberatory struggle.

## Conclusions and Recommendations

Freire made a distinction between systemic education and educational projects. Freire argued that until the oppressed have the political power to control the educational system and thereby implement a systemic education for liberation, the efforts by individuals and groups within the system of oppression to implement education for liberation should be conceptualized as projects and distinguished from systemic education. Freire's distinction highlights the importance not only of the content and intent of our educational practices but also the context in which those educational practices exist. My experiences in the practice of embodied transformative education have demonstrated to me the profound truth in that distinction (Freire, 1993).

I have consistently employed a systemic, reflective approach to embodied transformative education. Black Mama Sauce has always existed in opposition to and antagonistic to the operating sociopolitical mechanisms of the systems of European supremacy and cultural hegemony. All the groups that I have worked with have been targets of European supremacy and cultural hegemony. As work (with the exception of my work with "Our Bodies, Our Wisdom ") progressed, the self-sustaining mechanisms of European supremacy and cultural hegemony were triggered to fight against that which was perceived as a threat to the survival of the system. Those who wish to use Black Mama Sauce, TO, an Afrocentric paradigm, or other forms of liberatory, nonbourgeois, non-

Eurocentric transformative educational enterprise must be mindful of the possible ways the mechanisms of self-preservation of European supremacy and cultural hegemony will act to maintain the system. Fear, money, authority, and geographic distance can all be utilized as weapons in the struggle to maintain the systems of oppression that persist. Frequently, I have been confronted with the question of how much compromise compromises the integrity of the work. Ultimately my decisions to stay on a project or amend the design of a project have been based upon the degree to which I felt I could persist in doing the work to which I was committed from the beginning.

The critical examination of the ways in which power, privilege, and disadvantage have been socially distributed based upon the social identities of race, gender, sexual identity, and class have been essential to my work. As such I cannot avoid applying that analysis to reflection upon my work. When embodied transformative education is implemented by a working-class man of African ancestry in the United States as a liberatory practice, a political problem is raised within the framework of European supremacy and cultural hegemony that my middle-class, White colleagues working on bourgeois terms are not obliged to confront in their work.

Inherently, the spirit of my work has been dangerous, revolutionary, and contrary to the interests and aims of European cultural life in its current configuration as European supremacy, cultural hegemony, and world domination. My practice of transformative education puts my life and livelihood in greater danger than does the result of being Black and male in the United States. I have had contracts dissolved because Black Mama Sauce was getting into areas that those in control of the money did not expect, intend, or desire as they were confronted by profoundly transformative work taking place. I have learned, too, often, through experience that when transformation, at the very deep structural levels of personal and collective experience, emerges, it is at that very point of transformation, spontaneous evolution, and revolution (that word that dare not speak its name in the hollowed halls of the White middle-class academy) that reactionary forces of conservatism and hypocritical liberalism seek to squash, quell, and disrupt the "liminal experiences" so often lauded in White middle-class transformative education circles.

One of the reasons for my investment in the development of "Our Bodies, Our Wisdom" was my desire to practice Black Mama Sauce in a context that was as conducive to and supportive of the work as possible. In my work up to that point, I was frustrated with the pressures and limitations of conducting projects inside of systems of oppression. "Our Bodies, Our Wisdom," as a methodology, provides the space, the breathing room, to do the kind of work that I know is necessary in the way that I have come to know is essential. That is an important lesson for transformative education practitioners. We must allow the work to transform us and to act based upon that transformation. We cannot act as if we are unaware of the structural inequalities and the social injustices that provide the context for our work.

"Our Body, Our Wisdom" enlists the body, the mind, and the spirit in their collective struggle for liberation from the systems of repression and oppression that persist. The body, mind, and spirit collaborate to interrogate social reality, to rehearse the remaking of social reality, and to act toward the transformation of social reality. Because "Our Bodies, Our Wisdom"—the closest I have come to a true practice of Black Mama Sauce—honors the power of body-mind-spirit-community in transformation, it ruptures the status quo through a political sensuality that is profane and engrossing, ritualistic and beautiful, and erotic and critical.

Black Mama Sauce is the nectar that comes from the fertile Black Madonna. Black Mama Sauce is sensual and Black. It is sexual and gendered. Black Mama Sauce is also the slave stew that Black women made to nourish their families through slavery and bondage. Black Mama Sauce is what Mississippi Blues players drank at 3 in the morning to keep playing on into the dawn. Black Mama Sauce is what freedom-fighting maroons shared with each other as they sat and had ritual around the fire. Black Mama Sauce was what initiates took to begin their rites of passage. Black Mama Sauce could be a poison or a healing elixir depending on who you were and what was within your heart.

It is with authority and honor that I position Black Mama Sauce as a contribution to transformative education. Although I present my work as an example of Black Mama Sauce, it should not be concluded that Black Mama Sauce is unique to my work. There are thousands of African people who have used Black Mama Sauce for millennia to bring about transformation and healthy development of the individual and the society. It is to all those who have gone before me to whom I owe my gratitude and my epistemological allegiance.

# References

Boal, A. (1979). *Theatre of the oppressed*. New York: Theatre Communications Group.

Boal, A. (1992). *Games for actors and non-actors*. London: Routledge.

Boal, A. (1995). *The rainbow of desire: The Boal method of theatre and therapy*. London: Routledge.

Boal, A. (1998a). Invisible theatre. In J. Cohen-Cruz (Ed.), *Radical Street Performance: An International Anthology*, pp. 121–124. London: Routledge.

Boal, A. (1998b). *Legislative theatre: Using theatre to make politics*. London: Routledge.

Bynum, E. B. (1999). *The African unconscious: Roots of ancient mysticism and modern psychology*. New York: Teachers College Press.

Christian, B. (1990). The race for theory. In G. Anzaldua (Ed.), *Making Face, Making Soul: Hacienda Caras*, pp. 334–345. San Francisco: Aunt Lute books.

Cranton, P. (1994). *Understanding and Promoting Transformative Learning*. San Francisco: Jossey-Bass Inc.

Farajaje-Jones, E. (2000). Holy fuck. In K. Kay, J. Nagle, & B. Gould (Eds.), *Male Lust: Pleasure, Power, and Transformation*, pp. 327–335. New York: Harrington Park Press.

Freire, P. (1993). *Pedagogy of the oppressed*, 20th anniversary edition. New York: Continuum.

Freire, P. (1997). *Education for critical consciousness*. New York: Continuum.

Hilliard, A. G. (1998). *Sba: The awakening of the African mind*. Gainesville, Florida: Makare Publishing.

hooks, b. (1994). *Teaching to transgress: Education as the practice of freedom*. New York: Routledge.

Lorde, A. (1992). Uses of the erotic: The erotic as power. In M. Decosta-Willis, R. Martin, & R. P. Bell (Eds.), *Erotique Noire: Black Erotica*, pp. 78–83. New York: Anchor Books/Doubleday.

Mezirow, J. (1978a). *Education for perspective transformation: Women's re-entry programs in community colleges*. New York: Teachers College, Columbia University.

Mezirow, J. (1978b). Perspective transformation. *Adult Education* 28, 100–110.

Mezirow, J. (1989). Transformation theory and social action: A response to Collard and Law. *Adult Education Quarterly, 39*(3), 169–175.

Moses, R. (1990). Bob Moses. In H. Hampton & S. Fayer (Eds.), *Voices of freedom: An oral history of the Civil Rights Movement from the 1950s through the 1980s*, p. 194. New York: Bantam Books.

Myers, L. J. (1993). *Understanding an Afrocentric worldview: Introduction to an optimal psychology*, 2nd edition. Dubuque, Iowa: Kendall/Hunt Publishing Company.

Newton, H. P. (2002a). Statement: May 1, 1971. In D. Hilliard & D. Weise (Eds.), *The Huey P. Newton Reader.* New York: Seven Stories Press.

Newton, H. P. (2002b). The correct handling of a revolution: July 20, 1967. In D. Hilliard & D. Weise (Eds.), *The Huey P. Newton Reader.* New York: Seven Stories Press.

Newton, H. P. (2002c). Intercommunalism: February 1971. In D. Hilliard & D. Weise (Eds.), *The Huey P. Newton Reader,* pp. 181–199. New York: Seven Stories Press.

O'Sullivan, E. (2004a). Education and transformative learning: The need to choose between global visions. http://tlc.oise.utoronto.ca/insights/education.html

O'Sullivan, E. (2004b). Integral education: A vision of transformative learning in a planetary context. http://tlc.oise.utoronto.ca/insights/integraleducation.html

Rachal, J. R. (2000). We'll never turn back: Adult education and the struggle for citizenship in Mississippi's freedom summer. *Adult Education Quarterly, 50*(3), 166–196.

Williams, H. S. (2006). Our bodies, our wisdom: Engaging Black men who experience same-sex desire in Afrocentric ritual, embodied epistemology, and collaborative inquiry. *Dissertation Abstracts International, 67.*

# Section 3 Summary

## Animating Awareness Through the Expressive and Performative Arts

*Beth Fisher-Yoshida*

The unique contribution the authors of this section's chapters make is to explore fostering transformative learning in ways that are extrarational. The field of transformative learning has been noted as having a more developed cognitive, rational approach. More recently, scholars and practitioners have identified the need for other ways of understanding and fostering transformations when considering that we are more than just our minds and have human processes that are more than just cognitive.

The contributors in this section take a holistic approach: mind, body, spirit, and emotion/feeling. They use physical activities that engage the body as in dance, tai chi, yoga, theater, and meditation. They address emotions and feelings through reflective processes that can be individual mindfulness, journaling, or group dialogues. They focus on ways to become more attuned to their spiritual development through meditation, storytelling, and ritual practices and by stimulating liminal states that allow participants to engage their unconscious or spiritual mind.

The differences in their approaches are in the techniques they use to support transformative learning focusing on several levels of intervention with individual change being at the core as it stimulates larger-scale social changes to raise consciousness, be rid of oppression, and foster deeper understanding across cultures and develops ways in which humans can sustain themselves and the planet. We will address the five themes that were present in their methods, touching on the points they considered important and that generated their beliefs that influenced their approaches. All four authors were very clear that their role and the (1) *use of self* in their work were critical; (2) they talked about transformation coming from *relationship and sense of connectedness*; (3) their approaches and methods had *steps or stages* that were critical to follow; (4) they used a *multisensory* or *multimodal* approach; and (5) they took people *out of their everyday experiences to other spaces of being*.

The contributors are all educators or practitioners, who work with others. In their role as facilitators of transformation, they are an integral part of the process and, therefore, a critical *use of self* is a key part of the work they do. Annabelle Nelson, in her chapter, *Storytelling and Transformational Learning*, talks about the role of storytelling as a way of developing identity and cultural affiliation and emphasizes that the role of the storyteller is critical. "Storytelling communicates from the heart of the storyteller to the heart of the listener," not only communicating the story but also showing empathy and being a guide, thus making it so impactful for the listener. In *Bodymindfulness for Skillful Use of Self*, Adair Nagata's approach was developed to address intercultural communication and the power of nonverbal communication from her own experiences communicating across cultures. "We need to be mindful that we use our whole self when we communicate." We have a much larger impact on others with more than just the spoken word. Tiffany von Emmel in *Dreamscape: A Multimedia Collaboration Method* states that, "'use of self' refers to how the practitioner consciously acts in a relationship in order to facilitate growth and development." The practitioner makes choices throughout the interaction to foster ways in which she can help increase awareness for the participants to have transformative learning experiences. In *Black Mama Sauce: Embodied Transformative Education*, Hameed (Herukhuti) S. Williams says, "I subversively deviated from the standard staff development formula designed by RCCP because I felt that the spirit of RCCP, peace and diversity reform in schools, would be better served by doing something beyond the standard intervention." He took a risk in challenging what was prescribed and went with what he sensed the participants would find more beneficial.

The second theme in common is how *transformation takes place in relationship and connectedness*. In the context of the indigenous roots of storytelling, Nelson describes the spiritual connectedness with community and nature. There is a belief in the reciprocity between people, nature, other living forms around them, the cosmos and the give and take that exists. Nagata talks about the relationship that is fostered amongst people through intercultural communication done holistically, with body, mind, spirit, and emotion/feeling. She focuses on nonverbal communication and what she terms "intuitive inspirations" that connect us to "larger frames of meaning." Von Emmel refers to building community and to the idea that "relationship is the ground of *Interactivism*" and "*Connect*, the foundation of improvisation," this idea is the first dimension in the interactivist model in which opening the heart and relaxing into the feeling sensation is key. Williams points out that through the *Image Theater* technique of the *Theater of the Oppressed*, the participants discovered that their individual frustrations were shared with others. "The technique allowed the group to develop an understanding of the collective nature of their personal experiences," and for many this resulted in a sense of resolution and empowerment.

*Steps or stages*, the third theme, was common to the approaches highlighted in this section. In Nelson's storytelling, there were stages of the hero's journey. These stages were normal life, separation, tests of character, and the return home. Each stage was critical to complete before the next stage could take place effectively. In Nagata's bodymindfulness approach, there are steps to the practice: being present in the moment, tune into your breathing, breathe more deeply and evenly, set your intention, and use all the elements of bodymindfulness to "Be here now!" Von Emmel's *Dreamscape* has five phases: create the environment, use interaction tools and costumes, interactivism, community finale, and digital engagement. Each phase has different techniques open to the participants to select how they want to engage. Williams mentions a *"Four-Part Meeting"* used effectively with a particular support group. These steps are personal affirmations, personal self-critique, action planning, and a moment of silence. This personal growth work spreads from the individual to the larger community.

The fourth theme highlights the unique contributions of this section and that is a *multisensory/multimodal approach to transformative education and learning*. All of the contributors discuss the mind, body, emotion/feeling, and spirit levels of engagement in holistically addressing the person, group, and community. Nelson discusses the storytelling connection between storyteller, listener, and hero of the story. There are challenges to the mental, physical, emotional, and spiritual well-being of the hero, challenges that lead to his transformation. This is a metaphor for the same challenges the listener experiences through connecting with the hero. Nagata adapted Jung's Quaternity Model of human development in constructing bodymindfulness in herself and others. The center of the circle is *being*, surrounded in four directions by *spirit, mind, body* and *emotion/feeling*, which are situated in the context of *consciousness*. Awareness of all elements is critical in developing bodymindfulness. The performative turn as compared to the linguistic turn is what von Emmel refers to in her work with *Dreamscape*. The five phases in Dreamscape use multimedia approaches, such as auditory recordings, creation of visual objects, kinesthetic activities as dance and performance, and the creation of digital artifacts. These assorted media stimulate different ways of knowing so that a holistic engagement of mind, body, spirit, and emotion/feeling is enjoyed. Williams situates *Black Mama Sauce* as an embodied, decolonizing tradition of transformative education. "Embodiment within Black Mama Sauce also refers to the integrated understanding of the mind-body-soul in the process of liberatory transformation," shifting from embodied systemic oppression to a transformation of what is being embodied.

The fifth theme that was apparent in this section addressed the *liminal* or *out-of-everyday experiences* that permitted transformative learning. The contributors supported the participants' need to be free of the cognitive frames that were trapping them. Nelson stated that "storytelling promotes spiritual development through metaphoric knowledge and expanded intelligence, allowing intuition in the unconscious to be active in conscious awareness. . . . Therefore, through storytelling, a person can experience an expanded intelligence allowing the possibility of spiritual insight." This fuels transformation. Nagata in reference to bodymindfulness says, "Attention to and care for our bodymind affects our internal state" and state is a source of influence on our interpersonal behavior and relationships. Von Emmel refers to Vygotsky's zone of proximal development when she says that "Liminality can frame a zone for new behavior." Dreamscape was designed to be attentive to the margins of the space the participants inhabited—such as the beginnings, endings, early morning and twilight hours, and the transitions between activities—in which interactivists can stimulate transformative moments. Williams discusses a Black men's group he helped form and how in that space they were "creating space for the examination of our lives, the critical analysis of our social world; at the same time, we were creating space for us to love each other." The experience was so profound "many of us had never experienced such deep connection with other men."

These approaches to transformative education and learning take our experiences to new levels as we engage the rational mind and cognitive focus with the extrarational body, spirit, and emotion/feeling.

# Chapter 14

## Conclusion: Educating for Transformative Learning

*Beth Fisher-Yoshida, Kathy D. Geller, and Steven A. Schapiro*

In the introduction, we established the purpose of this book, which is to collect and share approaches to transformative learning from those actively engaged in the field. The focus is on the practice and application of transformative learning principles to create environments that are more likely to foster transformation in the people with whom we engage. The methods go beyond the rational and use alternative processes with diverse populations. The contributors all hail from Fielding Graduate University, which, as Stephen Brookfield wrote in the foreword, is an educational institution that puts into practice the tenets of adult learning across its three schools and assorted certificate programs.

We approach transformative learning as educators and as learners, as facilitators and as guides. The contributors work in a variety of domains—higher and graduate education communities, in and with organizations—on a global scale. We understand and are committed to lifelong learning and making our social worlds, communities, and the planet better places to live. In striving for these goals of social justice, we think about and experiment with ways in which we can foster more collaboration and understanding amongst the groups with whom we work. These can be in small teams, organizations, or communities, or the whole global village, as we reach out and embrace diversity.

We believe that using a critically reflective process as a regular practice plays a key role in transformative learning. In all our interactions with others, we are part of the learning process. We use ourselves as instruments of change and are in turn changed. It is an iterative cycle that we experience and try to stimulate in others.

At the end of each section of the book, we integrated the four chapters within to draw attention to the synergies amongst the approaches under each section theme: thus creating the space for transformation, difference, and diversity and for the expressive and performative arts. In this concluding chapter, we highlight some of the interconnections amongst the three sections to deliberately synthesize and make explicit that there are many facets to transformative learning. There are seven points of synergy amongst the contributions.

First, all of the contributors take a very hands-on practical approach to their practice. At the same time, all of their practices are grounded in theory, which enriches and adds meaning to their efforts. In other words, we employ a scholar-practitioner approach, blending the best of both worlds in bringing the richness of these different worldviews to our clients and students.

A second key integration point across this book is that transformative learning may happen independently of any of our efforts as practitioners and educators. At the same time, there are occurrences that take place in which we may miss opportunities to have transformative moments. This is why it is important to highlight the criteria conducive to enabling transformative education. We can induce the situation by creating environments that allow people to learn the skills and engage in the practices that are likely to lead toward transformative learning. We also want to be able to recognize moments of dissonance that with proper support we can turn into transformative learning moments.

A third important aspect across the practices is that the whole person is engaged in the learning process. The practices highlighted in this book show many creative applications to the principles of transformative education building on what is currently in the literature, which tends to be dominated by a rational, cognitive approach. We are entering into a new phase of engagement and expansiveness in that approaches here highlight the extrarational. In creating learning spaces, we understand that people enter into learning situations at all different stages of development and emotional readiness. We take people where they are and support them in moving to where they can go, to levels that they can reach in that moment in time. In the section highlighting culture and diversity, we describe the experience difference in a variety of ways: cognitive dissonance, physical discomfort, emotional upset, and spiritual disharmony. The section on expressive and performative arts describes how the authors deliberately engage participants in activities that call on physical activity, emotional expressiveness, and spiritual connectedness.

The fourth synergistic element is the role that relationship plays. In order to foster transformative learning, we need to create a supportive environment that allows it to take place. Some of the contributors talked about relationship in the form of communication used, which they refer to as being dialogic. The parties engage with one another in an open and honest way that is respectful and possibly challenge assumptions and worldviews, which can be transformative. Cultural differences and other aspects of diversity bring forth the feelings of comfort in seeking out those who are similar to us and in managing our unease with those who are different. It is when we open ourselves up to being in relationship with others who are different that we can build transformative relationships. The performative arts may be done in relationship with others as in improvisational theater, where each performer reacts to and responds to the other performers.

The fifth element concerns the use of self by the facilitators as a key ingredient in the learning process. This element overlaps in practice with all of the others. One example of this is the facilitator taking up the role of asking a provocative question to stimulate critically reflective thinking among the participants about a certain point or interaction. The facilitator may also make a statement revealing something more sensitive and profound than what had been revealed thus far in an effort to lead the way by example toward more disclosure.

The sixth element that runs across the book concerns the learner-centered nature of the process, which is reflected in a variety of ways. All of us emphasize the importance of engaging participants in an inquiry process involving their real questions, concerns, or problems, not the transmission of a predetermined curriculum. It is such engagement that makes transformation possible. We also share a belief that participants need to share some control of the learning space and the learning process. With such control comes more investment and more opportunity for transformative action. The practice of learner-centered education is also reflected in the dictum that "culture matters" and the need to create culturally sensitive learning environments appropriate to the needs and sensibilities of the particular learners involved. In all of these respects, we can never prescribe a particular template for a transformative learning experience but must develop that experience in response to and in collaboration with a particular group of learners.

A seventh element involves the need to take people out of their regular environments and into a liminal space in which they have the time and space to relate to others and themselves in different ways. This principle is reflected in the emphasis on turning encounters with cultural difference into opportunities for different forms of dialogue and communication, in the use of such nonrational processes as improvisation, movement, and art to engage our creative energies and our subconscious needs, in the use of retreats and other offsite learning experiences, and in the recognition that transformative learning must often expand beyond the time and space of the formal educational experience.

The overall implications of this book for the field can be found in each of the chapters individually, as well as in the themes and elements that they have in common. Each of the twelve individual chapters describes particular approaches to the theory and practice of transformative learning that others may learn from and apply in their own settings. The themes that we discerned among the chapters in each section point to key elements, in theory and practice, in regard to creating transformative learning spaces, making use of cultural differences as catalysts for such learning, and using the expressive and performative arts in the process. The seven integrative elements found across all of the chapters in the book, as described above, point to an expanded and integrated model of transformative education. Demonstrating how transformative learning principles are being utilized outside of traditional classroom environments and in combination with other theories and models of change, this book will inform the ongoing development of the field, which, in Mezirow's words, continues to be a "theory in process." In describing innovative practices in diverse settings, and in distilling from those practices new theoretical propositions, this book does much to advance both the theory and practice of transformative education.

# Notes on the Editors and Contributors

**Beth Fisher-Yoshida, Ph.D.,** is the Academic Director of the Masters of Science in Negotiation and Conflict Resolution and is on the faculty for the Continuing Education and the Social and Organizational Psychology Program at Teachers College, Columbia University. She is Managing Director of Fisher Yoshida International, a global consulting firm providing customized responses to organizational needs. Beth is coauthor of *Transnational Leadership Development* (2009).

**Kathy D. Geller, Ph.D.,** is Director of Organizational Effectiveness for Stanford University. Prior to joining Stanford, Kathy lived in Asia for 10 years serving as Global Head of Management Development for Standard Chartered Bank and as Managing Director for Areté Leadership International. She has served as adjunct faculty at Columbia University's Teachers College and Nova Southeastern University. Geller is coauthor of *Transnational Leadership Development* (2009).

**Steven A. Schapiro, Ed.D.,** is a professor at Fielding Graduate University's School of Human and Organization Development, where he coordinates the doctoral concentration in Transformative Learning for Social Justice, which brings together his interests in liberatory education, adult development, and social change. Among his publications are "From andragogy to collaborative critical pedagogy," *Journal of Transformative Education*, 1(2), 2003; and *Higher Education for Democracy* (Peter Lang, 1999).

## Contributors

**Ann Davis, Ph.D.,** has a passion for communication and culture. An agent for social change, Ann focuses her teaching and facilitation on cultural competency training with the goal to successfully raise awareness of the self/other orientation. She is adjunct faculty for Alliant International University and San Diego University for Integrative Studies. Ann's dissertation was titled *Cross Cultural Experiences of Intercultural Expatriate Teachers: From Cultural Difference within Disorienting Dilemmas to Shared Meaning* (Fielding Graduate University, California, 2005).

**Placida Gallegos, Ph.D.,** is a professor at Fielding Graduate University and a facilitator and consultant working to create healthier, more inclusive cultures where people may achieve their fullest potential. She provides organizational consulting with a specialty in implementing diversity change initiatives. Recent co-authored publications include: "Latino identity orientations: Implications for leaders and organizations," *The Business Journal of Hispanic Research* , 2008; and "Latinas at work: An untapped resource for organizational success," *The Diversity Factor*, 2008.

**M. Sue Gilly, Ph.D.,** has a diverse background in business and academia that includes such things as business consulting, doing research for a university nonprofit organization, and teaching. Currently she is a freelance scholar in the Dallas, Texas area. Her publications include her dissertation, *The Heart of Adult Peer Group Learning: Living the Learning Together* (Fielding Graduate University, California, 2003); and "Experiencing transformative education in the 'corridors' of a nontraditional doctoral program," *Journal of Transformative Education*, 2 (3), 2004.

**Charlene Green Fareed, Ph.D.,** is a human and organizational development consultant who specializes in delivering coaching, program development, and consulting services to nonprofits. She is the founder and director of Genesis Life Development Center for Women. Her work related to Black women's health and wellness has been published in conference proceedings and in her dissertation, *Strong Black Woman: A Collaborative Study on Understanding, Experiences, and Relationship to Health and Wellness* (Fielding Graduate University, California, 2006).

**Martin Leahy, Ph.D.,** is president of Falcarragh Institute, Ltd., a consulting firm. His primary interest is in relational approaches to dialogue (the space-between-us) where he helps groups to create the time and space for struggling with questions that matter. Martin is adjunct faculty in Research Methods at Capella University. His doctoral dissertation, *The Heart of Dialogue* (Fielding Graduate University, California, 2001) used a heuristic research approach to study the life of an exceptional group whose lived experience contributes to relational dialogue theory and practice.

**Pamela Meyer, Ph.D.,** is president of Meyer Creativity Associates and works with leaders who want to create dynamic workspaces that inspire creative collaboration and learning. She teaches at DePaul University where she also serves as associate director of the Center to Advance Education for Adults. Pamela is the author of *Quantum Creativity: Nine Principles to Transform the Way You Work.* (Contemporary, 2000), and *From Workspace to Playspace* (Jossey-Bass, in press).

**Adair Linn Nagata, Ph.D.,** has pursued careers in international education, corporate training, communication, organizational development, and university teaching. Most recently professor of Intercultural Communication at the Graduate School of Rikkyo University in Tokyo, Japan, her teaching, facilitation, scholarly activity, and publications emphasize integrative transformative learning through intercultural communication. Two recent publications from 2006 include "Cultivating researcher self-reflexivity and voice using mindful inquiry in intercultural education," *Journal of Intercultural Communication, 9,* and "Transformative learning in intercultural education," *Rikkyo Intercultural Communication Review, 4.*

**Annabelle Nelson, Ph.D.,** is a professor at Fielding Graduate University and founder of the *WHEEL*—Wholistic Health Empowerment and Health for Life Council. Annabelle has her Ph.D. in Developmental and Child Psychology from the University of Kansas. Some of her publications include *Living the Wheel* (Samuel Weiser, Inc., 2003); "Multicultural model of HIV prevention for youth," *International Journal of Learning,* 2005, and, with S. Wisner, "The spacious mind: Using archetypes for transformation toward wisdom," *The Humanistic Psychologist,* 35, 2007.

**Tiffany von Emmel, Ph.D.,** is the founder and CEO of Dreamfish, a pioneering social venture which enables people and organizations who are changing the world to facilitate change with collaborative social software, environments and organization development processes. She is also a group facilitator for Stanford Graduate School of Business, Her Ph.D. dissertation was titled *Somatic Performance: Relational Practices and Knowledge Activism of Bodies Improvising* (Fielding Graduate University, California, 2005).

**Ilene Wasserman, Ph.D.,** consults with leaders and teams engaging the whole system to leverage multiple dimensions of diversity through enhanced communication. Ilene is adjunct faculty at Columbia University Teachers College and the Haub School of Business, St. Joseph's University. She is co-author of "Moral conflict and engaging alternative perspectives," in *The Handbook of Conflict Resolution* (Jossey-Bass, 2006), and "Dancing with resistance: Leadership challenges in fostering a culture of inclusion," in *Diversity Resistance in Organizations,* (Taylor & Francis, 2008).

**Hameed (Herukhuti) Sharif Williams, Ph.D., M.Ed**, is a sociologist, consultant, cultural worker, author, educator, community activist, theorist, and African shaman. Currently a faculty member at Goddard College, he is the founder of Black Funk: The Center for Culture, Sexuality, and Spirituality and author of the book, *Conjuring Black Funk: Notes on Culture, Sexuality, and Spirituality, Volume I,* published by Vintage Entity Press in 2007.

**Front row:** Adair Nagata, Charlene Green Fareed, Steve Schapiro, Pamela Meyer, Placida Gallegos

**Center Row:** Kathy Geller, Beth Fisher-Yoshida, Ann Davis, Ilene Wasserman, Annabelle Nelson

**Back Row:** Sue Gilly, Tiffany von Emmel, Martin Leahy, Hameed (Herukhuti) S. Williams

# Index

## Studies in the Postmodern Theory of Education

*General Editors*
*Joe L. Kincheloe & Shirley R. Steinberg*

Counterpoints publishes the most compelling and imaginative books being written in education today. Grounded on the theoretical advances in criticalism, feminism, and postmodernism in the last two decades of the twentieth century, Counterpoints engages the meaning of these innovations in various forms of educational expression. Committed to the proposition that theoretical literature should be accessible to a variety of audiences, the series insists that its authors avoid esoteric and jargonistic languages that transform educational scholarship into an elite discourse for the initiated. Scholarly work matters only to the degree it affects consciousness and practice at multiple sites. Counterpoints' editorial policy is based on these principles and the ability of scholars to break new ground, to open new conversations, to go where educators have never gone before.

For additional information about this series or for the submission of manuscripts, please contact:

Joe L. Kincheloe & Shirley R. Steinberg
c/o Peter Lang Publishing, Inc.
29 Broadway, 18th floor
New York, New York 10006

To order other books in this series, please contact our Customer Service Department:

(800) 770-LANG (within the U.S.)
(212) 647-7706 (outside the U.S.)
(212) 647-7707 FAX

Or browse online by series:
www.peterlang.com